Fred Leong
Department of Psychology
Southern Illinois University
Carbondale, Illinois 62901

CAREER DEVELOPMENT:

A Life-Span Developmental Approach

VOCATIONAL PSYCHOLOGY

A series of volumes edited by:
Samuel H. Osipow

CAREER DEVELOPMENT:
A Life-Span Developmental Approach

Fred W. Vondracek
Richard M. Lerner
John E. Schulenberg
The Pennsylvania State University

 LAWRENCE ERLBAUM ASSOCIATES, PUBLISHERS
1986   Hillsdale, New Jersey   London

Lawrence Erlbaum Associates, Inc., Publishers
365 Broadway
Hillsdale, New Jersey 07642

Library of Congress Cataloging-in-Publication Data

Vondracek, Fred W.
    Career development.

    (Vocational psychology)
    Includes index.
    1. Vocational guidance. I. Lerner, Richard M.
II. Schulenberg, John E. III. Title. IV. Series.
HF5381.V59 1986 371.4′25 85-29379
ISBN 0-89850-828-1

Printed in the United States of America
10 9 8 7 6 5 4 3 2 1

TO
Katherina and Paul Vondracek
Jacqueline, Justin, and Blair Lerner
and
Barbara A. Schulenberg

Contents

Preface

The unprecedented high standard of living enjoyed by Americans and by the rest of the Western industrialized world is not only a consequence of the wealth of the land or of good fortune. Although these factors can certainly facilitate the development of wealth, they do not create it. People who work create wealth. Work and the act of working thus represent the very lifeblood of the culture and the society in which we live. It has always been that way, although the conditions and circumstances of work and the people who perform the work have certainly changed over time. Thus, the focus of our book is the presentation of a framework for examining and understanding the work careers of developing individuals in a changing environment.

Many changes in the conditions of work have occurred in just the past few decades. Work has become less physically demanding and less dangerous to health and well-being; it has become less time consuming and more rewarding, and by and large it has become more diverse and interesting. The people who work also have changed dramatically. Women have entered the labor force in increasingly greater numbers, and both women and men view work as something from which they expect not only the satisfaction of their most basic physical or financial needs, but also as an activity from which they hope to gain personal satisfaction. Moreover, they see work as the means by which they can elevate their status in society and community. Most importantly, perhaps, they see their work—their careers—as something that is part of them; their careers can grow, change, and develop with them throughout their lives. Ultimately, work thus represents an integral component of life-span human development.

Unfortunately, the field of study concerned with life-span human development has scarcely paid any attention to the career development of people. Vocational psychologists, on the other hand, have not viewed career development from a perspective that would facilitate the integration of their findings into a broader theory of development, one that goes beyond the world of work. We have attempted with this book to demonstrate the applicability and utility of a life-span developmental perspective to the phenomenon of career development. Our presentation does not purport to be a theory, and strictly speaking, it is not a model. It is merely intended to be an adaptation of the developmental-contextual framework (articulated previously by R. M. Lerner) to a most appropriate but hitherto neglected area, namely career development.

It is unlikely that this book could have been written without the stimulating and supportive context provided by our colleagues in the Department of Individual and Family Studies at The Pennsylvania State University. We are grateful.

We also would like to thank the following people who have helped to shape the ideas presented in this book, some through encouragement and others through specific comments or both: Urie Bronfenbrenner, Harry Beilin, Orville G. Brim, Jr., Cathleen M. Connell, Ann C. Crouter, David L. Featherman, Donald Ford, Harold Grotevant, Edwin Herr, Christopher Hertzog, David Jepsen, Stanley Cramer, Jacqueline V. Lerner, John R. Nesselroade, Samuel H. Osipow, Linda M. Peterson, Elizabeth Vondracek, Alan S. Waterman, and Joachim Wohlwill.

Kathie Hooven did a superb job of typing the entire manuscript and, in the process, deciphering handwritten sections that would have taxed the ability of any expert. Without her help writing of this book would have been a much more difficult task. Richard M. Lerner's work on the book was supported in part by grants from the John D. and Catherine T. MacArthur Foundation and from the William T. Grant Foundation. He is grateful for this support.

Finally, we want to thank our families for the warmth and encouragement they provided throughout this project. Their devotion was a constant support to us, and we are deeply grateful.

1 Vocational Behavior and Career Development: An Introduction

Industrialized Western societies have been built on a foundation represented by the work and productivity of their populations. The success of industrialized nations in producing great wealth and economic rewards for their citizens was possible only because these same citizens—for whatever reasons—accepted work as their central occupation in life. Today, work is viewed as an imperative not only for socioeconomic well-being but also for physical and psychological well-being. Moreover, recent statistics suggest that in the United States individuals tend to make a more permanent commitment to their work than to their first marital partner. Havighurst (1982) commenting on the meaning and importance of work, put it this way:

> The job . . . orients and controls the behavior of those persons who participate in it. It sets a goal for the worker, determines the manner in which the goal may be attained and the reward offered for its achievement, and affects the whole range of his/her participation in the society of which s/he is a member. Its influences extend even beyond the actual work life of the individual. We also find that the part of his/her adult life not spent in work is, nonetheless, affected. . . . In short the job in our society exerts an influence which pervades the whole of the adult life span. (p. 780)

Not surprisingly, then, there is a growing interest among social and behavioral scientists, business and industry, and policymakers at all levels of government to develop a more thorough understanding of the processes that govern individuals' selection of occupations as well as their subsequent

1

performance in those occupations. There also is great interest in how and why people change occupations, and how they eventually disengage from their occupation to—at least in some cases—develop a leisure career or other means of benefiting from the fruits of their work life. There is growing concern about the consequences of working in one occupation or another for the general well-being of the individual. Finally, there is great interest in how vocational and career development proceeds as part of the process of life-span human development in general.

All of these issues and concerns can and have been addressed from a number of different perspectives. They cut across social, psychological, and biological levels of analysis. Ultimately, they can be understood fully only when studied within a model that recognizes the interaction of multiple relevant characteristics of individuality with multiple contexts and environments across the life-span of the individual. Clearly, this represents a most comprehensive and extremely complex requirement, one that inevitably must lead to the conclusions that the study of vocational and career development must not be isolated from the study of other domains of human functioning and must take place from an interdisciplinary perspective.

A number of different disciplines have, in fact, made major contributions to our understanding of vocational and career development. Crites (1969) defines vocational psychology as "the study of vocational behavior and development" (p. 16), but goes on to note that vocational psychology overlaps significantly with (a) *industrial psychology,* which focuses on solving work-related problems in order to achieve efficiency and productivity; (b) *occupational sociology,* which sees the occupation as a social institution and uses it as its unit of analysis; and (c) *vocational guidance,* which facilitates and assists the individual in choosing and adjusting to an occupation (pp. 19–23). Other emphases, especially within psychology, have been concerned with vocational and career development. For example, Bandura's (1969) social learning theory became the basis of a social learning approach to career development, proposed by Krumboltz and his associates (Mitchell, Jones, & Krumboltz, 1979). In turn, developmental psychology represented the most important knowledge base for the influential theories of Ginzberg, Ginsburg, Axelrad, and Herma (1951), Tiedeman and O'Hara (1963), and Super (1953, 1957), whereas various types of personality theory provided the bases for Roe's (1956) theory of career choice and Holland's typology theory of vocational behavior (Holland, 1959, 1973).

None of these theories have succeeded in integrating completely current knowledge on vocational and career development. Many have concerned themselves primarily with occupational choice rather than career development (Super, 1980), and most have been unable to present a theory sensitive to the historically and ontogenetically changing contexts of life, as well as to the multidimensional nature of the individual's vocational and career development (Markham, 1983; Vondracek, Lerner, & Schulenberg, 1983a).

More specific criticisms of the major, current career theories recently have been summarized by Sonnenfeld and Kotter (1982). First, although acknowledging that occupational sociologists have made an important contribution in demonstrating the relationship between parental occupation, status, and wealth, on the one hand, and the income attained by their children, on the other, they note that researchers in this area often have neglected to take into account important changes over time in the social status of occupations, in the distribution of the population in different occupations, and in individuals themselves. Second, Sonnenfeld and Kotter, in reviewing trait/type career theories indicate that researchers in this area, most notably Holland (1959, 1973), have succeeded "somewhat" in establishing relationships between individuals' personality traits and the occupations they chose. Nevertheless, they point out that at the same time trait/type researchers are unlikely to take account of the fact that traits and the demands of the workplace change. They also note that trait/type researchers tend to utilize "unrealistically simple and static" conceptualizations of the occupational environment. Third, regarding career stage theories, Sonnenfeld and Kotter decry the lack of attention to the "dynamic interaction" between the work and nonwork aspects of life and to the individual's prior life history. Focusing on the work of Super (Super, Crites, Hummel, Moser, Overstreet, & Warnath, 1957) and Schein (1971), they acknowledge that these stage theories reflect more dynamic formulations than those of the occupational sociologists and the trait/type researchers; nevertheless Sonnenfeld and Kotter indicate that these stage theorists still fall short in the sense that they view the individual as rather passive.

The final category of career theory reviewed by Sonnenfeld and Kotter is described as a life-cycle approach. It is the most recent addition to the career theory field, and the position most akin to the one we take in this book. The main features of life-cycle approaches include concern with almost the entire life-span and a more comprehensive focus on what Sonnenfeld and Kotter (1982) call "the three major aspects of life: Work, family, and the individual" (p. 30). Interestingly, this approach, much more than any other, has focused on adult vocational behavior rather than on the focus of most other research, that is, vocational choice. Key studies by Gould (1972), Levinson, Darrow, Klein, Levinson, and McKee (1974), and Vaillant (1977), all focusing on adults, have been credited with being instrumental in the development of the life-cycle approach. The main criticism leveled at this approach by Sonnenfeld and Kotter is that it has not fully realized its potential. Thus, although this approach acknowledges that a large and complex set of factors interact dynamically in determining the course of careers, empirical studies have been too limited in scope, have suffered from sample limitations, have frequently ignored nonwork behaviors, have focused on male subjects only, and have used longitudinal time frames that are too short to appraise the full, life course patterning of career development.

These criticisms of life-cycle approaches raise the issue of whether it is necessary or even desirable to approach vocational and career development in its full complexity. One answer to that question has recently emerged in a number of articles that represent an innovative approach in the field of vocational psychology. For example, Markham (1983) has recently called for more complex models, noting that the simpler, typically normative models, such as that of Holland (1973), are unable to cope with idiographic variation or with what Markham calls the *social milieu*. He also points out that the popularity of simpler models may well be due to the fact that they lend themselves to simpler research designs or easy approaches to measurement.

The most eloquent advocacy of a comprehensive, "life-span, life-space approach to career development" has come from Super (1980) in the form of a major expansion of his conception of career development. Although not a detailed revision of his self-concept stage theory of career development, Super's (1980) more recent statements (see also Super & Knasel, 1981) have been made "in the hope that [they] . . . will lead to theories which are more comprehensive than the segmental theories which now dominate the field" (p. 283). In another paper Super (1981) states that:

> Theorists still tend to focus, perhaps legitimately in view of the size of their problem, on segmental theories. Each is thus generally considered to neglect other aspects of theory, other aspects of career development, and career behavior. Those who do seek to encompass more suffer from the appearance of superficiality. But some day global theories of career development will be made up of refined, validated, and well assembled segments, cemented together by some synthesizing theory to constitute a whole that will be more powerful than the sum of its parts. (p. 39)

Consistent with Super's endorsement of comprehensiveness and complexity, Sonnenfeld and Kotter (1982) have presented, in outline form, a model of career development that accounts for the life space of the individual by recognizing both the individual/personal space (ontogenetic development) and the work and nonwork contexts within which the individual functions. They state emphatically that more attempts need to be made to account for the entire life space of the individual, with all its complex interrelationships, and that more needs to be done to integrate findings and concepts from all existing theories of career development. (In Chapter 4 another version of just such a model, originally developed by Lerner and Lerner, 1983, is presented.)

The present authors (Vondracek & Lerner, 1982; Vondracek, Lerner, & Schulenberg, 1983a, 1983b) also have proposed that a new conceptual view of vocational and career development is needed. Specifically, we have urged the development of a conceptual model that recognizes and incorporates important advances in our understanding of the concept of life-span development. Furthermore, we have urged the inclusion of a developmental contextual perspective that recognizes the changing character of the individual's social, physical, and cultural milieus. Thus, we have argued that vocational and career development can be fully understood only from a relational perspective that focuses on the dynamic interaction between a changing (developing) individual in a changing context.

In sum, recently numerous authors have stressed a number of themes that, in our view, may indeed presage what Sonnenfeld and Kotter (1982) have called the *maturation of career theory*. First, there appears to be a growing recognition that vocational and career development is a *life-span phenomenon*. This is probably due in part to the emergence of life-span developmental psychology as a subspecialty of psychology and its emergence as a prominent influence within the broader multidisciplinary field of human development (Baltes, Reese, & Lipsitt, 1980). In part, however, it is very likely also due to the fact that changes in Western society have produced conditions that focus attention on adult career development, such as late career commencement in women with older children, mid-life career changes, and the career contingencies and decisions faced by older people. In other words, the career decisions of youth are viewed as only early, and perhaps not even the initial ones, in a series of career decisions made during a lifetime. As a consequence there is a growing recognition that vocational and career development need to be understood within the framework of a life-long developmental phenomenon, characterized by both continuity and discontinuity. Just as life-span developmental psychology has deemphasized the study of development in segmented (usually age-determined) periods, such as infancy, childhood, and adolescence, and has articulated the need to study processes in a time-extended fashion, so must vocational psychology progress toward conceptualizations of time-related change in vocational behavior across the life-span.

A second theme that appears to be emerging is that vocational and career developments are properly studied from a *multidisciplinary perspective*. For example, Garbin and Stover (1980) state that "the complexities of vocational behavior are of such enormity that fuller understanding is more likely if interdisciplinary studies are undertaken" (p. 124). Osipow (1983) has noted that "fruitful career development theory will take shape within the larger context of human development . . . " (p. 324; which itself is a multidisciplinary field). This emerging shift toward a multidisciplinary approach to vocational and career development may well be a function of a more general paradigm shift in the scientific community toward synthesis and integration (Schwartz, 1982). Writing specifically about issues in the study of health and illness, Schwartz notes that single-category, single-cause, single-effect models are being replaced by multicategory, multicause, multieffect models. The same appears to be true in the career development field, as evidenced by recent attempts to formulate complex multivariate conceptual perspectives (Markham, 1983; Sonnenfeld & Kotter, 1982; Super, 1980; Vondracek & Lerner, 1982; Vondracek et al., 1983a).

The move toward a life-span perspective also underscores the necessity for the integration of multidisciplinary approaches into a unified interdisciplinary theory. Lerner and Hultsch (1983) have noted that such integration requires merging ideas from within those disciplines that focus primarily on the individual (e.g., molecular biology/genetics, physiology, and psychology) with those that focus primarily on the group (social psychology, sociology, and anthropology). Osipow (1983) sees such integration as occurring as part of an emerging "systems view of career behavior" (p. 314). More specifically, he noted that such a systems view:

> explicitly recognizes that various situational and individual factors operate to influence career behavior in a broad way. With a highly sophisticated systems approach to career development, questions about the role of the biological, social, and situational factors in occupational behavior would become more explicit and . . . understandings of the interactions between these views would be more likely to emerge. (p. 314)

The ultimate result of embracing an interdisciplinary, systems theory-type view of career development will be a shift from simplicity to complexity, from relatively simple models (e.g., Holland, 1973; Super, 1953) to more complex ones (e.g., Holland & Gottfredson, 1981; Super, 1980). Of course, as Markham (1983) notes, complex models do not lend themselves to simple research designs or easy approaches to measurement. In our view they are not inherently better than simple models unless they can be shown to lead to empirically unique and more useful information. Nevertheless, there appears to have been a tendency in the field of vocational behavior in recent years to favor those approaches that have operationalized concepts via the introduction of measurement instruments. This may be cause for concern if it inhibits the development of theories that are more rather than less complex. Theory ought to lead to the development of measures, and one's theorizing ought not to be limited by the well-known difficulties involved in operationalizing and measuring complex concepts, nor should theory be confined to using concepts for which well-designed measurement instruments happen to be available.

A third theme that has been emerging rather strongly during the last few years is a *contextual perspective,* which is now viewed as essential for gaining an understanding of vocational and career development. Thus, in their review of vocational behavior and career development, Fretz and Leong (1982) conclude by observing that "understanding both the unique and interactive contributions of environmental and organizational, as well as organismic, variables to the development and implementation of careers may well be a challenge we can meet in the 1980s" (p. 152).

Fretz and Leong's optimism may well be justified by recent work in the field. For example, Super (1980) has proposed that career development be conceptualized as taking place as the individual chooses and shapes a variety of work and nonwork related roles in essentially four theaters (environments): the home, the community, the school, and the workplace. Moreover, he recognizes that situational determinants may play an important part alongside personal determinants in shaping the individual's life career. Among the situational determinants Super differentiates between those he classifies as remote determinants (i.e., social structure and economic conditions) and those he classifies as intermediate determinants (i.e., community, family). This explicit attention to the impact of the environment on career development represents a major (and from our perspective welcome) expansion of Super's original conceptualizations.

Sonnenfeld and Kotter (1982) have recognized the impact of the environment by constructing a model of the individual's life space, made up of Work/Occupational Space (Educational Environment, Work History, and Current Work Situation) and Nonwork/Family Space (Childhood Family Environment, Adult Family/Nonwork History, Current Family/Nonwork Situations). In their model, these two sets of environments represent the context for the Individual/Personal Space that includes all of the person's characteristics of individuality, including genetic factors, personality, adult development history, and current perspectives. Moreover, Sonnenfeld and Kotter have gone to considerable length in suggesting the various kinds of interactions that occur among the various individual and contextual factors.

Finally, Vondracek and Lerner (1982) have urged that the social (including political and economic), physical, and cultural milieu must be considered in studying vocational and career development. Vondracek and Lerner (1982) stress that:

> this contextual focus also needs to be developmental . . . in order to discern the altering character of the context in regard to (1) the extant array of vocations available for people in general and (2) the array specifically open to [individuals] with particular characteristics of individuality. . . . Thus the indi-

vidual characteristics of the developing [person] must be considered in relation to the particular features of the context within which the person is developing. (p. 604)

Most noteworthy is the fact that Vondracek and Lerner see both the individual and the context as changing interdependently over time, which thus requires a *dynamic interactional* view of career development.

The foregoing examples are not meant to be exhaustive of the many recent appeals for a contextual perspective. Krumboltz (1981), for instance, has listed the environmental conditions and events that influence career development: number and nature of job opportunities; number and nature of training opportunities; social policies and procedures for selecting trainees and workers; rate of return for various occupations; labor laws and union rules; physical events such as earthquakes, droughts, floods, and hurricanes; availability of and demand for natural resources; technological developments; changes in social organization; family training experiences and resources; educational system; and neighborhood and community influences (pp. 45–46). This list clearly suggests the variety and complexity of environmental influences on career development. As Krumboltz acknowledges, some of the influences are clearly outside the control of the individual, whereas others may involve conscious choices by the individual. What is also apparent from the list is the point we are trying to make: The context within which career development takes place must have a central position in any conceptual scheme purporting to further our understanding of career development.

The themes of an interdisciplinary, life-span developmental, and contextual framework for understanding vocational and career development can thus be seen to have considerable contemporary currency, and they constitute the core of the framework we present in the remaining chapters. Most importantly, we attempt to show how our developmental-contextual perspective is useful for understanding career development in its ecologically valid context; thus, we indicate how, for example, social changes do, in fact, affect the career development of individuals and of whole classes of individuals.

A major case in point is the changes that have occurred in the career development of women. Recent reviews (Fitzgerald & Crites, 1980; J. Lerner & Galambos, (1985a, 1985b); Osipow, 1983) have noted that current theories of career development are limited in their applicability to women. There is, of course, no dispute about the assertion that women's career development is different from men's. A developmental perspective would be least likely to dispute such differences, and it would be most likely to incorporate these differences into any theoretical formulations or models. After all, developmentalists have a long history of concern with sex differences in development (Maccoby, 1966; Maccoby & Jacklin, 1974). Moreover, a dynamic interactional perspective that focuses on the relationship of a changing (developing) individual to a changing context is likely to attend to changes in the relation of gender to vocations—an alteration that Osipow noted could make any theoretical proposals about women's careers premature at this time (1983, p. 271).

THE PLAN OF THE BOOK

Our discussion thus far has attempted to show that the field of study concerned with vocational behavior and career development is complex and thus, understandably, has contributions by scholars and practitioners from a variety of disciplines. We believe that future advances may rest upon an integration of these multidisciplinary contributions and that such an integration must be able to deal with the actual complexity of career development.

We also have observed that there are a number of problems with current theories. However, there also are a number of emerging prototheories that offer the promise of leading to genuine theoretical and practical advances in the field of vocational behavior and career development. Hence, it is our intention to move the field (if only a bit) in the direction of what we consider to be the emerging themes of a life-span developmental emphasis, an interdisciplinary approach, a contextual perspective, and a greater awareness of individual differences in vocational behavior and career development. Of course, we do not claim to have originated the concepts represented by these themes. However, these ideas are represented in our earlier work (Lerner, 1979, 1981, 1982, 1984; Lerner & Busch-Rossnagel, 1981a; Lerner & Hultsch, 1983; Vondracek & Lerner, 1982; Vondracek et al., 1983a).

In the first four chapters of the book we discuss the relative merit of taking a developmental approach to career development. Most importantly, we reiterate and further expand on an argument we have recently stated elsewhere (Vondracek et al., 1983a, 1983b), namely that developmental concepts must be used in vocational or career theory in more than a superficial manner, and that the conceptual, empirical, and methodological problems inherent in developmental concepts must be properly recognized. Moreover, we demonstrate that the state of the art in developmental theory in the early 1950s, when Ginzberg and his colleagues and Super formulated their respective developmental theories of career development, was substantially and importantly different from the state of developmental formulations today. Thus, we examine whether stages (Super, Crites, Hummel, Moser, Overstreet, & Warnath, 1957), critical transitions

(Levinson et al., 1974), or developmental tasks (Havighurst, 1951) are the most tenable concepts in developmental theory today.

One of our objectives in Chapter 2 is to examine some of the more controversial issues that have been the subject of much recent discussion by developmental theorists (for example, see Collins, 1982; Lerner, 1976, 1985; Overton & Reese, 1973). In accord with our conviction that career development theory must be based on more than a superficial understanding of developmental concepts, a discussion of the philosophical roots of various concepts of development follows. As part of that discussion the basic features of the mechanistic, organismic, and contextualist models of development are presented along with an analysis of the scientific implications of embracing one or the other model. Finally, we introduce the concept of probabilistic epigenesis that represents the essence of what we believe to be the most powerful way of conceptualizing development: *developmental contextualism.*

Chapter 3 is devoted to the presentation and analysis of our conceptualization of the context of career development; this discussion relies heavily upon Urie Bronfenbrenner's *Ecology of Human Development* (1979). We argue that contextual factors are important contributors, along with a person's characteristics of individuality, to behavior, to human development, and thus to career development. Moreover, we maintain that because both the individual and the context are constantly changing they can be fully appreciated only from a dynamic interactional perspective (Lerner, 1978, 1979, 1984, 1985; Lerner, Lerner, Windle, Hooker, Lenerz, & East, 1986). Substantively, the focus of Chapter 3 is on the family, and to a lesser extent, on the school and the workplace, as well as on the relationships among them. In addition, neighborhood, community, and organizational contexts are considered. Finally, the overarching contexts of the sociocultural milieu and of the public policy arena are discussed.

The first part of the book concludes with Chapter 4, an articulation of what we call a life-span developmental approach to career development. Specifically, we discuss the concepts of embeddedness and dynamic interactionism and their attendant implications for considering: (a) the plasticity of development; (b) the person as a producer of his/her own development; and (c) the potential for intervention. Integrating the considerations of the nature of development from Chapter 2 and of the nature of the context of development from Chapter 3, Chapter 4 proposes a model of career development that is derived from the goodness-of-fit model of development proposed by Lerner and Lerner (see, for example, J. Lerner, 1983; J. Lerner, Baker, & R. Lerner, 1985; J. Lerner & R. Lerner, 1983). The principal feature of this model is its focus on the relationship (or the degree-of-fit) between characteristics of individuality (such as personality or vocational interests) and the demands of the person's contexts (such as the school or the workplace). We propose that such a goodness-of-fit model will be able to account for career development in a more satisfactory way than models focused on an assessment of personological features alone.

In the second part of the book (Chapters 5-9) we examine how the concepts explored in the first four chapters can serve as a means to organize and explain research evidence obtained to date and serve as a guide for future research in the field of career development. In order to demonstrate the applicability of our model, Chapter 5 is devoted to a discussion of vocational role development in adolescence, a period in the life-span that has attracted a majority of the attention of vocational theorists and researchers. Examining some representative studies from the extant research literature, we point out that many of them suffer from serious methodological and design limitations. Moreover, we observe that many variables that are important in the study of development in general, such as biological, cognitive, personality, and motivational variables, are underrepresented in the study of career development.

In Chapter 6 we address in greater detail the methodological issues raised by our developmental-contextual view of career development. In the area of measurement and assessment, we point out that measures of individuality, or measures of personal characteristics, which are not contextually sensitive, are of limited value. As J. Lerner et al. (1985) stress, a goodness-of-fit model requires measures not only of the individual but also of the contextual properties and demands within which the individual is operating. Thus, they note that the "unit" of analysis in such research must be a relational one—because the focus of inquiry is the relationship or "fit" between individual and context. In the area of research design we focus on two areas deemed essential in the study of career development: longitudinal designs and the study of change. Viewing the progression of individual careers as human developmental phenomena makes the use of longitudinal designs more than desirable: It makes their use essential. Furthermore, such research designs must be contextually sensitive. We thus propose the use of sequential longitudinal strategies, pioneered by Schaie (1965), Baltes (1968), and Nesselroade and Baltes (1974). The advantages of a sequential longitudinal design include efficiency (shorter time periods are possible than for traditional longitudinal designs), the inclusion of control groups and the potential disentanglement of age-related, time of measurement-related, and historical (cohort)-related, influences on change (see also, Dusek & Flaherty, 1981).

Although such longitudinal designs obviously address issues in the study of change, they do not, by and large, examine intraindividual change. This is a serious omission, as pointed out by Cattell (1952), and more recently by Nesselroade (1983) and by Schulenberg (1984). In fact, Cattell (1952) stated: "Some psychologists have been prone thoughtlessly to assume that day-to-day variations in measurement on an individual are largely experimental error of measurement" (p. 104). In this connection we point out the danger inherent in basing career interventions on the one-time administration of vocational interest or other similar measures.

Although we are proposing a general model of career development within the broader perspective of human development, we would be amiss to not recognize the significant differences that exist in most cultures, including our own, in the career development of males and of females. Chapter 7 presents a discussion of issues related to the career development of females, at least insofar as our developmental-contextual perspective is concerned.

Chapter 8 addresses the relationship between career development and health across the life-span. Some features of this relationship, especially pertaining to work and health, have received substantial attention in the past. For example, occupational safety and health are mandated concerns of the government with an entire agency, the Occupational Safety and Health Administration (OSHA), dedicated to supervising the enforcement of pertinent laws and regulations. Other areas, however, such as stress in the workplace and stress involved in making career transitions, require more focused attention from researchers. We attempt to show that our developmental-contextual model is capable of accounting for the dynamic interaction between the individual and health implications of his or her career. Moreover, we show how this conceptualization leads to the identification of heretofore neglected areas. Thus, for example, virtually no research exists on how stress, experienced by adolescents as a result of the initial career decision process, impacts on subsequent career development. Yet, clinical evidence suggests that many adolescents experience their initial career decisions as more stressful than other, much more researched life events, such as the onset of puberty or their initial heterosexual experiences.

The facilitation of career development is the principal objective of most career interventions across the life-span. Chapter 9 reviews the implications of a developmental-contextual perspective for career interventions. Particular features of intervention from this perspective include a focus on optimization and a concern with the whole person and his or her context and life circumstances. In addition we emphasize that developmental intervention can be most effective if preceded by a properly conducted developmental assessment.

Any endeavor that attempts to be broad in scope rather than narrowly focused and tries to serve an integrative function is likely to be criticized for being too inclusive on the one hand and for having serious omissions on the other. In our case we would like to acknowledge from the start that we have neglected certain areas in order to emphasize others. This was not done because we considered the neglected areas to be unimportant; rather, it was done because we felt that other scholars would be more qualified, by virtue of their interests and expertise, to pursue them. One such area is the career development of minorities in the United States. Although research on minority career development has greatly expanded in the past decade, such research has produced conflicting results, in part because American minorities do not represent a monolythic group (Smith, 1983). Moreover, Smith observes that research on minority career development has suffered from lack of a clear conceptual basis. We hope that the developmental-contextual model presented in this book can represent the basis for a more satisfactory conceptualization of career development, including that of minorities.

Another shortcoming in our coverage of career development phenomena is the relative lack of attention given to the impact of sociocultural factors on career development. Naturally, Chapter 3, which deals with the context of career development, includes discussion of the cultural context of career development. We must stress, however, that our conceptualizations are based on our understanding of career development as it is known in the United States and, to a large extent, in other Western industrialized societies. Career development as we know it may not take place similarly for individuals in China, in Uganda, and in many other countries around the world.

Finally, we would like to acknowledge that, even though we profess to have a life-span orientation, we have not given equal emphasis to various periods throughout the life-span. This is due in part to the fact that adolescence (our main focus) has received the most attention in the career development literature to date. We do not view this as a major deficiency, however, because our principal intent has been to present a viewpoint and to demonstrate its utility rather than to provide a comprehensive review of the literature across the life-span.

In spite of its limitations, it is our hope that this book will stimulate developmental psychologists and human developmentalists to recognize the centrality of the career development process in human development. At the same time we hope that vocational psychologists will look at life-span developmental psychology as offering an exciting body of theory, research findings, and methods, which can make an important contribution to their work. Ultimately, only a truly multidisciplinary effort can substantially advance the field of career development. We will consider our efforts successful if this book makes a contribution toward this end.

2 The Concept of Development

Within vocational psychology, the terms *vocational development* and *vocational role development* are used frequently. This use is not remarkable, because few, if any, scholars would contend that an adolescent's or young adult's adoption of a vocational role occurs without antecedents or precursors. However, does the seemingly obvious and ubiquitous observation that vocational role choices in one's youth are influenced by prior events in life suffice to say that a developmental sequence has occurred?

An answer to this question is difficult to formulate, because it depends initially on what is meant by *development,* and the term is one steeped in controversy (e.g., see Harris, 1957; Lerner, 1985; Overton & Reese, 1973; Reese & Overton, 1970, for reviews). In vocational or career theory (see Osipow, 1983, for a review), explicit use is made of developmental notions such as *stages* (e.g., Ginzberg, Ginsburg, Axelrad, & Herma, 1951; Gottfredson, 1981; Super, 1953, 1957), the *life cycle* (e.g., Levinson, Darrow, Klein, Levinson, & McKee, 1978), or the *life-span* (Super, 1980); however, these terms are no less controversial than is the term *development* (see Baltes, Reese, & Lipsitt, 1980; Lerner, 1985; Lerner & Hultsch, 1983, for reviews).

We believe that the use of the term *development* in vocational and occupational psychology needs to be an informed one; in other words, when *development* is used in these fields, it should be done with explicit recognition and articulation of the nature and implications of the particular meaning attached to the term. For instance, when the term *stage* is forwarded, we should be aware that within some views of development (e.g., Erikson, 1959; Freud, 1954; Piaget, 1950, 1970), but not all (e.g.,

15

Bijou, 1976; Brainerd, 1979), the term implies a universal and invariant sequence of qualitative changes through which all people pass and that there are rather strict formal criteria (in the Aristotelian sense; see Pepper, 1942) that have to be met in order to establish such a sequence (e.g., see Kohlberg, 1969, for a discussion of such criteria in regard to cognitive developmental stages). Thus, when the term *development* is introduced without any explicit indication of the particular theoretical conception underlying its use (as, for example, in Gottfredson, 1981), the potential for confusion and misapplication is substantial. In addition, when authors borrow either particular developmental concepts or entire developmental theories (e.g., that of Erikson, 1959) to advance a notion of vocational role or career development, it is not clear whether: (a) they see vocational roles or careers developing in a manner isomorphic with the process the original theorist spoke of (e.g., ego development in the case of Erikson, 1959); or (b) they see vocational roles or careers as only an outcome or correlate of the more general process discussed by the original theorist.

In this chapter we discuss the key philosophical and theoretical issues that have been involved in attempts to use the term *development* in a meaningful manner. Our goal is to provide, within the context of our concern with vocational theory, an overview of the sorts of conceptual concerns with which one must deal when using the term *development* and/or concepts related to it (e.g., stage, life course). Our presentation is evaluative, however. We often indicate the positions we take in regard to the philosophical and theoretical issues we review, and in so doing we reach, by the end of the chapter, a presentation of the concept of development to which we adhere. Our conception of development is informed by what we term a developmental-contextual (Lerner & Kauffman, 1985) or a probabilistic-epigenetic (Gottlieb, 1970, 1983) model. This conception leads us to see vocational role development as part of a more general developmental process linking the person reciprocally to his or her context. This view is recognized as consonant with the life-span, life-space approach to career development forwarded by Super (1980), but it also is seen to be different by virtue of our emphasis on the reciprocities between developing people and their changing worlds and on the active contributions individuals make to their own development.

ISSUES IN DEFINING THE TERM DEVELOPMENT

The meaning of the term *development* has been the subject of lively philosophical and theoretical debate by psychologists, sociologists, and other social and biological scientists (Collins, 1982; Harris, 1957; Kaplan, 1966, 1983; Lerner, 1984, 1985; Overton & Reese, 1973; Reese & Overton,

1970). The existence of the debate is itself indicative of a key feature of the meaning of the term; that is, development is not an empirical concept. If it were, then inspection of a set of data would simply indicate to any observer whether development was present.

However, different scientists can look at a set of data and disagree about whether development has occurred. This is because development is a theoretical concept. It is, as Kaplan (1966, 1983) has put it, a concept of postulation. Conceptual differences exist because different scientists are committed to distinct philosophical and theoretical beliefs about the nature of the world and of human life. For instance, some scientists find it useful to view the world as a machine and to study humans in terms of the energies needed to set the parts of the machine in motion. Other scientists do not find it useful to see humans as machines made up of discrete parts. Instead, they conceive of humans as integrated wholes and study how the structure or the organization of this whole changes over time.

Despite the philosophical and theoretical differences that exist among scientists in their conception of development, there is some agreement about the minimal features of any concept of development. In its most general sense, development refers to change. But clearly, change and development are not equivalent terms. If they were, there would hardly be need for the more abstract term *development,* and there would seem to be little reason for the philosophical and theoretical debates about the meaning of the term. Thus, although it is the case that whenever development occurs there is change, not all changes are developmental ones. For example, random, chaotic, completely disorganized, or totally dispersive changes cannot readily be construed to be developmental ones. Changes must have a systematic, organized character for them to be labeled as *developmental changes.*

But even systematic or organized change does not suffice to define development. An office organized by one head secretary may run by one system, whereas another office, organized by another head secretary, may run by a completely different system. If the first secretary leaves his or her job and is replaced by the second secretary, the latter may change the former's system into the one he or she prefers. At both points in time (during the tenure of the first secretary and then during the tenure of the second) a system, an organization, existed. Yet, the system at the second point in time was not an outgrowth of the system at the first point in time; there was no necessary connection between the two types of systems. In fact, if Secretary One returns to his or her job, the first system can be reinstated and, in such a case, there would again be no necessary connection between the two organizations. Thus, although change occurred, and although at the two points in time across which change was observed a system existed, there was no connection between the two systems. The character of System One did not in any way influence the character of System Two. Accordingly, the change in the office from time one to time two was not a developmental one, although it did involve an organized, systematic structure.

For organized, or systematic changes to be developmental ones they must have a successive character. The idea of successive changes indicates that the changes seen at time two are, at least in part, influenced by the changes that occurred at time one, if only to the extent that the range of changes probable at time two are delimited because of time one occurrences. In short, in a most general sense, the concept of development implies systematic and successive changes over time in an organization.

Virtually without exception, however, developmental psychologists go considerably beyond this "minimum" definition. For instance, the concept of development is historically a biological one (Harris, 1957). As such, the "unit" of concern (or analysis) for most psychologists is typically an individual organism. Furthermore, because the intellectual roots of the concept of development lie in biology, developmental changes are held to be only those systematic, successive changes over time in the organization of an organism, which are thought to serve an adaptive function, i.e., enhance survival (Schneirla, 1957).

As another instance, other developmental psychologists postulate that there must be a specific form to organized, successive changes in order for one to say that a *developmental progression* exists. In other words, only when the structure of an organization changes in a particular sequence is development said to occur. For example, Werner (1948, 1957), Werner and Kaplan (1963), and Kaplan (1983) postulate that development exists when a system changes from being organized in a very general or global way (wherein few, if any, differentiated parts exist) to having differentiated parts that are organized into an integrated hierarchy. Werner and Kaplan label this concept of development the *orthogenetic principle* and indicate that only those structural changes that coincide with this sequence of globality to differentiated and integrated parts fulfill the requirements for a developmental progression (Werner & Kaplan, 1963).

The point to be drawn from the aforementioned examples is that despite a relatively high degree of consensus that development is a theoretical concept, which connotes systematic and successive change in an organization, there is a good deal of difference among developmental psychologists about what particular ideas need to be added in order to adequately define the term. As just indicated, these differences in definitions are associated with theoretical differences that also divide scientists. The theoretical differences among scientists are, ultimately, based on their commitments to different philosophical positions (Kuhn, 1970; Pepper, 1942). As a consequence, it is of use to discuss the different philosophical positions that influence developmental psychologists.

Before proceeding with this discussion, we should note that in the career development field a number of theories have been profoundly influenced by the different theories of development—and hence different conceptions of development—that inspired them. As Ginzberg (1984) recounts, the theory put forth by him and his colleagues (Ginzberg, Ginsburg, Axelrad, & Herma, 1951) reflects a substantial indebtedness to both psychoanalytic and genetic formulations on the nature of development. Similarly, Tiedeman's theory (Dudley & Tiedeman, 1977; Tiedeman & O'Hara, 1963) is based, in several important ways, upon the developmental theories of Erikson and Piaget (see, for example, Erikson, 1963; Inhelder & Piaget, 1958; Piaget, 1970). Super (1953) acknowledges his reliance on the developmental formulations of Bühler (1959), whereas Levinson et al. (1978) state that "On the psychological side, our thinking about adult development . . . grows out of an intellectual tradition formed by Freud, Jung, and Erikson" (p. 5).

As noted earlier, we applaud efforts to view career development from a developmental perspective, and we understand the desire of vocational psychologists to capitalize on the work of developmentalists, especially in the area of developmental theory. Elsewhere we have noted, however, that vocational psychologists have often adapted key constructs from developmental theory without proper attention to the conceptual, empirical, and methodological problems involved (Vondracek, Lerner, & Schulenberg, 1983a). Consequently, a thorough examination of different conceptions of development, including their philosophical roots, is an essential prerequisite for the successful integration of developmental and vocational psychology.

PHILOSOPHICAL MODELS OF DEVELOPMENT

Scientists generally initiate their research with both implicit and explicit assumptions. Often, these assumptions take the form of theories that guide the selection of hypotheses, methods, data analysis procedures, etc. In addition to these relatively empirical features of science, scientists also hold preempirical beliefs, i.e., beliefs not open to empirical test. These assumptions may be also explicit or implicit (Watson, 1977); they may take the form of a presupposition about the nature of a specific feature of life, for example, that there is an inevitable connection between early experience and behavior in later life (Kagan, 1980, 1983). In addition, these beliefs may take the form of a more general "paradigm" (Kuhn, 1962, 1970), "model" (Overton & Reese, 1973; Reese & Overton, 1970), "world view" (Kuhn, 1962, 1970), or "world hypothesis" (Pepper, 1942), that is, a philosophical system of ideas that serves to organize a set, or "family" (Reese &

Overton, 1970), of scientific theories and associated scientific methods. Thus, these philosophical models of the world have a quite pervasive influence on the scientific positions they influence: They specify the basic characteristics of humans and of reality itself and thus function to either include or exclude particular features of humans and/or of the world's events in the realm of scientific discourse.

Three philosophical models or world views are of particular importance as bases for the formulation of developmental theories: mechanism, organicism, and contextualism. The mechanistic and organismic world views have been the subject of a series of essays by Overton and Reese (Overton, 1984; Overton & Reese, 1973, 1981; Reese, 1982; Reese & Overton, 1970) in which they explored ways in which these views have shaped theories of development. There have also been repeated efforts to examine the potential of the contextual world hypothesis (Pepper, 1942) for the derivation of developmental concepts and theories (Baltes, 1979; Lerner, 1984, 1985; Lerner et al., 1983; Lerner & Kauffman, 1985; Lerner, Skinner, & Sorell, 1980; Overton, 1984; Reese, 1982). However, Overton (1984) has argued that if contextualism is to prove useful for such derivations it will have to be integrated with either mechanism or organicism. We argue for a somewhat similar position, but we add the following points: (a) Only organicism, and therefore not mechanism, is useful for such an integration; (b) the organismic view alone has too many conceptual limitations for use as a model of development; (c) just as contextualism needs organicism to enhance its use, so does organicism need contextualism. To begin to develop this argument we turn to a presentation of the mechanistic, the organismic, and the contextual models.

The Mechanistic Model

As explained by Reese and Overton (1970), the mechanistic model

> represents the universe as a machine, composed of discrete pieces operating in a spatio-temporal field. The pieces—elementary particles in motion— and their relations form the basic reality to which all other more complex phenomena are ultimately reducible. In the operation of the machine, forces are applied and there results a discrete chain-like sequence of events. These forces are the only efficient or immediate causes; purpose is seen as a mediated or derived cause. Given this, it is only a short trip to the recognition that complete prediction is *in principle* possible, since complete knowledge of the state of the machine at one point in time allows inference of the state at the next, given a knowledge of the forces to be applied. (p. 131)

For instance, from a mechanistic, behavioristic perspective—which constitutes the major "translation" of this model into an approach to psychological development—organisms differ across their life-span only in the quantitative presence of qualitatively identical behavioral units, i.e., elements of the behavioral repertoire, such as stimulus–response connections, acquired by the causally efficient laws of conditioning (e.g., Bijou, 1976; Bijou & Baer, 1961). As such, the organism is seen as a host (Baer, 1976) of these elements, and even the most complex human behavior is believed reducible to these identically constituted units (Bijou, 1976). The only constraint on behavior change in a "consequent" period of life is imposed by past (antecedent) reinforcement history. Thus, the repertoire of behaviors available to the organism at any point in time may moderate the efficiency by which current stimuli can extinguish or otherwise modify any particular behavior.

As a consequence, from the mechanistic, behavioral perspective no "strong" view of development is present. Instead, the concept of development is reduced to a concept of change in the elements of the behavior repertoire; the means by which change is brought about consists of adding to or subtracting from the behavioral repertoire via conditioning. Change at any point in life thus becomes largely a technological matter always occurring with regard to past reinforcement history and pertaining to such issues as management of stimulus contingencies and of reinforcement schedules (e.g., in regard to building up, reducing, or rearranging a behavioral chain).

Although not explicit about the philosophical bases of their conception of development, it would appear that the social learning approach to career development usually associated with Krumboltz (Mitchell, Jones, & Krumboltz, 1979) comes closest to representing a mechanistic model. Its emphasis on conditioning histories and contingencies in shaping the individual's self-views, occupational preferences, career decision making, and career planning skills is certainly consistent with a largely mechanistic view of development. As we see in the next section the organismic model also is represented, in its essence, in career development theory.

The Organismic Model

As explained by Reese and Overton (1970), the organismic model has as its basic metaphor "the organism, the living, organized system presented to experience in multiple forms" (p. 132). Reese and Overton (1970) go on to note:

> the essence of substance is activity rather than the static elementary particle proposed by the mechanistic model. . . . In this representation, then, the *whole* is organic rather than mechanical in nature. The nature of the whole,

rather than being the sum of its parts, is presupposed by the parts and the whole constitutes the condition of the meaning and existence of the parts ... the important point here is that efficient cause is replaced by formal cause (i.e., cause by the essential nature of a form). (p. 133)

When the organismic model is translated into a set of ideas pertinent to psychological development an "active organism" model of humans has resulted. From this perspective, the human is inherently active; that is, it is the human who provides a source of its behaviors in the world, rather than the world providing the source of the human's behaviors. Humans, by virtue of their structure, give meaning to their behavior; that is, they provide it with organization—with form—by virtue of integrating any given behavior into the whole. By virtue of their activity and their organization, they are *constructors* of the world, rather than passive responders to it. Moreover, as a consequence of the inherent activity of humans, change, or development, is accepted as given (Reese & Overton, 1970). The organismic approach is thus a holistic one, one in which formal cause, and in its "purest" philosophical formulation also final (teleological) cause (Nagel, 1957; Pepper, 1942), provide the basis of developmental explanation. This explanatory orientation, especially when it is cast within an idealized view of developmental progression, has important implications. Material and efficient causative agents—for instance, as derived from the context enveloping the organism—are seen as irrelevant to the sequence of development and as such to the form the organism takes at any point in this sequence. The context can inhibit or facilitate, that is, speed up or slow down, developmental progression, but it cannot alter the quality of the process or its sequential universality. If a contextual variable does alter the quality or sequence of an organism's progression, then, by definition, that feature of functioning was not a component of development.

Gottlieb (1970) has labeled this version of organicism as *predetermined epigenesis.* Victor Hamburger's (1957) organismic position epitomizes this view:

the architecture of the nervous system and the concomitant behavior patterns result from self-generating growth and maturation processes that are determined entirely by inherited, intrinsic factors, to the exclusion of functional adjustment, exercise, or anything else akin to learning. (p. 56)

An examination of theories of career development reveals that just as there is no theory that completely embraces a mechanistic conception of development, there is no theory that completely and formally adheres to the propositions of the organismic conception. Levinson, Darrow, Klein, Levinson, and McKee (1974, 1978) represent the most recent example of an essentially organismic theory of career development. Dannefer (1984), in a recent review, has criticized the work of Levinson et al. for its underlying organismic assumptions, including the notion that "developmental periods" represent universal sequences in human experience, independent of the social context in which they take place. Another theory of career development that is basically organismic is Super's original formulation of his theory (1953, 1957). As is well known, Super's approach was based in part upon the theory presented by Ginzberg et al. (1951), a position that also reflects an organismic bias. Most important in both approaches is the concept of stages of (vocational) development that represent an idealized model of developmental progression, characteristic of organismic conceptions. Interestingly, Super's more recent statements on his theory incorporate important departures from the organismic perspective and move closer to the contextual model that is discussed next.

Contextualism

According to Pepper (1942), the main metaphor of contextualism is neither the machine nor the whole organism. It is the historic event. "The real historic event, the event in its actuality, is when it's going on *now*, the dynamic dramatic active event" (p. 232). In contextualism, every behavior and incident in the world is an historic event, and therefore change and novelty are accepted as fundamental. Thus, a contextual model assumes: (a) *constant change* of all levels of analysis; and (b) *embeddedness* of each level with all others; changes in one promotes changes in all. The assumption of constant change denotes that there is no complete uniformity or constancy. Rather than change being a to-be-explained phenomenon, a perturbation in a stable system, change is a given (Overton, 1978); thus, the task of the scientist is to describe, explain, and optimize the parameters and trajectory of processes (i.e., variables that show time-related changes in their quantity and/or quality).

The second assumption of contextualism is thus raised. It stresses the interrelation of all levels of analysis. Because phenomena are not seen as static, but rather as change processes, and because any change process occurs within a similarly (i.e., constantly) changing world (of processes), any target change must be conceptualized in the context of the other changes within which it is embedded. Thus, change will constantly continue as a consequence of this embeddedness.

There is an organism in the contextual perspective; but the organism, conceived of as an "organism in relation" (Looft, 1973), or an "organism in transaction" (Dewey & Bentley, 1949; Pervin, 1968; Sameroff, 1975) with its context, is the focus of developmental analysis. The timing of the interaction between organism and context is critical in contextualism. Indeed, the fact that the timing of interaction plays a central role in contextualism serves to provide a key distinction between it and organicism. As Pepper (1942) explains:

> Organicism takes time lightly or disparagingly; contextualism takes it seriously. ... The root metaphor of organicism always does appear as a process, but it is the *integration* appearing in the process that the organicist works from and not the *duration* of the process. When the root metaphor reaches its ultimate refinement the organicist believes the temporal factor disappears. (p. 281)

However, a major problem arises with the use of contextualism as a paradigm from which to derive a concept of development. Contextualism is, at its core, a dispersive paradigm (Overton, 1984). In other words, a purely contextual approach sees the components of life as completely dispersive (Pepper, 1942). Indeed, Pepper (1942) believes that it is the dispersive character of contextualism that is the key idea making it a world view distinct from the organismic one, which is marked by integration. As we have argued already, if the term *development* is to have meaning beyond that of mere change it must imply, at the very least, systematic and successive changes in the organization of an organism or, more generally, a system. Thus, a world view that stresses only the dispersive, chaotic, and disorganized character of life would not readily lend itself to the derivation of a theory of development.

But, although contextualism may not suffice in and of itself as a model from which an adequate concept of development may be derived, there is a way to combine features of this model with organicism—with which we see it is closely aligned (Pepper, 1942)—to forge such a concept. To better appreciate the need for, and the potential use of, such an integration it is necessary to examine how each of the three models we have discussed speak to key issues of development.

MECHANISM, ORGANICISM, CONTEXTUALISM, AND ISSUES OF DEVELOPMENT

The mechanistic model stresses the continuous applicability of a common set of laws or principles. Continuity exists because even quite complex behavior may be reduced to common elements (e.g., stimulus–response connections in S–R, behavioristic theories), elements whose linkage is controlled by forces external to an essentially passive, reactive organism. Thus, the task of developmental psychologists, from this perspective, is to identify the efficient antecedents (e.g., the stimuli) controlling consequent behaviors.

The organismic model stresses the integrated, structural features of the organism. If the parts comprising the whole become reorganized as a consequence of the organism's active construction of its own functioning, the structure of the organism may take on new meaning; thus, qualitatively distinct principles may be involved in human functioning at different points in life. These distinct, or new, levels of organization are termed *stages* in this view (Lerner, 1985; Reese & Overton, 1970). The task of developmental psychologists, from this perspective, is to assess the different functions of the organism that are associated over time with its changing structure.

Contextualism stresses the current, historic event and emphasizes that the *relation* among all elements comprising the event and not the elements themselves should be the focus of analysis. The task of a developmental analysis becomes one of depicting the changes that exist in the relation among elements over time as a consequence of the timing of the interactions among the elements.

These general distinctions between the three models lead to the identification of several other issues pertinent to understanding development. Reese and Overton (1970), Overton and Reese (1973), and Lerner (1985) have discussed several of these. These issues serve to highlight the distinctions we have drawn already.

Elementarism Versus Holism.   The mechanistic model is an elementaristic one. Human functioning is reduced to its core, constituent elements (e.g., S-R connections) and in turn, the laws that govern the functioning of these elements are applicable continuously across life. As a consequence, there is no true qualitative discontinuity—no newness, no emergence (i.e., no epigenesis)—within this perspective. Only quantitative differences may exist.

The organismic model is a holistic one. As Reese and Overton (1970) explain:

> The assumption of holism derives from the active organism model. More particularly, it derives from the representation of the organism as an *organized* totality, a system of parts in interaction with each other, such that the part derives its meaning from the whole. (p. 136)

Reese and Overton note also that the idea of holism within organicism has been most clearly articulated by Werner and Kaplan (1963), who indicate that the idea "maintains that any local organ or activity is dependent upon the context, field or whole of which it is a constitute part: its properties and functional significance [meaning] are, in large measure, determined by the large whole or context" (p. 3). In contextualism a similar stress is made on the role of the context in providing meaning for the parts which comprise it.

Antecedent-Consequent Versus Structure-Function Relations. The mechanistic model stresses efficient (and material) causes and, as we have already explained, is thereby concerned with identifying the necessary and sufficient antecedents of a behavior. Behavior is reduced, then, to an analysis of a qualitatively unchanging, continuous, and unbroken chain of cause–effect (e.g., S–R) relations. In organicism, however, the emphasis is on determining the functions associated with the actively constructed structures of the organism. Qualitative changes in structures can occur, as the active organism constructs—or better, reconstructs—its organization. Thus, novelty, newness, qualitative discontinuity, or epigenesis—occur as a consequence of changing structure–function relations. Here again, contextualism is quite compatible with organicism, although there is stress in contextualism on the *relation* between structure and function rather than on either alone.

But, if structure leads to function, what accounts for structure? One answer is simply function. The active organism shapes its structure, which in turn influences the organism's function, and so on, in a continuous and bidirectional (reciprocal) manner. However, this answer is only one of several possible replies to this question and is, in fact, quite controversial. Kohlberg (1968), Reese and Overton (1970), Overton (1978), Gottlieb (1976a), and Lerner (1985) have noted the existence of several formulations about the *source* of an organism's structure. These formulations divide on the basis of their relative emphases on nature-based processes (e.g., genes, heredity, maturation) or on nurture-based processes (e.g., conditioning, the physical ecology of one's context, the social events of one's context) in accounting for structure. As such, these formulations divide in respect to perhaps the key issue of human development—the nature–nurture issue, i.e., the controversy surrounding the source of any facet of human development.

Mechanistically derived formulations about the nature of psychological structure have tended to emphasize the role of nurture processes (e.g., the laws of classical and operant conditioning) in building up a response repertoire (and/or mediation processes) within the organism (e.g., Bijou, 1976; Bijou & Baer, 1961). Thus from this perspective, structure is imposed from outside the organism.

Several formulations regarding this issue are associated with the organismic model. Some of these views stress the role of nativistic variables in exerting a predetermined influence on an organism's structure, an influence independent of any nurture variables. Examples here are Chomsky (1965, 1966) and McNeill (1966), who maintain that psychological structures are completely present at birth, and Hamburger (1957), whom we cited earlier as maintaining that in the genome lies the basis for the architecture (structure) of the nervous system, which in turn directly determines various behavioral functions. Because the basic character as well as the course of changes in such structure is believed to be so thoroughly shaped by nativistic variables, it is apparent why Gottlieb (1970) has labeled such views *predetermined epigenetic.*

Other formulations associated with the organismic view emphasize that an *interaction* between nature and nurture variables provides the basis of structure. However, the concept of interaction is itself a complex and controversial one. Indeed, one's concept of interaction determines whether one remains committed to an exclusively organismic model or a position that integrates organicism and contextualism. For instance, Piaget (1968, 1970) maintained that although there existed an innate (congenital) structure, or organization, subsequent structures develop through an interaction between the present organization and the ongoing activity of the person (Reese & Overton, 1970). Note, however, that this concept of interaction sees the focal point, the locus, of interaction *within* the organism. The interaction is between the extant organization and the active organism's constructionist functions on (with) that organization.

Although Piaget's organismic, internal version of interaction is the converse of the mechanistic, more extrinsic notion of interaction discussed earlier, it is also distinct from the *strong* concept of organism–environment interaction (Lerner & Spanier, 1978, 1980; Overton, 1973), transaction (Sameroff, 1975), or dynamic interaction (Lerner, 1978, 1979), that is associated with a contextual perspective. This concept stresses that organism and context are always embedded, each in the other (Lerner, Hultsch, & Dixon, 1983); that the context is composed of multiple levels changing interdependently across time (i.e., historically); and that because organisms influence the context that influences them, they are efficacious in playing an active role in their own development (Lerner & Busch-Rossnagel, 1981b).

Because of the mutual embeddedness of organism and context, a given organismic attribute will have different implications for developmental outcomes in different milieus; this is the case because the organism's attribute is only given its functional meaning by virtue of its relation to a specific context. If the context changes, then the same attribute of the organism will have a different import for development. In turn, the same contextual condition will lead to alternative developments when different organisms interact with it. Thus, to draw a quite subtle distinction in somewhat strong terms, a given organismic attribute only has meaning for psychological development by virtue of its timing of interaction, i.e., its relation to a particular set of time-bound contextual conditions. In turn, the import of any set of contextual conditions for psychosocial behavior and development can only be understood by specifying the context's relations to the specific, developmental features of the organisms within it. This central role for the timing of organism-context interactions in the determination of the nature and outcomes of development provides a probabilistic component of epigenesis (Gottlieb, 1970; Scarr, 1982; Scarr & McCartney, 1983). In short, a distinctive feature of a contextual approach is its treatment of the concepts of time and timing.

But, although issues associated with the contextual treatment of the concepts of time and timing give the perspective its potential for providing an approach to developmental theory distinct from organicism, it can only do this by building on organicism. This point is brought to the fore with the next developmental issue we discuss.

Behavioral Versus Structural Change.   What is it that develops, that changes, with development? Does this development have any necessary directions? As Reese and Overton (1970) explain, answers to these questions provide perhaps the most important distinctions between the mechanistic and the organismic (and, we may note here too, the contextual) positions.

With the mechanistic model (qualitatively identical) elements may be added to, or subtracted from, the machine. For instance, in the behavioral translation of the model, lawfully identical S-R connections may be added to, or subtracted from, the response repertoire. Development is thus a matter of quantitative constancy or change, with elements being added to or subtracted from the organism's repertoire in accordance with the laws of conditioning (Bijou & Baer, 1961).

With decreases or increases possible in the number of S-R connections in the repertoire, development may be said to be multidirectional within this perspective. In short, within this exemplar of the mechanistic model in developmental psychology, what changes in development is the number of S-R connections in the organism's repertoire, and there is no a priori necessary direction to such change.

Quite a different set of ideas characterizes the organismic model. Reese and Overton (1970) note that in this model changes in structures and functions are emphasized, and that these changes are specified a priori to move toward a final goal or end state. Thus, development is *teleological* within this view; it is goal directed. Indeed, Reese and Overton (1970) indicate that within the organismic model the definition of development is "changes in the form, structure, or organization of a system, such changes being directed towards end states or goals" (p. 139).

Reese and Overton (1970) explain that development within this view is an a priori concept; that is, the general function of development—the end state or goal (e.g., "maturity," "ego integrity," "genital sexuality," or "formal operations")—is postulated in advance and acts as a principle for ordering change. In short, within the organismic perspective structure-function relations develop, and these changes are, in a final sense, unidirectional: they move toward a final end state. This goal directedness is not found in contextualism. Indeed, the disavowal of a telos in development is a key feature of contextualism, and this stance is a central distinction between it and organicism (Dixon, Lerner, & Hultsch, in preparation).

Although development is thus seen in organicism to be an a priori, idealized ordering of structure-function relations, and development is therefore continuous in the sense of always being directed by the final end state, there may be—and typically are—qualitative changes in structure-function relations over the course of development. Contextualism also admits of the possibility of discontinuity. The possibility of structure-function changes of a qualitative character raises two other key developmental issues on which the models provide divergent perspectives.

Continuity Versus Discontinuity.   Continuity means constancy or a lack of change in some feature of development. For example, a given personality "trait" (e.g., aggression, dependency) may be continuously present within a person across his or her life, or a child's growth rate (e.g., 2 inches a year) may remain constant across the childhood years. Discontinuity means change. Dependency may be altered or transformed into independence, and with puberty, and the adolescent growth spurt, a child's growth rate may increase dramatically.

All three models speak of continuity and of discontinuity. In mechanism the number of S-R connections (elements) in the response repertoire may be continuous; in organicism a given structure-function relation may be continuous for a specific period of the person's life and in contextualism there will be continuity for the duration of the event. Thus, from all models ideas of continuity may be derived.

However, the models divide clearly when the issue of discontinuity is raised. As we have implied already, only quantitative discontinuity is possible in the mechanistic conception of development. However, within organicism and contextualism there is an active organism that may construct or revise its structure and, in so doing, create a *new* structure-function relation. Thus, in organicism and contextualism qualitative discontinuity is possible. Such a change constitutes not just more of a previously or already existing structure; rather, it constitutes something new, something that cannot be reduced to a prior state or status of the organism. Such changes are said to be emergent ones, and such qualitative discontinuity is termed epigenesis.

The possibility that life is characterized by qualitatively distinct phases of structure–function relations raises one last developmental issue we may treat here. This is the issue of stages.

Stages of Development.   Like many of the other concepts we have been discussing, the concept of stage is a complex and controversial one (e.g., Brainerd, 1978; Flavell, 1970; Kessen, 1962; Lerner, 1980; McHale & Lerner, 1985; Overton & Reese, 1973; Reese & Overton, 1970; Wohlwill, 1973). Here we need to note only that the models clearly divide on the basis of the way the term *stage* is used as a theoretical construct. In mechanistically derived, behavioristic positions (e.g., Bijou, 1976), a *stage* summarizes the presence of some quantity of S–R connections. However, there is nothing qualitatively different about organisms at one or another stage of life.

In organismically derived theories and in positions compatible with contextualism (Lerner, 1980), however, a *stage* denotes a qualitatively distinct level of organization (e.g., Reese & Overton, 1970; Schneirla, 1957), i.e., an organizational structure qualitatively discontinuous with those of prior or later periods. As Reese and Overton (1970) explain:

> Within the active organism model, change is in structure–function relationships or in organization. As organization changes to the extent that new system properties emerge (new structures and functions) and become operational, we speak of a new level of organization which exhibits a basic discontinuity with the previous level. (p. 143)

Further Implications of the Organismic, Mechanistic, and Contextual Views

The foregoing can best be summarized as follows: The mechanistic model stresses a passive organism in an active world and emphasizes reductionism, continuity of laws governing development, only quantitative behavioral change across life, potential multidirectionality of change, elementarism, antecedent-consequent relations, and it eschews the idea of stages as qualitatively distinct periods of life. The organismic model stresses an active organism in a relatively passive world and emphasizes emergence, qualitative change in structure–function relations across life, unidirectional, teleological, goal-directed change, holism, and the appropriateness of the idea of stages as qualitatively distinct levels of organization. In contextualism, there is a stress on the active organism in an active world and on the relation between the developing organism and its changing context. Although not teleological in orientation, contextualism shares with organicism other important ideas: Key examples are the view that there may be both quantitative and qualitative continuity and discontinuity and the notion that qualitatively distinct stages may exist.

The mechanistic and organismic models have led to a set of theories—what Reese and Overton (1970) term a *family of theories*—of use in the study of all or part of the life-span. For instance, the behavioristically oriented, functional analysis approach of Bijou and Baer (1961), Bijou, (1976) exemplifies the translation of the mechanistic model into a theory of development. However, other "family members" include the social learning theories of Miller and Dollard (1941), Davis (1944), and McCandless (1970). The theories of Werner (1948), Piaget (1950, 1968, 1970), Freud (1954), and Erikson (1959, 1963, 1968) exemplify the translation of the organismic model into developmental theories. No theory of development has been derived from a completely contextual view, however. Indeed, this absence may be a key basis for the claims that contextualism in and of itself cannot (because of its key, dispersive, character) provide a model for developmental theories (Lerner & Kauffman, 1985; Overton, 1984).

But, both mechanistically and organismically derived theories encounter problems when attempting to formulate a useful concept of development. Mechanistically derived conceptions cannot, as we have noted, deal directly with novelty, or with qualitatively distinct levels of being. In the former case, novelty must be interpreted as reducible to common constituent elements; in the latter case, the influence of cultural, sociological, and physical ecological variables, for instance, must also be reduced to common (e.g., behavioristic) principles in order for their influence to have a place in the continuity perspective of mechanism. For these and other reasons (for example, see Bell, 1968; Bell & Harper, 1977; Lerner, 1982; Lerner & Busch-Rossnagel, 1981a; Lewis & Rosenblum, 1974; Schneirla, 1957; Tobach, 1981; Tobach & Schneirla, 1968), we are oriented more to formulating an organismically derived concept of development rather than a mechanistically derived one. However, as we have implied also, there are major conceptual problems with organicism that diminish its usefulness for derivation of a concept of development.

As Pepper (1942) has pointed out, the key features of "pure" organicism fail to deal with the point that the timing of interaction of causal developmental variables is probabilistic (Gollin, 1981; Gottlieb, 1970, 1976a; Scarr, 1982; Scarr & McCartney, 1983; Schneirla, 1956, 1957; Tobach, 1981; Tobach & Schneirla, 1968). As a consequence, there is a lack of concern with the implications that such differences in timing may have. For example, although the process of development may remain invariant across history (e.g., although an orthogenetic progression in structure–function relations may exist), the ongoing features of developmental trajectories may show considerable interindividual variability and there may be no universally inevitable end state of a developmental progression. In other words, there may be a probabilistic rather than a predetermined pattern to epigenetic change. Evidence for this view comes from attempts to account for changes pertinent to the adult and aged years (Baltes et al., 1980; Baltes & Schaie, 1973). Findings in regard to intellectual performance during these periods have not been consistent with the unidirectional conception of change required by a "pure" organismic conception of development (e.g., Cumming & Henry, 1961). Thus, increasingly greater between-people differences in within-person change were evident in several studies (Baltes, 1983; Baltes & Schaie, 1974, 1976; Schaie, Labouvie, & Buech, 1973). Simply, as people developed into the adult and aged years intellectual differences between them were increased.

DEVELOPMENTAL CONTEXTUALISM

Given the earlier evidence we consider it to be appropriate to propose a conception of development that interrelates features of organicism and contextualism. Clearly, "pure" contextualism, which is completely dispersive, would not be useful as a philosophical model from which to derive a concept of development. After all, such a dispersive model would lead to a concept of development in which the behavior of the organism is predicted entirely on the basis of the immediate contextual conditions within which it happens to exist at the time. "Pure" organicism, on the other hand, is equally unsatisfactory in that it considers contextual and temporal variables irrelevant in determining the quality and sequencing of the developmental progression. Overton (1984) has suggested the term *contextual-organicism* to describe the merger of contextualism and organicism, a merger that in our view appears necessary to circumvent the problems inherent in their "pure" formulations; Gottlieb (1970, 1976a, 1976b) has used the term *probabilistic epigenesis* for this merger.

Our own preference is to use the term *developmental contextualism,* as long as we can add the admonition that one must keep in mind that the concept is still intended to refer to an organismic, epigenetic process. Moreover, developmental contextualism incorporates the notion that the context does not simply produce alterations in development, but that the context itself is influenced and constrained by the organism's characteristics. This, then, leads to a conceptualization of development in terms of reciprocal organism-context relations or dynamic interactional relations (Lerner, 1978, 1979, 1982, 1984, 1985). In sum, the heart of the developmental contextual paradigm is created by synthesizing two key ideas from contextualism and organicism, respectively: that contextual change is probabilistic in nature, and that development proceeds according to the organism's activity.

In elaborating upon this position Gollin (1981) has explained that probabilistic, developmental change is not dispersive because the living system—the organism—has organization and internal coherence, and these features constrain the capability of the *developmental context* to affect the system. Gollin (1981) says that:

> The determination of the successive qualities of living systems, given the web of relationships involved, is probabilistic. This is so because the number of factors operating conjointly in living systems is very great. Additionally, each factor and subsystem is capable of a greater or lesser degree of variability. Hence, the influence subsystems have upon each other, and upon the system as a whole, varies as a function of the varying states of the several concurrently operating subsystems. Thus, the very nature of living systems, both individual and collective, and of environments, assure the presumptive character of organic change.
>
> Living systems are organized systems with internal coherence. The properties of the parts are essentially dependent on relations between the parts and the whole (Waddington, 1957). The quality of the organization provides opportunities for change as well as constraints upon the extent and direction of change. Thus, while the determination of change is probabilistic, it is not chaotic. (p. 232)

Gollin's position illustrates that one needs to understand that development occurs in a multilevel context and that the nature of the changes in this context leads to the probabilistic character of development; but one needs to appreciate too that the organism as much shapes the context as the context shapes it.

A final point about the developmental-contextual (probabilistic epigenetic) view needs to be highlighted. Although both developmental-contextual and mechanistic-behavioral perspectives make use of the context enveloping an organism in attempts to explain development, it is clear that they do so in distinctly different ways. Developmental-contextual theorists do not adopt a reflexively reductionistic approach to conceptualizing the impact of the context. Instead, because of a focus on organism-context transactions, and thus a commitment to using an interlevel, or relational, unit of analysis (Lerner, Skinner, & Sorell, 1980), the context may be conceptualized as composed of multiple, qualitatively different levels, e.g., the inner-biological, the individual-psychological, the outer-physical, and the sociocultural (Riegel, 1975, 1976). Moreover, although both the mechanistic and the developmental-contextual perspectives hold that changes in the context become part of the organism's intraindividually changing constitution, the concept of "organism" found in the two perspectives is also quite distinct. The organism in developmental contextualism is not merely the host of the elements of a simplistic environment. Instead, the organism is itself a qualitatively distinct level within the multiple, dynamically interacting levels forming the context of life. As such, the organism has a distinct influence on the multilevel context that is influencing the organism. As a consequence the organism is, in short, not a host, but an active contributor to its own development (Lerner, 1982; Lerner & Busch-Rossnagel, 1981b).

CONCLUSIONS

In developmental-contextualism behavioral development becomes, at least in part, a matter of self-activated generation. In this view development arises essentially by the strong interaction of organism and context (or, in other words, of nature and nurture, or of heredity and environment). Hence it is a logical next step to focus on the meeting place of those factors lying primarily within the organism (hereditary) and those lying primarily outside (environment). This meeting place is of course the organism itself. By focusing on the contributions that the organism's own characteristics (e.g., its cognitive attributes, its type of behavioral style, or its physical attractiveness) make towards its own further development, developmental-contextual theorists are essentially studying the continual accumulations of the interacting contributions of nature and nurture. This focus brings about a concern with how particular features of a complex and changing context influence and are influenced by a complex and developing organism.

In Chapter 3 we discuss features of the context we believe are particularly important to focus on, given the current state of knowledge in the vocational role development and career development literature. In Chapter 4 we present the general features of a life-span developmental perspective that we believe is useful for studying vocational role and career developments, a perspective that we see as quite consonant with the developmental-contextual perspective for which we have argued in this chapter.

3

The Context of
Career Development

With a few recent exceptions (e.g., Schein, 1978; Sonnenfeld & Kotter, 1982; Super, 1980), consideration of the context of career development has been relatively sporadic in the career development literature, and research and theory on the context of career development has usually not been integrated into the work of personologically or developmentally oriented scientists. This is somewhat surprising in view of the fact that it is universally acknowledged that the various environments in which people develop, both as humans and as workers or professionals, exert a very significant influence on their careers. There are, of course, some theorists and researchers who have paid considerable attention to the impact of the social environment on career choice (e.g., Blau & Duncan, 1967; Blau, Gustad, Jessor, Parnes, & Wilcock, 1956; Hollingshead, 1949; Miller & Form, 1951; Mortimer, 1976; Mortimer & Kumka, 1982). Osipow (1983) classified such approaches as sociological approaches, indicating that their central point is that "societal circumstances beyond the control of the individual contribute significantly to career choices and . . . the principal task confronting a person is the development of techniques to cope effectively with the environment" (p. 10). Unfortunately, these sociological approaches have generally focused only on the social context to the virtual exclusion of the physical environment on the one hand and the cultural context on the other. In spite of these limitations, the work of sociological theorists and researchers in explicating the impact of social variables, especially socio-economic status, on career development has had far reaching implications for much career development research and for career interventions.

Wohlwill and Heft (in press) have recently proposed a differentiation between the physical (inanimate) and the social environment based on relative responsivity. The animate or social environment is seen as providing truly interactive feedback, whereas the inanimate environment provides only very limited interactive feedback as is the case with computers, for example. Indeed, concerning the development of the child in the social environment, Wohlwill and Heft (in press) write: "One of the signal features of the child's social environment is its *interactive* nature. . . . The child's interaction with the social environment has a more open-ended and generative quality than the closed response feedback loop characteristic of the child's relationship with the physical environment, where feedback is strictly contingent on the child's behavior." Nevertheless, the apparently greater importance of the social environment does not justify ignoring the physical environment. In addition, as Stokols (1978, 1981a, 1981b) points out in his discussions concerning the advances within the domain of environmental psychology over the past few decades, the physical environment is a salient but often neglected component of person–environment transaction. Simply put, the physical environment literally "sets the stage" for the social environment; physical structures and their properties (e.g., lighting, space, noise levels) can facilitate or delimit certain social interactions, behaviors, and attitudes (e.g., Alessi, Brill, & Fowles, 1979). In terms of the impact of the physical environment on career development, there is an extensive body of literature, for example, concerning the links between the physical characteristics of the work setting and job satisfaction and productivity (e.g., Alessi et al., 1979; Barnaby, 1980; Brookes & Kaplan, 1972; Finnegan & Soloman, 1981; Maier & Ferguson, 1983; Leibson, 1981). Clearly, as we attempt to illustrate throughout this chapter, the physical features of the environment need to be considered when unraveling the impact of the context on career development.

The overarching and ever-changing cultural, economic, and technological features of the context, features that undoubtedly influence career development, have also been typically ignored by career developmentalists. As Osipow (1973) stated:

> Social and economic conditions have changed drastically in the United States between the 1930s and 1970s and so has career development. Thus, it is not unreasonable to expect significant changes in the economy and culture in the years ahead, bringing about concomitant changes in career development. . . . Often our theories, seeming to assume that career development is static, appear designed to describe career development only in the context of mid-twentieth century America. (p. 293)

Over the past few decades, the work of several life-span developmentalists and life-course sociologists has underscored the link between macrolevel societal change and individual development (e.g., Baltes, Cornelius, & Nesselroade, 1978; Elder, 1974; Featherman & Lerner, 1985; Nesselroade & Baltes, 1974; Riegel, 1976; Schaie, 1982); that is, the course of one's development is dependent, to some extent, on one's location in historical time (i.e., birth-cohort membership). For example, the difference between the career development of two females, one born in 1900 and the other born in 1960, is likely to be due to differences in the overarching cultural context between the two time periods. Hence, a comprehensive conceptualization of the context of career development must be sensitive to the overarching and historically changing cultural, economic, and technological features of the context.

Even if there were a comprehensive theory of career development sensitive to the social, cultural, and physical features of the environment, however, it would still not satisfy the requirements of the developmental contextual view proposed in the previous chapter unless it also incorporated the notion of dynamic interaction (Lerner, 1978, 1979). In other words, to simply acknowledge that the various features of the context impact the development of the organism is not enough; dynamic interaction means that context and organism are inextricably embedded in each other, that the context consists of multiple levels changing interdependently across time, and that because organisms influence the contexts that influence them, they are able to play an active role in their own developments (Lerner & Busch-Rossnagel, 1981).

From these introductory comments, it should be clear that the context of career development entails far more than simply one's immediate social environment. Furthermore, the individual is not a passive recipient of contextual forces; rather, the impact of the context on an individual's career development is conceived of as a result of the dynamic interaction between the developing individual and the ever-changing context. In this chapter, we present what we believe are important points to consider in conceptualizing the context of career development. Our notions are not entirely new; rather they represent a reordering and integration of past conceptualizations and empirical findings. In keeping with our focus on organism-context interactions, we start by considering the concept of affordances (J. Gibson, 1979), essentially a functional view of the context, as it relates to career development. Then we turn to a discussion of the "ecology of human development," which represents a conceptual framework devised by Bronfenbrenner (1979) to order and describe various portions of the context salient to human development. Bronfenbrenner's key concepts are presented and adapted to illustrate our views concerning the ecology of career development. Finally, we draw upon Bronfenbrenner's framework of ecological subsystems to portray the various components of the context that need to be considered when conceptualizing and studying career development.

CONTEXTUAL AFFORDANCES
AND CAREER DEVELOPMENT

To illustrate how a given attribute of the organism has different implications for developmental outcomes depending on the context within which development takes place, consider the following example. A young boy who is unusually gifted in mathematics and who belongs to a middle-class American family, is almost certain to be encouraged to prepare for a career in academics or in engineering; thus the functional significance of his special talent would be derived from the fact that his context (i.e., family, school) recognizes and fosters it. Another boy with a similar talent, growing up in an inner-city ghetto is not as likely to receive the same encouragement and recognition. His talent may thus not be developed, and one could say that the nature of his context greatly reduced the functional significance of his talent.

What should be apparent at this point is that this conceptualization of person (organism) and context interaction is sensitive to all features of the context. For example, the physical environment gives functional meaning to the ability to tolerate great heights—important in Utah but much less so in Kansas; the social environment gives functional meaning to mathematical ability, as discussed earlier, and the cultural context gives functional meaning to physical attractiveness—a person considered very attractive in Western Europe may be considered unattractive in Uganda. Such a "functionalist" conception of the context of development is not without precedent. Eleanor Gibson (1982) claims that the spirit of functional psychology "man acting in reciprocity with his environment, keeping in touch with a real world, and perceiving the utility of what that world offers" (p. 60)—is represented in the notion of affordance promoted by J. J. Gibson (1979).

The concept of affordance centers on the idea that environments offer, provide, and/or furnish something to the organism as long as the organism can perceive "it" as such. Gibson (1982) states that "The properties that define the affordance have unity only 'relative to the posture and behavior of the animal being considered'" (p. 56). According to Gibson, objects, places, events, other people and man-made symbols all offer affordances. Applied to the world of work and careers, objects may be perceived to have affordances as tools; places may have affordances: a conference room affording a meeting, an operating room affording the practice of surgery. Events can also be viewed as affordances, such as an event affording the making of an occupational choice (e.g., a job interview or receiving a job offer). Gibson (1982) points out that "other people have affordances of immensely varied kinds, and we acquire considerable skill in perceiving what another person's behavior or expressive gestures may afford" (p. 63). Finally, symbols have affordances (e.g., information contained in written words or in the blinking of a yellow light).

What is offered by a conceptualization of the context of career development as a set of affordances? First of all, it is an approach which, as Gibson (1982) points out, has important implications for human development, and hence, by implication, for career development. Affordances must, of course, be perceived as such. Thus, one individual, at a given point in his/her developmental trajectory may perceive an affordance in a given event or object whereas another person may not—even though he/she is looking at the same event or object. How people come to perceive affordances may depend in part on their developmental status. This underscores the point made in the previous chapter, namely, that both the individual and the environment should be viewed from a developmental perspective. At a more mundane level this perspective may provide some answers to the question of why some people perceive great opportunities for career development in situations that others perceive as offering none.

Apart from its implications for the study of development, Wohlwill and Heft (in press) point out that affordances are ecologically real and not merely mental representations of the environment. Thus, they conclude that the concept of affordances "provides a possibility for the formulation of an objectively specifiable *and* psychologically meaningful taxonomy of the environment." To illuminate this point E. Gibson (1982, p. 56) quotes J. J. Gibson (1979) as follows:

> An important fact about the affordances of the environment is that they are in a sense objective, real, and physical, unlike values and meanings, which are often supposed to be subjective, phenomenal, and mental. But, actually, an affordance is neither an objective property nor a subjective property; or it is both if you like. An affordance cuts across the dichotomy of subjective–objective and helps us to understand its inadequacy. It is equally a fact of the environment and a fact of behavior. It is both physical and psychical, yet neither. An affordance points both ways, to the environment and to the observer. (p. 129)

It is this apparent mutuality of person and environment that makes the concept of affordances so compatible with the developmental-contextual perspective discussed in the previous chapter. Ultimately, however, it is the functionalism represented by the concept—its practical applicability to the real world—that may prove to be of premier importance in its use in career development theory. Such use must also await the development of an appropriate and meaningful taxonomy such as that referred to by Wohlwill and Heft (in press; see also, Stokols, 1978, 1981a).

IMPLICATIONS OF AN ECOLOGY
OF HUMAN DEVELOPMENT
FOR CAREER DEVELOPMENT

There is yet another conceptualization of the environment that is quite compatible with the developmental-contextual view presented in the previous chapter. Bronfenbrenner (1979), in introducing his "Ecology of Human Development" stated that his "perspective is new in its conception of the developing person, of the environment, and especially of the evolving interaction between the two" (p. 3). It may be of interest to note that Young (1983) and two of the present authors (Vondracek & Lerner, 1982), as well as Campbell (1969) and Scheller (1976) before them have suggested an "Ecology of Career Development" as the potentially most promising framework for conceptualizing career development in its full complexity, that is, as properly embedded in the stream of human development. It is no accident, therefore, that the three components of Bronfenbrenner's conceptualization, the developing person, the environment, and the interaction between the two, coincide with the substantive content of Chapters 2, 3, and 4, respectively. It is also no accident that career development theory suffers from a deficiency similar to that described by Bronfenbrenner (1979) as affecting the behavioral sciences in general: Most would agree with the assertion that human development is properly viewed as a product of the interaction between the developing person and the environment, *but* in practice there is an overwhelming focus "on the properties of the person and only the most rudimentary conception and characterization of the environment in which the person is found" (Bronfenbrenner, 1979, p. 16).

Although the present chapter is concerned primarily with the context of *career development,* Bronfenbrenner's conceptualizations are quite applicable. Moreover, we find ourselves in substantial agreement with many of his major points. Thus, the remainder of this chapter relies heavily on Bronfenbrenner's characterization of the ecology of human development, which we see as offering a major framework for ordering and integrating differing viewpoints regarding the context of career development. To quote Bronfenbrenner (1979):

A theoretical conception of the environment extending beyond the behavior of individuals to encompass functional systems both within and between settings, systems that can also be modified and expanded, contrasts sharply with prevailing research models. These established models typically employ a scientific lens that restricts, darkens, and even blinds the researcher's vision of environmental obstacles and opportunities and of the remarkable potential of human beings to respond constructively to an ecologically compatible milieu once it is made available. As a result, human capacities and strengths tend to be underestimated. (p. 7)

Needless to say, if Bronfenbrenner is right, adaptation of his position would be of substantial interest to anyone interested in the optimization of career development (see, for example, Vondracek & Lerner, 1982). Indeed, the full utilization of human capacities is important not only for positive career adjustment but also for worker productivity.

A number of Bronfenbrenner's key concepts deserve special mention because they are particularly germane to career development. For example, Bronfenbrenner (1979) defines an *ecological transition* as occurring "whenever a person's position in the ecological environment is altered as the result of a change in role, setting, or both" (p. 26). Bronfenbrenner's own examples of ecological transitions include such things as "finding a job," "changing jobs," "losing jobs," "changing careers," and "retiring." Ecological transitions can thus be seen as occurring across the entire life-span, and as including every major milestone of career development. They are also viewed as consequences of both organismic and environmental changes and as representing examples of the mutual accommodation between organism and environment.

Bronfenbrenner (1979) stresses that ecological transitions constitute "both a consequence and an instigator of developmental processes" (p. 27). In the next chapter a discussion of the life-span perspective of human development reveals a closely related concept, namely, the person as producer of his/her development (see, also, Lerner, 1982; Lerner & Busch-Rossnagel, 1981b). Although these concepts are quite compatible, it should be noted that whereas Bronfenbrenner maintains his largely descriptive emphasis in depicting ecological transitions, Lerner and Busch-Rossnagel invoke feedback mechanisms to account for the processes by which individuals act as producers of their own development.

Just as the concept of ecologial transitions has a closely related counterpart in life-span developmental theory so has Bronfenbrenner's *principle of interconnectedness.* In short, Bronfenbrenner's framework envisions a number of nested, interconnected systems as representing the structure of the ecological environment. The interconnectedness holds true both within and between systems, and it is such a central part of Bronfenbrenner's conceptualization that Bronfenbrenner (1979) goes as far as to state that his theory is "a theory of environmental interconnections and their impact on the forces directly affecting psychological growth" (p. 8). In the life-span perspective the concept of dynamic interaction (Lerner, 1978, 1979, 1985) represents similar concerns. Dynamic interaction assumes that the most important phenomena of human development occur at multiple, interrelated levels of analysis and that development can be understood only by examining the interaction among the various levels as they impact the person's developmental trajectory. This, of course, has special significance in career development because multiple contexts contribute to career development throughout the life-span.

For example, both structural and functional features of the family context impact career development in relatively predictable ways (for a recent review see Schulenberg, Vondracek, & Crouter, 1984). Social class membership (Blau & Duncan, 1967) and the structure of the organizations in which people work (Schein, 1978) are other examples. The need for both a taxonomy and a conceptual framework for ordering the multiplicity of contexts becomes readily apparent when it is realized that the various levels of context are interconnected and interact dynamically with one another as they affect and are affected by the developing person.

It may be appropriate to present one additional consideration that has special implications for career development. Bronfenbrenner (1979) points out that the traditional views concerning the relationship between basic science and public policy are in need of revision. Specifically, he argues that "in the interest of advancing fundamental research on human development, *basic science needs public policy even more than public policy needs social science*" (p. 8). Moreover, he argues that researchers in human development must be aware of and knowledgeable about public policy because public policy constitutes an important element of the context in which human development occurs and of the context within which research on human development is carried out.

Perhaps no area of human development is more persistently affected by public policy than is career development. Krumboltz (1981, pp. 45–46) enumerates some public policy-related environmental conditions that influence the career development of individuals: number and nature of job opportunities, number and nature of training opportunities, social policies and procedures for selecting trainees and workers, labor laws and union rules, changes in social organizations, the educational system, and neighborhood and community influences. Obviously, career development research ought to be influential in the making of public policy decisions, but the researcher in career development must be aware of public policy that influences the behavior of his or her dependent variables. Bronfenbrenner's point is well taken: Public policy and research should be "functionally integrated" in the interest of improving both. Viewing public policy as a legitimate and important part of the context may be a step in the right direction.

Our discussion, thus far, of Bronfenbrenner's concept of ecological transitions, of his principle of interconnectedness, and of his call for the integration of basic science and public policy has focused on pointing out compatibilities between Bronfenbrenner's conceptualizations and those proposed within the life-span developmental perspective. In addition, examples were presented to demonstrate the relevance of these ideas for career development theory and research. In the section that follows, Bronfenbrenner's analysis of ecological space as consisting of the micro-system, mesosystem, exosystem, and macrosystem is discussed as offering a framework for the simultaneous consideration of the multiple contextual influences on career development.

Before proceeding with this discussion it is necessary to briefly mention two points of departure between Bronfenbrenner's position and that of the present authors. First and foremost is Bronfenbrenner's conception of development. In contrast to the probabilistic epigenetic conception of development presented in the previous chapter, Bronfenbrenner (1979) is concerned with *development-in-context.* "Development is defined as the person's evolving conception of the ecological environment, and his rela-tion to it, as well as the person's growing capacity to discover, sustain, or alter its properties" (p. 9). The emphasis in this view appears to be more on the context of development rather than on development as such. In devel-opmental contextualism (that, as we have noted, is another term used to describe the probabilistic epigenetic conception of development) develop-ment arises out of the strong interaction between organism and context, of nature and nurture. Thus, the emphasis is more on the organism, as it is the meeting place of those factors contributing to development that lie inside the organism, namely, heredity, and those lying outside the organism, namely, the environmental context. Through focusing on the organism's characteristics of individuality and their contributions to the organism's own further development, a developmental-contextual perspective leads to an examination of the continual accumulation of the interacting contribu-tions of nature and nurture. This, in turn, raises the possibility of formulat-ing questions concerning *how* particular features of a complex and changing context influence and are influenced by a complex and developing organism.

The second departure from Bronfenbrenner's position concerns his virtually exclusive emphasis on the social environment, recently also criti-cized by Wohlwill and Heft (in press) and by Stokols (1981b). This omission in Bronfenbrenner's position does not appear to be a fatal flaw and, indeed, it appears that more explicit recognition of the impact of the physical environment on development could be accommodated by his framework with only minor changes. Nor does Bronfenbrenner's omission appear to be unique. Dannefer (1984), in an article focused on criticizing, among others, life-span developmental theory for its lack of explicit attention to contex-tual variables, fails to even mention the physical environment in spite of purporting to present a new, sociogenic paradigm for understanding human development. Our own focus on career development leads to the recognition that the physical environment plays an important role, along with the social environment, in influencing the course of career development.

In spite of some minor departures from Bronfenbrenner's position, we feel that the context of career development can be conceptualized and examined by using his ideas and concepts of the ecological environment. Consequently, the ecology of career development may be described by Bronfenbrenner (1979) as a "nested arrangement of concentric structures, each contained within the next" (p. 22). Each of the structures is related to the others and to the developing person. We turn now to a consideration of the ecological structures and relationships as they pertain to career development.

THE ECOLOGY OF CAREER DEVELOPMENT

It should be clear at this point that we view career development as a complex life-span process whose substance is determined by the developing person in interaction with his/her environment (see also Schein, 1978; Super, 1980). The environment may either directly contain the developing person, such as the family and the place of work, or it may exert its influence indirectly and without containing the developing person, as would be the case with the parents' place of work or the larger cultural context. Bronfenbrenner (1979) has defined four ecological structures to describe the environment: the *microsystem,* which most directly contains the developing person (e.g., one's family, one's workplace); the *mesosystem,* which represents the interrelations among various microsystems (e.g., links between a child's family and school); the *exosystem,* which does not directly contain, but nevertheless does impinge upon, the developing person (e.g., one's spouse's or parent's workplace); and the *macrosystem,* which is the "blueprint" representing overarching cultural belief systems and ideologies that are prevalent in the form and content of the other subsystems (e.g., sex-role prescriptions, child-labor laws).

In our view, ordering the context according to Bronfenbrenner's ecological framework permits an examination of the context as it affects career development in a manner that is far more comprehensive than has been possible thus far. The remainder of this chapter focuses on documenting this assertion. In integrating several divergent domains of literature, our purpose is to point out the specific ecological subsystems important to career development, as well as to discuss how certain features of the more salient ecological subsystems may influence career development. Rather than providing an extensive review of the literature, we draw examples from the literature to illustrate the utility of viewing the context of career development in ecological terms. Where it is appropriate, we point out gaps in the literature. In later chapters, when examining specific issues relevant to the career development of individuals at certain points along the life-span, the literature is discussed in greater detail.

In the following discussion it is important to keep two points in mind. First, as mentioned earlier, Bronfenbrenner (1979) stresses the interconnectedness of the ecological subsystems. One implication of this interconnectedness is that any discussion of one subsystem is somewhat artificial in that the properties of the subsystem under discussion depend on its relationship to, and the properties of, the other subsystems. For example, the impact of the racial/ethnic features of the family on career development, specifically on occupational opportunities, depends in part on the posture of overarching attitudes and legislation aimed towards certain racial/ethnic minorities (characteristics of the macrosystem). To take the example a step further, prior to the civil rights movements and equal opportunity legislation initiated in the 1960s, the economic and occupational opportunities for minorities were far more limited (see Blau & Duncan, 1967) than they were afterwards (see Jaffee, Adams, & Meyers, 1968). Thus, not only is it necessary to understand that the meaning of the features of one subsystem for vocational and career development depend on features of the other subsystems, it is imperative also to acknowledge the nonstatic quality of the ecological subsystems and of the interrelations among the subsystems. This view is in accord with Pepper's (1942) conceptualization of contextualism in which the focus is on *constant change* at all levels of analysis and the *embeddedness* of each level with all levels (see Chapter 2).

The second point to keep in mind when discussing the four ecological subsystems is that all considerations depend on the point of focus. Specifically, as we emphasized when considering the concept of affordance, the impact of the context (or of a given ecological subsystem) depends on the characteristics of the person in focus. When viewing the context in ecological terms, the most important personological characteristic may well be the given individual's location along his or her developmental path. For example, as the child develops, his or her self-regulatory abilities are enhanced and the abstractness of his/her perceptual and cognitive abilities increase (Bandura, 1978; Kopp, 1982); thus, he or she becomes better able to transform, manipulate, conceptualize, or otherwise modify the microsystems (e.g., the classrooms) in which he or she functions. Furthermore, implicit in the ecological view is that depending on one's developmental status, the ecological subsystems *themselves* are different. For example, a parent's workplace, which is a microsystem for him or her, is one of the child's exosystems. Later, with this point in mind, we discuss the ecology of career development from the perspective of the developing child and adolescent who has not yet assumed a worker role. This discussion serves as an example of the type of ecological analysis needed. Another equally important analysis would examine the ecology of career development from the perspective of the adult who has assumed a major role as a worker.

We start with an illustration. When viewing the context of the child or adolescent as it relates to career development, one of the most powerful and consistent environmental predictors of one's occupational aspirations and attainments is the socioeconomic status (however it may be defined) of his or her family of orientation; that is, as two of the present authors observed in a review of the literature (Schulenberg et al., 1984), "the general pattern that emerges is that SES begets SES" (pp. 130–131). With a few notable exceptions (which are later discussed in detail), the research in this area has typically studied groups of children, adolescents, and sometimes adults from families of different socioeconomic backgrounds, found consistent differences in occupational outcomes, and interpreted the findings according to class-theoretical explanations (cf. Lewin, 1935). There is no doubt that this type of research is important in its own right. Nevertheless, as Bronfenbrenner (1982) stated in reference to such research,

> no explicit consideration is given in research operations to intervening structures or processes through which the environment might affect the course of development. One looks only at the *social address*—that is, the environmental label—with no attention to what the environment is like, what people are living there, what they are doing, or how the activities taking place could affect the child ... observed differences in children from one or another setting are "explained" simply as attributes of the child in a given context. (p. 151)

What is lacking, according to the ecological model, is a delineation of the structures, forces, and processes that link social class, which derives meaning from the overarching sociocultural-economic context (macrosystem), to the developing individual. The primary contexts in which the child develops, or the microsystems, need to be examined to discern differences in such factors as interpersonal relations, role models, opportunities, and resources that may covary with social class. In this case, one would be most interested in the family of orientation (but it should be clear that other microsystems, such as the school, peer group, and part-time work settings deserve recognition): What work-related values are being stressed within the home? What are the parent–child relations like? Are there resources to send the child to college?

It also is necessary to look at the relations among the child's several microsystems (i.e., the mesosystems): What is the attitude of the family towards education? Are the activities and expectations consistent across the school and family? Are there similarities between the adolescent's peers and parents according to beliefs and desires regarding the world of work? In addition, it is essential to examine the contexts that do not directly contain the child but nevertheless influence his or her career development (i.e., the exosystems): What is the impact of the type of work a parent does on parenting practices that affect the child? How does the closing of the local steel factory and the consequences that follow impinge upon the adolescent's career plans? If the parents' co-workers are also close friends and frequent visitors to the home, what does the child learn about the world of work?

Finally, it is important to consider the macrosystem and its contribution to the "SES begets SES" link: When the child is ready for college, what is the government's policy towards providing academic loans and grants? What is the cultural or subcultural work ethic? What are the economic situation and the labor market conditions pertaining to the type of occupation that the adolescent aspires to enter? The list of questions could go on, but it should be clear that taking an ecological perspective entails far more than viewing the context simply as the child's social address. As we discuss later, many of the earlier stated questions have been posed in the literature, and there appear to be some rather consistent findings confirming the applicability of the ecological model to career development.

The Microsystem

The microsystem represents that portion of the context that contains the developing person him or herself, and which thus represents the most direct contextual influence on the individual. In acknowledging his indebtedness in the conceptualization of the microsystem to Kurt Lewin's (1935) construct of the life space, Bronfenbrenner (1979) offers the following definition: "A microsystem is a pattern of activities, roles, and interpersonal relations experienced by the developing person in a given setting with particular physical and material characteristics" (p. 22). Activities, interpersonal relations, and roles, which are the "elements" of the setting, provide the links between the developing person and the given context. Activities are defined as forms of *lasting* behaviors, which may or may not have a perceived aim, and, which vary in degree of complexity. Activities can be performed by the individual in focus alone (e.g., a child cleaning his or her room), in relation with others (e.g., a worker and his or her co-workers performing a task together), or by others directed towards the individual in focus (e.g., a teacher providing instruction to the student).

Interpersonal relations refer to dyads, as well as higher order (e.g., N +

2, N + 3) interactions. According to Bronfenbrenner (1979) dyads are "formed whenever two persons pay attention to or participate in one another's activities" (p. 56), and exist in three functional forms: (a) observational dyads, in which one observes the other perform, who in turn acknowledges (at least) the observer; (b) joint-activity dyads, which are characterized by reciprocity, balance of power (not necessarily equal), and affective relations; and (c) primary dyads, which are characterized by strong emotional bonds and continue to be influential even when the two persons are apart. These three forms of dyads are not mutually exclusive; indeed the impact of the dyad may be more powerful for the developing person if it exists in more than one form, which would be the case, for example, when a father trains his son to take over the family business. In addition, dyads themselves develop, which would be represented in the aforementioned example by a gradual change in the balance of power from the father to the son. Of course, dyads do not exist alone, and in any microsystem analysis it is important to consider second order effects. For instance, in continuing with the aforementioned example, the form and development of the father–son dyad may be influenced by the mother–father relationship or by a son–sibling relationship.

Roles are defined by Bronfenbrenner (1979) as sets of "activities and relations expected of a person occupying a particular position in society, and of others in relation to that person" (p. 85). With roles, of course, come role expectations. An examination of roles and role expectations that exist in a given setting may be particularly salient to understanding the context of career development, especially when considering work settings. However, roles in other settings are also important to consider. For example, the role one holds in a peer group, whether it be "leader," "follower," or "peacemaker," may have certain implications for one's career development. Along with these elements of the setting, a microsystem analysis would include a consideration of the physical, material, and structural features of the setting, especially as these features impinge upon the elements of the setting.

There are several microsystem settings that appear to be relevant to understanding the career development of children and adolescents, including the family of orientation, the school setting, the peer group, and the "part-time work"/"odd-job" setting. To illustrate a microsystem analysis, we focus only on the family of orientation. However, the importance of the other microsystems should not be underestimated. Indeed, the school context is perhaps second only to the family in terms of its influence on the career development of children and adolescents. The activities, both coursework related and extracurricular, the interpersonal relations with teachers, other students, and guidance counselors, the various roles and role expectations, and the physical, structural, and material features of the school context, all combine to make the school a salient microsystem. It is through the school that the child is provided with his or her first structured social arena within which to encounter and realize the consequences of social and academic competence, competition, and power relationships (cf. Minuchin & Shapiro, 1983), which may be extremely important to career development. In addition, students experience several important ecological transitions as they progress through the grade levels, transitions that entail movement into progressively and sometimes drastically more complex contexts; the student's ability to master these transitions may well set the stage for the future school-to-work transition.

Peer groups, perhaps the most fluid and least defined microsystems, are also important to career development. The activities that friends engage in allow for the discovery and practice of various skills and interests. Through their peer groups, children and adolescents may be exposed to conceptions about the world of work that may be concordant or discrepant with those of their parents. Finally, the "part-time work"/"odd-job" setting, microsystems that children sometimes encounter quite early (e.g., cutting the neighbors' grass, setting up a lemonade stand, baby-sitting), would obviously be important to career development. Through such settings, children and adolescents gain experience in the worker role (e.g., the exchange of services for money), as well as in potentially career-related skills and interests.

We begin our ecological analysis of the family microsystem with a quote by Bachman (1970):

> Family background is a powerful force—or, more accurately, a cluster of powerful forces—shaping an individual's capacities and accomplishments throughout his lifetime. The educational and occupational attainments of parents, the physical resources of the home, the personal relationships between parents and children—these factors and many more are what we mean by family background. The impact of this background is visible early in the life of a child; his intelligence and ability to perform in school are in part predictable from knowledge of his background. Later, in adolescence, his educational and occupational aspirations are predictable in part from the attainments of his parents. Still later, his own attainments reflect quite clearly the stamp of his family background. . . . (W)e tend sometimes to think of the family *environment* as the primary determinant of the effects mentioned above. But many factors that cause different family environments are also implicated in different *genetic* endowments. Thus we are dealing with both nature and nurture—and the two are closely intertwined in each individual's family background. (p. 1)

This quote by Bachman (1970) raises two important points. The first, of course, is the acknowledgement that the family context is a complex web of several powerful forces that influence the career development of children.

The second point concerns the recognition that the family's influence does not operate solely through environmental forces; that is, the family microsystem is unique in that its influence on children's career development is the product of a combination of environmental and genetic forces. The genotypic transmission of abilities, temperament, and physical stature (attributes whose expression would clearly depend on the individual's interaction with the environment) may be an important component of the family's impact on career development. It is likely that a son whose biological father is a professional basketball player (known for his ability to touch the net without jumping), and whose biological mother is a large woman with an active interest in suma wrestling, will not become a professional jockey. As obvious as this point may be, it is not typically recognized in the literature concerning family influence on career development (see, however, Roe, 1964).

In one notable exception, Grotevant (1979) found greater similarity between the vocational interests of adolescents and parents of biological families than between those of adolescents and parents of adoptive families. It is important to note that in this study the biological and adoptive families were similar along salient parental features (e.g., education, income, degree of husband–wife similarities in vocational interests), and that 92% of the adolescents from adoptive families were adopted before they were 6 months of age. Thus, although Grotevant's (1979) study leaves some issues unanswered (e.g., do parents in biological families expect their children to be more similar to them than do parents in adoptive families?), it seems reasonable that both environmental and hereditary forces must be recognized when delineating the family's influence on career development. This point should be kept in mind as we move on to a detailed consideration of the elements and features of the family context. The discussion that follows first focuses on the activities, interpersonal relations, and roles occurring within the family context, and then on structural, physical, and material features.

The Elements of the Family Setting.   Activities, interpersonal relations, and roles, can be viewed as the mechanisms of occupational socialization; that is, what the child learns about the world of work from the parents (and siblings) takes the form of: (a) activities the child is taught, encouraged, or disciplined to do (or not to do); (b) interpersonal relations through which learning occurs; and (c) the roles the child views and is taught to participate in.

As is the case within the larger domain of human development, very little is empirically known about the molar activities that children engage in, alone or with others, which may be important to their career development (cf. Bronfenbrenner, 1979). It is not unreasonable to assume, however, that the games young children play or the chores they perform, for example, have implications for career development. As Goldstein and Oldham (1979) observed in their study on children's socialization towards work, "children's work and learning experiences (1) typically start in early childhood on a *very* small scale; (2) are extremely widespread; and (3) apparently are subject to age-related increments" (p. 169). Depending on the goals of various activities, children are exposed to notions of competition, cooperation, rewards as the result of accomplishments, or more generally, "the rules of the game." As a function of age, or more correctly, of experience and development, children may be provided with or seek out more complex activities (e.g., increased temporal sequences, incorporation of a wider conception of the ecological terrain), which in turn may provide lessons in responsibility and practice in manipulating the environment to produce desired outcomes.

As noted previously, activities that also need to be considered are those directed at the child or adolescent. Of major concern here are child-rearing practices, which are activities with explicit, as well as implicit, purposefulness. In discussing the literature on the effects of parenting practices on children's work orientations, Lueptow, McClendon, and McKeon (1979) state that there is considerable evidence demonstrating the link between: "(1) socialization emphasis upon achievement and independence training; and (2) acquisition of achievement orientations (in children). . . . Achievement, and especially independence training in families of egalitarian relationships or low parental dominance, results in higher levels of achievement orientation, educational and occupational aspirations and achieving performances" (p. 465) (see also Anderson & Evans, 1976). Parents' actions can also take a more direct course, which would be the case when they actively attempt to foster a specific type of career in their child.

It would be expected that interpersonal relations occurring within the family context, particularly parent–child relations, are important to the child's career development. If the parent–child dyad is characterized by a strong emotional bond (i.e., a primary dyad), then the parent may have more influence on the child's behavior and development (and, as well, the child would have more influence on the parent). As Bronfenbrenner (1979) stated:

> Such dyads are viewed as exerting a powerful force in motivating learning and steering the course of development, both in the presence and absence of the other person. Thus, a child is more likely to acquire skills, knowledge, and values from a person with whom a primary dyad has been established. (p. 58)

Indeed, there is considerable evidence suggesting that parent–child relations serve as mediators of the occupational socialization process. For example, Mortimer and Kumka (1982) have demonstrated that a close relationship between father and son is a crucial component of the "occupational linkage hypothesis" (Kohn, 1969; Lueptow et al., 1979; Mortimer, 1976; Mortimer & Kumka, 1982, Spenner, 1981)—which is essentially a conceptual model linking characteristics of father's occupation with child's psychological attributes via father's psychological attributes and socialization practices (see the following discussion concerning the exosystem influences of parent's work on children's career development); that is, the similarities between fathers' and sons' occupations along both vertical (e.g., prestige) and nonvertical (e.g., extent of work autonomy, extrinsic or intrinsic rewards) dimensions were found to be greatest when fathers were occupationally successful and when sons reported a close and supportive relationship with their fathers (see also Mortimer, 1976).

Additional evidence for the importance of family relationships to career development comes from the Youth in Transition project, which was a longitudinal investigation of career development in a national sample of males as they progressed from high school through young adulthood. Using the first wave of data, Bachman (1970) found a positive and moderate correlation between the quality of parent–son relations (as measured by the son's reports of closeness with mother, closeness with father, parental consultation with son, and parental punitiveness) and occupational and educational aspirations. Parenthetically, it should be noted that a causal direction cannot be inferred from this study, nor from Mortimer and Kumka's study (their results were based on a conceptually derived, fully recursive causal model); that is, it is possible too that the son's choice to aim for higher status occupations and more education, or to follow in his father's occupational foot steps, led to greater harmony with parents.

One component of parent–child relations that appears to be particularly salient to the child's career development is parental support. Parental support can take many forms, including financial support for college or other educational opportunities, as well as encouragement and favorable attitudes towards the child's choice of career. Although both types of support are important, and probably at least moderately interrelated, we are referring here to the latter form of parental support. Consistent with Bronfenbrenner's notions of dyads and their development, when members of the dyad take an active interest in each others activities, the dyad becomes more powerful and the members become more influential to each other's development. This notion appears to be especially relevant when considering females' career development. Males are automatically socialized into the worker role; parental support for engaging in occupationally relevant activities is a given in most cases. For females, however, even though the past two decades have witnessed a dramatic rise in women's labor-force participation, parental support of a career for their daughter is not as automatic (e.g., Hauser, 1971; Peterson, Rollins, Thomas, & Heaps, 1982). Of related interest, there appears to be a rather consistent finding that women aspiring to or engaged in nontraditional occupations tend to report receiving support for their career decisions from one or both parents (e.g., Cartwright, 1972; Hennig, 1974; Standley & Soule, 1974; Tenzer, 1977; Weitz, 1977). In a review of this literature, Auster and Auster (1981) concluded that women are more likely to enter nontraditional careers if *both* parents are supportive of their decision.

Although the literature appears to implicate the parent–child relationship as being quite salient to the child's career development, the familial interpersonal context entails many more interpersonal relations, which also may be important to career development. The child's relationships with his or her siblings, as well as higher order influences on parent–child or sibling–sibling relations (e.g., the influence of the mother–father relationship on the mother–son relationship) are potential but empirically untested sources of influence on the child's career development.

Roles and role expectations represent the last of the three elements of the family microsystem. There are many ways in which roles could be important to career development. For example, family roles can be viewed in terms of power relationships (e.g., "I'm the father, you're the son—that means you do what I say"). In addition, roles can be viewed as the part one plays in maintaining familial functioning patterns. In advocating a family system perspective when delineating the family's influence on career development, Bratcher (1982) stated:

> It is the family's rules and myths that influence the establishment and maintenance of roles for family members and the development and maintenance of family beliefs and values that in turn influence the development and maintenance of family traditions. It is these guiding or operating principles that provide the major link of the family to past and future generations.... This will be perhaps the most important variable to be considered when children begin to think in terms of a career choice. (p. 88)

Perhaps the most important way in which roles and role expectations link the family microsystem and children's career development entails the roles children *learn* in the context of the family setting. Parents are children's first, and perhaps foremost, work-role and sex-role models. Through the perception of, identification with, and practice in "playing" parental work and sex roles, children begin to grasp notions concerning societal role expectations and to fantasize about what work role they might eventually assume (Ginzberg, Ginsburg, Axelrad, & Herma, 1951; Nemerowicz, 1979). Indeed, Havighurst (1964) proposed that the major vocational developmental task for 5-to-10-year-olds is to identify with the worker role of parents (or of other significant persons).

In terms of females' career development, there is considerable empirical consensus that maternal employment is the single most powerful predictor of daughters' career salience and aspirations for nontraditional careers (see Auster & Auster, 1981; Huston-Stein & Higgins-Trenk, 1978; Lerner & Galambos, 1985b; Tangri, 1972, for reviews of this literature). Although simply positing the working mother as a significant role model for her daughter has limited explanatory value (Bronfenbrenner & Crouter, 1982; Schulenberg et al., 1984), the mother's role, whether it be homemaker or worker, is bound to affect the daughter's conception of her own role in the world of work. It is important to note that although children are generally viewed as aligning their roles in accord with those of the same-sex parent, cross-sex parents have also been found to be significant role models important to children's career development (e.g., Banducci, 1967; Crites, 1962; Hennig, 1974; Standley & Soule, 1974).

Clearly, an examination of the elements linking the family context to children's and adolescents' career development provides a richer and more complex view of the family's impact on vocational development. Although the preceding discussion was intended to be illustrative and not comprehensive, it should leave no doubt that the ecological model permits a highly differentiated view of the family context. Further differentiation is seen as we turn now to a discussion of the structural, material and physical features of the family setting.

Structural, Material, and Physical Features of the Family Setting.   The structural features of the family, including family size, birth order, and single parenthood, have been given a fair amount of attention in reference to their impact on occupational and educational aspirations and attainments in the sociological literature. As noted, however, most of this research depicts the structural features of the family in terms of the child's "social address." For example, it is fairly well documented that family size (i.e., number of siblings) is inversely related to both the status of children's occupational aspirations and attainments, as well as to their educational aspirations and attainments (e.g., Bachman, 1970; Bachman, O'Malley, & Johnston, 1978; Blau & Duncan, 1967; Duncan, Featherman, & Duncan, 1972; Featherman & Hauser, 1976; McClendon, 1976; Olneck & Bills, 1979; Rehberg & Westby, 1967). It should be noted that these relationships hold even when family SES (which tends to be negatively correlated with family size) is accounted for. However, from an ecological perspective, it would be necessary to consider how family size impinges on the elements of the setting that are important to career development; that is, it would be important to consider such factors as parental support, parent–child relations, socialization practices, roles, and activities, which covary with family size. For example, among male high school seniors, Schenk and Emerick (1976) found that those from larger families tended to perceive their parents as being less supportive and less able to be supportive (for time reasons) in terms of pursuing higher education than did those from smaller families.

Birth order explanations of career choice have long been a popular topic among the public and research community, which began, perhaps, with the work of Francis Galton in 1874. (In studying the family backgrounds of famous English scientists, Galton found that proportionally more were firstborns.) For the most part, studies in this area have attempted to demonstrate that, because firstborns tend to be more organizing, controlling, and directing, whereas laterborns tend to be more sociable, sympathetic, and empathetic, siblings would choose vocations consistent with these order-related traits; that is, birth order has been typically used to indicate children's social addresses. However, although birth order differences have been found in educational attainment (e.g., Blau & Duncan, 1967; see however, Bachman, 1970) and nontraditional career choices among women (Auster & Auster, 1981), the research concerning birth order differences for *specific* types of career choices (e.g., dentist, lawyer) has yielded inconsistent and contradictory results. In a review of the literature, Gandy (1974) argues that although methodological deficiencies are partly to blame for inconclusive findings in this area, much of the blame lies in the predominant focus on searching for birth order differences common across families; that is, Gandy asserts that if birth order differences exist for specific career choices, they are to be found within families. For example, in studying the career interests among siblings from three-sibling families, Verger (1968) found that the interests of the first and third siblings were more similar than were those of the first and second siblings. Verger explained these results in terms of sibling roles, activities, alliances, and rivalries (e.g., the first antagonizes the second, the second antagonizes the third, who in turn receives "protection" from the first). Gandy's argument and Verger's findings provide evidence for the necessity of going beyond using birth order as a social address and focusing on the elements of the family setting.

Sibling spacing, although not a topic explored in terms of career development, may nevertheless be an important structural feature of the family setting. Zajonc (1976; Zajonc & Markus, 1975) proposed a "confluence model", which posits sibling spacing as a mediator of intellectual functioning. Essentially, the model (which is based on data obtained from over 400,000 Dutch adolescents) predicts that the larger the spacing between the siblings, the more likely that older siblings will serve as "teachers" rather than rivals to the younger siblings. Thus the focus is on sibling roles and relationships. As a result, the "intellectual environment" of the home increases with the extent of spacing between siblings. Whether this confluence model has implications for career development is unknown. Nevertheless, it is useful in drawing links between sibling spacing (a structural feature) and the elements of the family setting.

Single parenthood has not been systematically studied in terms of its impact on career development. From research using single parenthood as an indicator of children's social address, it appears that males from single parent households tend to aspire to and attain less education and lower status occupations than do males from two parent families (e.g., Bachman, 1970; Bachman et al., 1978; Blau & Duncan, 1967). However, even as a social address variable, single parenthood may not be that useful, in that several mediating factors (e.g., age of child when one parent departs, financial and supportive resources available to the single parent) operate in determining the outcomes of single parenthood on the intellectual and career development of children (Biller, 1971; Schulenberg et al., 1984; Zajonc, 1976). Nevertheless, single parenthood may be a salient structural feature of the family setting, and again, exploiting this variable for its explanatory value would entail a consideration of how single parenthood impinges on the elements of the setting. For example, Weiss (1979) suggests that when divorce occurs, older siblings assume a more parental role in the family.

From our discussion of the structural features of the family it should be apparent that from an ecological perspective, the salience of these features for career development derives mainly from their impact on the activities, interpersonal relations, and roles occurring within the family microsystem. A similar statement could be made regarding the material and physical features of the family setting. Although neither the material nor the physical features of the family setting have been systematically studied in terms of their impact on career development, they nevertheless appear to be implicitly encompassed in family SES level; that is, the quality and quantity of the material and physical environment are assumed to covary with family SES. For example, the number and type of books in the family setting, the number of rooms in the family household, and the presence of radios, televisions, are sometimes included as measures of family SES (e.g., Bachman, 1970). In such cases, the physical and material features are considered as indices of, once again, the social address.

What is needed, of course, is a focus on how the material and physical features impinge on the elements of the setting. For example, how are sibling interactions that are important to career development affected by the physical layout of the home? (e.g., do the two siblings share a bedroom?). Research on proxemics (e.g., the impact of physical space and organization on social interactions), and environmental stressors (Stokols, 1978) may prove instructive in this respect. The noise level within the home, for example, has been found to be inversely related to children's reading achievement and auditory discrimination (Cohen, Glass, & Singer, 1973), as well as to children's proficiency on selective attention tasks and sensitivity to auditory distraction (Wohlwill & Heft, 1978). It may also prove useful to draw from the work of Barker and his associates (1968; Barker & Gump, 1964; Barker & Wright, 1955; see also Wicker, McGrath, & Armstrong, 1972) on behavior settings, particularly on the notion of under, adequate, and overmanning (i.e., the ratio of persons to activities) as it relates to roles and activities occurring within the family setting. For example, it would be important to discover whether the general finding that, in smaller schools (typically involving a situation of undermanning), students tend to experience greater involvement and responsibility, is a phenomenon which transfers to the family setting (e.g., Garbarino & Asp, 1981). The lack of empirical research in this area, however, precludes any conclusive statements concerning the impact of physical and material features of the family setting on career development.

From our illustrative analysis of the family microsystem, it should be apparent that viewing the primary contexts of career development according to an ecological perspective entails far more than simply delineating the "social address." Of course, comprehensiveness is gained at the expense of simplicity. Nevertheless, explicating the links between career development and primary contexts necessitates a conceptual basis, which does not deny the inherent complexity. We turn now to a consideration of the portion of the context beyond the microsystems. As we leave behind the focus on primary settings, we also leave behind most of the systematic research; that is, there are few empirical studies that have attended to the more distal components of the context as they relate to career development. Nevertheless, in drawing from the conceptual work of Bronfenbrenner (1979) and others, a framework for viewing the context of career development beyond primary settings can be devised.

The Mesosystems

Bronfenbrenner (1979) defines a mesosystem as "a set of interrelations between two or more settings in which the developing person becomes an active participant" (p. 209). The primary building blocks of the mesosystem are the same as those for the microsystem: molar activities, interpersonal relations, and role transactions. As Bronfenbrenner (1979) stated: "The difference lies in the nature of the interconnections involved. At the microsystem level, the (elements) . . . all occur within one setting, whereas in the mesosystem these processes take place across setting boundaries" (p. 209).

The interrelations among the settings can take several forms, with the most fundamental form entailing *multisetting participation,* which occurs when one individual participates in two or more settings (e.g., home and school, workplace and interpersonal network). Because settings are experienced sequentially, an important component of multisetting participation is the ecological transition (Bronfenbrenner, 1979). As we discussed earlier, ecological transitions occur when the developing person moves from one setting to another. Thus, in unraveling the effects of the transitions from school to work, from one position or occupation to another, or from work to retirement, a mesosystem analysis would be particularly instructive. Interrelations among the settings can also take the forms of: *indirect linkage,* which occurs when the individual is not an active participant in the two settings but is nevertheless joined to both settings through his or her relationship with an individual who actively participates in the two settings (e.g., the relationship between a parent and a teacher, in which the common link is the child); *intersetting communication,* which concerns the transmission of information from one setting to another (e.g., via a "report card"); and *intersetting knowledge,* which entails information or experience gained in one setting concerning another setting (e.g., school courses geared towards providing work-related information and experience) (Bronfenbrenner, 1979).

There are several mesosystems important to the career development of children and adolescents, including the various sets of interrelations among the family, school, peer group, and part-time work setting. Although empirical and conceptual work linking the various mesosystems to career development is lacking, it is possible to consider what knowledge might be gained through a mesosystem analysis. For example, it is rather apparent that academic success tends to be more likely to occur as one moves up the social-class ladder (cf. Schulenberg & Garbarino, 1985). Equally apparent is that many middle-class values are inherent in our educational system. Schulenberg and Garbarino (1985) state: "the academic culture tends to be rooted in value codes of adults that are associated with middle-class experiences, resources, and goals. But the connection (between background SES and school success) is not inevitable. The real issue is one of values rather than income". (p. 389) Hence, by focusing on the family–school mesosystem, it is possible to discover the extent of congruence between the educational values extant in both settings, thus adding explanatory information to the previously mentioned SES-begets-SES phenomenon. In a similar fashion, one could analyze the link between the family and peer network. For example, it has been found that adolescents are more likely to follow a given career path when both parental encouragement and peer aspirations are in accord (e.g., Kandel & Lesser, 1969; Simpson, 1962).

A particularly salient mesosystem for the career development of adolescents is the link between school and work. This mesosystem sometimes consists of the relationship between school and current work setting, which would be the case for the various government and school sponsored work programs (see Sherraden, 1980; Steinberg, 1983, for reviews of this literature). For the most part, however, the school–work link pertains to the inter-relations between school and the future work setting. According to Bronfenbrenner (1979) "Development is enhanced to the extent that, prior to each entry into a new setting... the person and members of both settings involved are provided with information, advice, and experience relevant to the impending transition" (p. 217). The school is a primary provider of "intersetting knowledge" for the student, as well as for potential employers.

For example, several high school courses (typically vocational or busi-ness courses) are aimed towards providing work-relevant information and experience. In addition, one of the primary functions of school guidance counselors is to provide information about future career prospects. Schools also provide the credentials (e.g., diplomas, certificates) necessary to pur-sue higher education or meet the minimal requirements of obtaining cer-tain jobs (cf. Schulenberg & Garbarino, 1985; Squires, 1979). The adequacy of these components of the school–work link in preparing the adolescent for the impending ecological transition into the world of work is crucial and has been of concern to educators, employers, and policymakers (e.g., Anderson & Sawhill, 1980; Princeton Manpower Symposium, 1968; Squires, 1979). In fact, the school is often viewed as the primary target for efforts to curb the youth unemployment situation. As Anderson and Sawhill (1980) stated: "The search for more effective strategies for dealing with youth employment problems in the years ahead will lead invariably toward a larger role for public school systems. Unquestionably, the schools will have to play a stronger role in preparing youth for the job market" (p. 151). Of course, there are problems associated with relying on the schools to solve the various social problems (cf. Schulenberg & Garbarino, 1985), and, as Squires (1979) points out, several employers prefer to train their own employees upon entry regardless of prior training. Nevertheless, it appears that a "strong" link between school and future work is imperative for a successful transition into the world of work. By viewing this link from a mesosystem perspective, it is possible to examine the extent of congruence between the elements of both settings and thus pinpoint the stronger and weaker portions of the link.

The Exosystems

Exosystems are defined by Bronfenbrenner (1979) as "consisting of one or more settings that do not involve the developing person as an active participant but in which events occur that affect, or are affected by, what happens in that setting" (p. 237). Again, the building blocks of the exosystems are the same as those for the two lower order systems: molar activities, interpersonal relations, and role transactions. As Bronfenbrenner indicates, to demonstrate that an exosystem is operating, it is necessary to establish causal sequences connecting external events to processes within the microsystem, as well as connecting these microsystem processes to changes in the developing person, a requirement that has not been met thus far in the career development literature.

There are several exosystems that may be important to the career development of children and adolescents. For example, events occurring within the community, over which the developing child or adolescent has little or no control (e.g., the school board's decision to hire two computer science teachers rather than two music instructors, or a major employer within the community attempting to create a better liason with the schools by instituting work study programs) may have significant implications for his or her career development. Another example of exosystem influences is apparent in a situation in which the focal individual's older brother is experiencing extreme behavioral difficulties in the school setting, and as a result the processes within the focal individual's home and/or school setting may change. This, in turn, may cause changes in his or her career development because of altered perceptions of the focal individual (perhaps through a process of "guilt by association") on the part of parents, peers, and teachers.

Perhaps one of the most important exosystems for the developing child or adolescent is the parents' workplace. The research by Kohn and Schooler (Kohn, 1969; Kohn & Schooler, 1973, 1978, 1983), as well as the research that has focused on the "occupational linkage hypothesis" (e.g., Lueptow et al., 1979; Mortimer, 1976; Mortimer & Kumka, 1982; Spenner, 1981) has provided some clear, but not conclusive, evidence demonstrating the causal link between characteristics of the parents' workplace and socialization practices, and the career-relevant processes and outcomes in the child.

Based on concepts forwarded by Aberle and Naegele (1952) and McKinley (1964) regarding the link between parental work autonomy and child-rearing practices, Kohn initiated a series of studies in an effort to explicate the link between occupations, the value of and orientation toward conformity, and socialization practices. In a 1964 nationwide sample of working-class and middle-class men, Kohn (1969) found that the men tended to hold values for themselves and about their children consistent with the demands of their jobs. Specifically, working-class men, whose jobs required compliance with authority, tended to value obedience and conformity in their children, whereas middle-class men, whose jobs depended more on self-direction, tended to value initiative and independence in their children. Furthermore, punishment practices tended to covary with these values and orientations, with working-class parents favoring physical punishment and middle-class parents favoring psychological punishment. In addition, the working-class parents tended to punish their children according to the consequences of the child's actions, whereas the middle-class parents focused more on the child's intentions in using punishment. Although Kohn was not able to separate the impact of education and occupational position on these values and practices, subsequent studies using the same cross-sectional data plus 10-year follow-up data (Kohn & Schooler, 1973, 1978), permitted an assessment of the independent effects of occupational characteristics. Specifically, Kohn and Schooler conducted causal modeling analyses to demonstrate the causal link between occupational self-direction (e.g., the extent to which a job requires autonomy and complex skills) and intellectual flexibility 10 years later.

Hence, they were able to draw causal links between characteristics of the job and parenting values. Nevertheless, as Kohn and Schooler (1983) recently pointed out, "we have not looked beyond parental values, as if the very fact of parent's valuing self-direction or conformity to external authority necessarily implied that parents would behave appropriately to their values and events that parents' values would be successfully transmitted to their children. We do not so believe" (p. 309); that is, although the causal sequence between characteristics of the job setting and intellectual flexibility and values was demonstrated, the causal link between parental intellectual flexibility and values and career developmental outcomes in their children was not demonstrated.

Nevertheless, Mortimer's work on the intergenerational transmission of vertical and nonvertical components of occupations suggests that a full causal sequence may indeed be operating. In a secondary analysis of longitudinal data collected from college males during 1962–1967, Mortimer (1974) found a strong tendency for college males to choose occupations similar to their fathers' occupations along vertical (e.g., prestige, income) and nonvertical (e.g., extent of work autonomy, intrinsic occupational rewards, job complexity) dimensions. In a subsequent analysis, Mortimer (1976) demonstrated that occupational transmission was mediated by the father–son relationship. Specifically, she found that the extent of occupational transmission (along vertical and nonvertical dimensions) was greatest when the sons reported a close father–son relationship, and when the father's occupational status was high.

Further information regarding specific types of occupations and intergenerational transmission is provided by Mortimer (1975) and Mortimer and Kumka (1982). From the 1962–1967 data set, Mortimer (1975) focused on male college seniors from business families and from professional families. She found that professional-family sons were more concerned about the intrinsic values of their expected occupation and less concerned about the extrinsic values (e.g., high income and advancement), whereas the opposite was true for business-family sons. Again, a close father–son relationship (as measured by sons' perception) was an important mediator of "people-oriented" values. Mortimer and Kumka (1982) conducted a 10-year follow-up on the aforementioned sample. In conclusion they stated: "In the business families, both the father's occupational success and parental support were found to intensify sons' extrinsic values and further income attainment. In the professional families, these variables instead encourage the development of people-oriented values and the attainment of work with high social content following college" (p. 13).

It should be noted that Mortimer's initial findings were not replicated by Lueptow et al. (1979). However, Mortimer and Kumka (1982) made a strong case that the missing link in Lueptow et al's. research (among other problems) was the father–son relationship. Specifically, as we mentioned before, the quality of the father–son relationship (e.g., warmth and support) mediates occupational transmission. This fits quite well with the pronounced ecological focus on the elements occurring within the settings. Nevertheless, even with the coupling of Kohn's and Mortimer's work, the existence of the two-part causal sequence required to confirm an exosystem is not demonstrated.

The work of Kohn and Mortimer and their associates (see also, Miller, Schooler, Kohn, & Miller, 1979; Spenner, 1981) is important in at least two respects. First, their work represents a large portion of the total research efforts that have sought to discover exosystem relationships (cf. Bronfenbrenner, 1979), and future research efforts would do well to follow their lead. Secondly, their work provides a strong foothold for delineating the origins of the SES-begets-SES phenomenon. Specifically, they go far beyond treating social class simply as a social address variable and delve into explicating the links between distal contextual forces and the developing individual.

The Macrosystem

The macrosystem represents the final and highest order ecological subsystem. Bronfenbrenner (1979) defines it as "the consistency observed within a given culture or subculture in the form and content of its constituent micro-, meso-, and exosystems, as well as any belief systems or ideology underlying such consistencies" (p. 258). Thus, the macrosystem is the overarching "blueprint" of cultures and subcultures. We may speak of the impact of the macrosystem on the career development of children and adolescents in several ways. For our purposes it is instructive to consider the macrosystem and its impact on career development according to: (a) cultural and subcultural influences; and (b) history-graded influences (cohort effects).

Because an entire volume could be devoted to the subject, it is well beyond the scope of this chapter to do justice to the topic of cultural and subcultural influences on career development. Rather, our intent is to illustrate the operation of macrosystem influences in shaping career development. In addition, it is essential to note that we do not consider crosscultural and subcultural differences in terms of a "deficit model." John Ogbu's (1981) discussion of human competence from a cultural ecological perspective is relevant here. Ogbu rejects the "universal model" of human development that attributes nonmajority failures in achieving majority competencies to deficiencies in nonmajority child-rearing practices. Ogbu (1981) argues that

> child rearing in the family and similar micro settings in the early years of life and subsequent socialization of adolescents are geared toward the development of instrumental competencies required for adult economic, political, and social roles. These cultural imperatives vary from one cultural group to another as do the required competencies. In the United States, they are different for the white middle class and for minority groups like urban ghetto blacks. (p. 413)

Ogbu further states that "in every relatively stable human population, instrumental competencies have prior existence before individual families which teach these competencies to their offspring through the process of childrearing" (p. 418).

A good example of crosscultural differences in career development is provided by Osuji's (1976) study of Nigerian adolescents. He found that Nigerian students tended to choose and commit themselves to careers much earlier than do students from more industrialized Western societies. In addition, he found that intergenerational transmission of occupational status was weaker than is typical in Western societies. Osuji attributed these differences between Nigerian and Western students to such factors as relative economic and technological underdevelopment, limited job opportunities, lack of vocational guidance, high job obsolescence, strong societal presses towards upward mobility, and strong extended family obligations (e.g., the use of elite relatives as liasons) extant in the Nigerian social–economic context.

Although Osuji's study highlighted cultural differences in career development, Osipow (1983, p. 251) notes that there are also many similarities in career development across national and cultural boundaries. The important point to be made is that through utilization of ecological analysis greater and more precise attention can be paid to cultural features important in career development.

In many countries the diversity of the population is such that important differences exist within a given cultural context. As an example of such subcultural differences in career development, Gross (1967) studied two Jewish middle-class groups, one Ashkenazic and the other Sephardic. The former group places a high value on intellectual development through verbally mediated interaction and conceptual language; in short, it strives to optimize the academic culture. The latter group does not stress traditional academic development and academic culture. The differences between the children from these two groups, with respect to the traditional academic culture, are as great as between any different social class groups. The Ashkenazic children are competent in the school setting (and its related standardized testing situations) whereas the Sephardic children (despite their affluence) do poorly. Nevertheless, because of their access to commercial opportunities and training in commercial competence, the Sephardic children can expect to replicate their parents' economic success. Social class and cultural values are separable and distinct here. Each tends to reproduce itself, so the affluent make money whereas the traditionally academically sophisticated do well in school and may make money as well.

In both of the aforementioned examples, and in line with Ogbu's (1981) notions concerning the cultural origins of human competence, the links between the macrosystem, or cultural "blueprint," and the developing individual are demonstrated quite clearly, showing that culture and subculture represent potent macrosystem influences on career development. It is necessary, however, to be mindful of Bronfenbrenner's emphasis on studying not just environmental or contextual differences but to examine the processes by which such differences impact the course of human development.

Another major macrosystem influence, historical change, is particularly important in the study of career development from a life-span developmental perspective. As we have previously noted, this perspective involves the simultaneous study of the changing individual in a changing context. The effects of historical change on the individual have been labeled *cohort* effects (e.g., Baltes, 1968; Baltes, Cornelius, & Nesselroade, 1978). One of the most illustrative studies of such cohort effects is Elder's (1974) influential study of two cohorts of children who experienced the Great Depression. The first cohort included those born in the early 1920s who grew up in Oakland, California, and the second cohort included those born in the late 1920s who grew up in Berkeley, California. Thus, the Oakland cohort were beyond childhood during the Great Depression years, whereas the Berkeley cohort experienced the Great Depression during their childhood. To detect the differential impact of the Great Depression on life patterns according to timing in the life course, Elder (1974, 1979) investigated differences between the two cohorts across their life-spans. In addition, to detect potential variations according to intracohort differences, such factors as the social class of the family, the extent of relative deprivation experienced by the family, the strength of the parents' marital relationship, and the sex of the child were considered. Of special interest here is the finding that the Berkeley cohort boys fared less well than their Oakland counterparts. Elder (1979) states: "On the basis of this study, the timing of economic deprivation in the course of preadult development has the greatest consequence for the well-being of boys; the earlier the event of economic loss, the more pathogenic its effect on male development" (p. 155). Furthermore, in the Berkeley sample, it was found that economic loss served to weaken the father–son bond and strengthen the mother–daughter bond, and that this pattern was exacerbated by a weak marital relationship prior to the Depression. This weakening or strengthening of parent–child bonds most likely influenced the career development of these children (especially in light of Mortimer's findings discussed earlier); however, Elder did not explicitly focus on the children's career development. He did find, however, that even though the Berkeley boys from deprived families were worse off than their non-deprived peers in terms of adolescent functioning, they did appear to reverse their prospects and experience a relatively productive and healthy adulthood.

Finally, we should note that Bronfenbrenner's appeal to scientists to study and participate in the formulation of public policy is particularly appropriate in examining the impact of the macrosystem on development. Changes in public policy toward minorities and women (e.g., the Economic Opportunity Act of 1964; the Civil Rights Act of 1964) have all but revolutionized the workplace in the United States. Labor laws, minimum wage laws, government sponsorship of training programs, and many other public policies are also responsible for other rapid and significant macrolevel changes that represent immensely powerful influences on career development across the entire life-span.

CONCLUSIONS

It has been our aim in this chapter to illustrate the complexity and variety of contextual influences on career development and to document, by relying heavily on Bronfenbrenner's (1979) ecological model of human development, how this orientation can lead to a more orderly, systematic, and comprehensive understanding of the context as it impacts career development. Out of necessity we have been selective in our discussion, focusing on the context of vocational or career development from the perspective of the child and adolescent. We noted that the same type of ecological analysis needs to be performed for other age-groups across the life-span. In the following chapter we make an attempt to present an integration of our conceptualization of development, presented in Chapter 2, and our views on the context, presented in the present chapter.

4

A Life-Span
Developmental Approach
to Career Development

In the introductory chapter the point was made that the proper conceptualization of career development required an understanding of developmental concepts; consequently, Chapter 2 was devoted to an explication of the mechanistic, the organismic, and the contextually oriented models of development. It was concluded that an integration of the organismic and contextual models into what was called a developmental-contextual model would be the most useful way of conceptualizing development. In Chapter 3 it was the context of development that was the focus of attention; it was concluded that the context, whether viewed in a global or specific way, from a proximal or a distal, or from a micro or a macroperspective, is an integral and necessary component of any explanatory scheme that tries to account for human development.

Career development, including the initial development of a vocational role as well as the progression of a career over time, can be conceptualized as one feature—albeit a very central one—of a person's development. As such, career development is properly examined with the same lens as cognitive development, moral development, or physical development: In each instance individual development can be shown to have important bidirectional links to a changing social context. For example, parents are clearly affected by the context of their work or career environment. This has potential ramifications for the development of children within the family, and children, in turn, influence the functioning of parents at work, and thus the parents' career development.

With individual development having such bidirectional links to a changing social context, two arguments may be raised. First, one must forego an exclusively psychological analysis of individual (career) development. Instead, one should seek models that emphasize the multilevel bases of human functioning and the connections among levels. Second, if the course of human development is responsive to variables from multiple levels of analysis, then the processes of development are "more plastic," more subject to change, than often previously believed.

There is a growing theoretical and empirical literature that supports these arguments. To a great extent this literature has been associated with a life-span view of human development, an orientation to the study of development, which is consistent with the developmental-contextual perspective presented in Chapter 2. The life-span perspective provides us with a developmental framework with which to approach the discussion of the individual-social context relations we see as involved in vocational and career development. As such, it is useful to present some of the key ideas and features of the perspective.

Before we proceed to take a closer look at the life-span human development perspective, it may be useful to observe that just as developmental psychology has moved toward a life-span perspective so has the field of career development. Friedman and Wallace (1968) stated the prevailing view of their time as follows:

> One of the major milestones in the life of a person is reached when he begins to contemplate job interests and opportunities and to make plans to obtain the education and skills required for the work of his choice. For most individuals in Western culture, this process is begun in late adolescence and completed soon thereafter. (p. 246)

This occupational choice view must be contrasted with a career development view that is being expressed much more frequently today. Super (1981) summarizes this view in the following way:

> studies of the life span and life space have made it clear that occupational choice or assignment is not something that happens once in a lifetime, on leaving school or the university . . . people and situations develop and . . . a career decision tends to be a series of minidecisions of varying degrees of importance. (p. 38)

Although it is gratifying to observe this apparent shift toward a life-span developmental perspective (see, for example, Levinson, Darrow, Klein, Levinson, & McKee, 1978; Schein, 1971; Super, 1980), a better understanding of the implications of the life-span human developmental perspective could significantly advance theory, research, and intervention in the field of career development (Vondracek, Lerner, & Schulenberg, 1983a; Vondracek & Schulenberg, (in press).

THE LIFE-SPAN VIEW OF HUMAN DEVELOPMENT

The "life-span view of human development" (Baltes, 1979a; Baltes, Reese, & Lipsitt, 1980) has become crystallized over the course of several conferences (Baltes & Schaie, 1973; Datan & Ginsberg, 1975; Datan & Reese, 1977; Goulet & Baltes, 1970; Nesselroade & Reese, 1973), the initiation of publication of an annual volume devoted to life-span development (Baltes, 1978; Baltes & Brim, 1979, 1980, 1982, 1983, 1984; Baltes, Featherman, & Lerner, 1986), and the publication of numerous empirical and theoretical papers (Baltes, 1979b; Baltes & Nesselroade, 1973; Baltes, et al., 1980; Featherman, 1983; Featherman & Lerner, 1985). From this scholarly activity, it has become clear that one may characterize the life-span perspective as a set of interrelated ideas about the nature of human development and change. In their combination these ideas present a set of implications for theory building, for methodology, and for scientific collaboration across disciplinary boundaries. This is particularly timely in the field of career development where, as we noted in Chapter 1, theory building has been relatively absent in recent decades, the application of change-sensitive methodologies is needed, and collaboration across disciplinary boundaries is essential.

There are two key propositions or assumptions that are central to the life-span view of human development. They have been labeled *embeddedness* (Lerner, Skinner, & Sorell, 1980) and *dynamic interaction* (Lerner, 1978, 1979, 1984) and they, in turn, have important implications regarding (a) the plasticity of individual development; (b) the capacity of individuals to play an active part in their own development; and (c) the potential for intervention across the life-span. Collectively, these propositions and implications constitute the core of current life-span thinking in human development.

Embeddedness and Dynamic Interactionism

The idea of embeddedness is that the key phenomena of human life exist at multiple levels of analysis (e.g., the inner-biological, individual-psychological, dyadic, organizational, social network, community, societal, cultural, outer physical-ecological, and historical); at any one point in time variables and processes from any and all of these multiple levels may contribute to human functioning. However, it is particularly important to have a perspective about human development that is sensitive to the influences of these multiple levels because the levels do not function in parallel, i.e., as independent domains. Rather, the variables and processes at one level influence and are influenced by the variables and processes at the other levels; that is, there is a dynamic interaction among levels of analysis, where each level may be both a product and a producer of the functioning and changes at all other levels. This idea is, as may be recognized by recalling the discussion in Chapter 2, a key component of the developmental-contextual (probabilistic epigenetic) view of development (Gottlieb, 1970, 1976a, 1976b; Lerner, 1978, 1979, 1984; Scarr, 1982).

To illustrate how the view of developmental processes promoted in the life-span perspective may be seen as consistent with the components of probabilistic epigenesis discussed in Chapter 2, we may note Gollin's (1981) statement that:

> The relationships between organisms and environments are not interactionist, as interaction implies that organism and environment are separate entities that come together at an interface. Organism and environment constitute a single life process. . . . For analytic convenience, we may treat various aspects of a living system and various external environmental and biological features as independently definable properties. Analytical excursions are an essential aspect of scientific inquiry, but they are hazardous if they are primarily reductive. An account of the *collective behavior* of the parts as an organized entity is a necessary complement to a reductive analytic program, and serves to restore the information content lost in the course of the reductive excursion. . . . In any event, the relationships that contain the sources of change are those between organized systems and environments, not between heredity and environment. (pp. 231–232)

A similar view has been expressed by Baltes (1979b). In regard to the life-span perspective Baltes (1979b) has indicated:

> Life-span developmental psychologists emphasize *contextualistic-dialectic* paradigms of development (Datan & Reese, 1977; Lerner, Skinner, & Sorell, 1980; Riegel, 1976) rather than the use of "mechanistic" or "organismic" ones more typical of child development work. There are two primary rationales for this preference. One is, of course, evident also in current child development work. As development unfolds, it becomes more and more apparent that individuals act on the environment and produce novel behavior outcomes, thereby making the active and selective nature of human beings of paramount importance. Furthermore, the recognition of the interplay between age-graded, history-graded, and non-normative life events suggests a contextual and dialectic conception of development. This dialectic is further accentuated by the fact that individual development is the reflection of multiple forces which are not always in synergism, or convergence, nor do they always permit the delineation of a specific set of endstates. (p. 2)

The developmental-contextual ideas found in the life-span view lead to the position that any level of analysis may be understood in the context of the biological, cultural, and ontogenetic changes of which it is a part (Tobach, 1978, 1981; Toulmin, 1981), and that the idea of "one level in isolation" as the "prime mover" of change is not a useful one. And if change on multiple, interrelated levels of analysis characterizes the human life-span, then neither specific ontogenetic outcomes (Baltes, 1979b) nor totally uniform features of development at any portion of ontogeny necessarily characterize the life course (Toulmin, 1981). Instead, a human life-span is characterized by the potential for individual flexibility as a consequence of multilevel, embedded plastic processes (Maier & Schneirla, 1935; Schneirla, 1957; Tobach & Schneirla, 1968), and human lives may differ in the incidence of flexibility because of interindividual differences in the progression of plastic processes.

The implications of these statements for career development are far reaching. Accepting the notion that no one level of analysis can be considered the "prime mover" of change means that neither cognitive development (e.g., Dudley & Tiedeman, 1977) nor socioeconomic upheavals (e.g., Elder, 1974), nor parents' occupational status (e.g., Blau & Duncan, 1967; Mortimer, 1974, 1976) can be considered to have preeminence in determining the nature and direction of career development. Moreover, the potential for individual flexibility, which characterizes not just the "formative" years but the entire life-span, accounts for the wide variety of career trajectories encountered among individuals of all levels of ability, motivation, or socioeconomic background and suggests the possibility of alteration of career paths across life.

In sum, a probabilistic epigenetic (developmental-contextual) view of development is consistent with the major ideas associated with the life-span perspective, a perspective that suggests that, as a consequence of dynamic interactions among multiple, embedded levels of analysis, there is a basis for human plasticity. As noted earlier, however, the key propositions associated with a life-span perspective may be discussed in regard to a set of interrelated implications derived from them.

IMPLICATIONS OF THE PROPOSITIONS OF THE LIFE–SPAN PERSPECTIVE

To briefly recapitulate the import of the two key assumptions of the life-span perspective, let us note that the ideas of embeddedness and dynamic interactionism together mean that, first, individual developmental phenomena occur in the context of the developmental and nondevelopmental change phenomena of other levels of analysis; and, second, that developments and/or changes on one level influence and are influenced by developments and/or changes at these other levels. There are at least three major implications of the joint consideration of the ideas of embeddedness and dynamic interactionism.

The Potential for Plasticity.   The first implication is the one perhaps most clearly involved in our preceding discussion. The idea that changes at one level are reciprocally dependent on changes at other levels suggests that there is always some possibility for altering the status of a variable or process at any given level of analysis. Simply, the character of the interaction among levels of analysis means that there is a potential to change the functioning of any target level (or target variable) and indeed of the system of interlevel relations itself. In short, there is a potential for plasticity within any level of analysis and across the system as a whole.

For example, take the career trajectory of a middle-aged oil company executive. A dramatic change in his career could occur because of a war in the Middle East (e.g., the price of oil could quadruple, making small, marginal oil companies profitable and inducing them to pursue top talent in the field at salary levels far above his current level). This would be a change produced because of the malleability (plasticity) of the macrolevel context. On the other hand the executive's career could change because his children are about ready to enter college, and accepting a long-standing offer to join the department of petroleum engineering would result in such important economic benefits (tuition remission and others) that the offer is no longer refuseable. This would be a change produced by the plasticity of the meso-system of the environment in interaction with the plasticity of the individual organism. In short, the potential for plasticity exists across all levels of analysis involved in life. The work on mid-life career changes and the work on creative retirement and postretirement careers represent important but limited demonstrations of this proposition.

However, this potential for plasticity is not construed by life-span developmentalists to mean that there are no limits or constraints on change. For instance, by virtue of its structural organization a system delimits the range of changes it may undergo (Brent, 1984) and such a structural constraint holds for any level of analysis. For example, the prior, developmental organization of a system constrains the potential of a later influence to as easily lead to a change in the system as would have been the case if that same influence acted earlier in development (Lerner, 1978, 1979; Schneirla, 1957). Thus, the oil company executive could not choose to be a professional ballet dancer, and it would be unlikely that he would choose to be a manual laborer.

In fact, the possibility that developmental and nondevelopmental phenomena at one point in life may influence functioning at later points is explicitly recognized by life-span developmentalists in the concept of *developmental embeddedness* (Parke, R. D., personal communication, December, 1982). This concept indicates that there may be links among periods of life and that for any target period of life prior developmental events may provide causal antecedents; in turn, functioning in the target period may have consequences for later developmental periods. Thus, as a consequence of the potential for developmental embeddedness, life-span developmentalists emphasize that one must consider not only the changes across life but the constancies as well. Indeed, a key issue within the life-span perspective is to understand the relation between processes that serve to promote constancy and those that serve to promote change (e.g., see Lerner, 1984); that is, life-span development is concerned with understanding the developmental syntheses between both continuous and discontinuous processes (Lerner, 1978, 1979).

Nevertheless, despite the recognition of the limits and constraints on change, and the emphasis on the concept of developmental embeddedness, the notion that there is a potential for plasticity means to life-span developmentalists that the system is never necessarily completely limited or constrained (Brim & Kagan, 1980), and that as a consequence of the dynamic interaction among multiple levels of analysis means may be found to reorganize or restructure a system—even in advanced periods of that system's development (Baltes & Baltes, 1980; Baltes et al., 1980; Greenough & Green, 1981).

Thus, in sum, many life-span developmentalists might agree with geneticist R. C. Lewontin's (1981) views about the issue of constraints. Lewontin points out that:

> It is trivially true that material conditions of one level constrain organization at higher levels *in principle*. But that is not the same as saying that such constraints are quantitatively nontrivial. Although every object in the universe has a gravitational interaction with every other object, no matter how distant, I do not, in fact, need to adjust my body's motion to the movement of individuals in the next room. The question is not whether the nature of the human genotype is relevant to social organization, but whether the former constrains the latter in a nontrivial way, or whether the two levels are *effectively* decoupled. It is the claim of vulgar sociobiology that some kinds of human social organization are either impossible, or that they can be maintained only at the expense of constant psychic and political stress, which will inevitably lead to undesirable side effects because the nature of the human genome dictates a "natural" social organization. Appeals to abstract dependencies (in principle) of one level or another do not speak to the concrete issue of whether society is genetically constrained in an important way.

> . . . in fact, constraints at one level may be destroyed by higher level activity. No humans can fly by flapping their arms because of anatomical and

physiological constraints that reflect the human genome. But humans do fly, by using machines that are the product of social organization and that could not exist without very complex social interaction and evolution. As another example, the memory capacity of a single individual is limited, but social organization, through written records and the complex institutions associated with them, makes all knowledge recoverable for each individual. Far from being constrained by lower-level limitations, culture transcends them and feeds back to lower levels to relieve the constraints. Social organization, and human culture in particular, are best understood as negating constraints rather than being limited by them. (p. 244)

The optimism inherent in this position should not be overlooked. The principle of plasticity means that no one may be irretrievably "over the hill." The system may be restructured—at least in part—at any time, and at a variety of levels. If the system is structured in such a way that desired changes cannot be accomplished at one level of analysis, it may be always possible, at least in principle, to accomplish the desired change at another level, even despite the fact that overall, plasticity tends to decline somewhat with age (MacDonald, 1985). The following, second implication of the life-span perspective reinforces this optimistic perspective by suggesting that individuals actually participate in shaping their own environment that, in turn, helps to shape them.

The Person as a Producer of His/Her Own Development.   A second implication of the two key propositions of the life-span perspective is that it is possible to view any level of analysis as an influence on the other levels of analysis that influence it. From the perspective of individual psychological development, this idea means that the person may affect the context that affects him or her. By influencing the context that influences him or her, the person provides feedback to himself or herself. Thus, in other words, the individual is a producer of his/her own development (Lerner, 1982; Lerner & Busch-Rossnagel, 1981a; Scarr & McCartney, 1983).

The individual may influence or act as a producer of his/her own development in a variety of ways. First, this influence can come about as a consequence of the individual's constituting a distinct stimulus to others (e.g., through characteristics of physical and/or behavioral individuality). For example, a young man may be identified as a prime candidate for a career in sports because he is big and has developed excellent athletic skills; a young woman may be encouraged to become a ballet dancer because of her excellent figure and because she has developed exquisite dancing skills since early childhood. Second, individuals may act as producers of their own development as a consequence of their capabilities as processors of the world (e.g., in regard to cognitive structure and mode of emotional reactivity). For example, research using the Holland (1973) typology has demonstrated that individuals who dislike structure, show relatively little self-control, and readily express their emotions gravitate toward artistic occupations. Third, individuals may produce their own development as a consequence of their own active behavioral intervention or "behavioral agency" (Bakan, 1966; Block, 1973); there is evidence to suggest, for example, that individuals, largely through their own efforts, have overcome tremendous problems to successfully pursue careers for which they seemed ill suited. Theodore Roosevelt is but one example that readily comes to mind. Indeed, it may be the developing competency of individuals to behaviorally shape and/or select their contexts (Bandura, 1978; Mischel, 1977) that represents ultimately the most flexible means by which they can act as producers of their own development (Kendall, Lerner, & Craighead, 1984; Snyder, 1981). This is particularly relevant in a mobile society like that of the United States. Indeed, stories of individuals who moved to "the city" or who went "west" to seek their fortunes abound in the folklore. Many success stories of this genre represent illustrations of individuals choosing a context that allowed them to maximally influence their development and thus to have enormously successful careers.

The emphasis of the life-span developmental perspective on recognizing the capabilities of individuals to be producers of their own development is quite compatible with the entrepreneurial approach fostered by a capitalist society. The focus in both is on self-regulation, self-efficacy, and control of one's own destiny. It is noteworthy in this context that, in contrast, communist, totalitarian governments focus on regulating and controlling individuals, thus undermining the ability of individuals to act as producers of their own (career) development. The economic consequences of this approach are well known; the developmental consequences for individuals can only be estimated.

The Potential for Intervention.   A final implication of the assumptions of a life-span perspective may be noted. This is that there is a potential for intervention across the entire life-span. Given the potential for plasticity, it follows that means may be designed to prevent or ameliorate undesired or nonvalued developments or behavior, as well as enhance desirable ones (cf. Baltes & Danish, 1980). Moreover, the multilevel embeddedness of any target of intervention, and the dynamically interactive character of change, means that one may approach the same intervention target from any one of several levels of analysis; this possibility underscores the use of a multidisciplinary approach to intervention and, of course, to the knowledge base from which interventions should derive.

In addition, the idea of developmental embeddedness suggests that one may take a historical approach to intervention, and, for instance, devise long-term preventative strategies (Lerner & Ryff, 1978). However, individual ontogeny is not the only aspect of history that may be considered here. Life-span developmentalists' awareness of the features of intergenerational transmission (e.g., see Bengtson & Troll, 1978) lead them to be sensitive to the possibility that one may intervene with future parents to prevent undesired outcomes in yet-to-be-conceived offspring. We return to this point later in the book, but an example that may be given here is of the possibility of changing the type of birth control precautions of sexually active young adolescents in order to prevent the conception and birth of a child who will be at risk for several health problems as a consequence of being born to a young adolescent mother.

Finally in regard to the implications of the life-span perspective for intervention, it needs to be stressed that although there is a potential for plasticity across the entire life-span, it does *not* mean one should ignore or neglect intervention in early life. In fact, just the opposite view is promoted. The life-span perspective indicates that although plasticity may exist across life, there are always constraints on change, and plasticity is not eqipotential across life. There is evidence to suggest that as the organism develops, the range of structures and functions within which the potential for plasticity may be actualized becomes narrower (cf. Baltes & Baltes, 1980; Clarke & Clarke, 1976; Greenough & Green, 1981). Thus, it may be easier, more efficient, and less costly to intervene earlier in life, i.e., when the system is being organized and when there are fewer constraints on the design, implementation, and likelihood of success of a given intervention than would be the case if the system had progressed to a more advanced point.

This perspective, as is easily recognized, represents a powerful rationale for early vocational and career education. This is not to suggest that young people should be "programmed" to pursue one career or another. Rather, it recognizes that young people are capable of considering more options, more alternative career development trajectories than older individuals who may be constrained by both limitations from within and external, contextual barriers. However, if such early intervention is not possible the implication of the life-span perspective is that all is not lost. There may be means, albeit more difficult and/or more costly ones (such as retraining or mid-life career changes), to effect a desired change.

Conclusions

We return at several places in this book to the implications of the life-span developmental view for intervening across life. Here, it is useful to note three points about the present status of the life-span perspective. First, in order to study the complex interrelations among organism and context, life-span developmentalists (e.g., Baltes, 1968; Schaie, 1965) promote the use of particular research designs and methodologies, such as sequential designs, P-technique factor analysis, multivariate statistics, and cohort analysis. (This is discussed in more detail in Chapter 6.) Second, they seek both methodological and substantive collaboration with scholars from disciplines whose units of analysis have traditionally been other than individual-psychological or personological ones. For example, the work of life-course sociologists has been important in advancing life-span developmental psychology (e.g., Brim, 1966; Brim & Kagan, 1980; Brim & Ryff, 1980; Elder, 1974, 1979; Featherman, 1983; Riley, 1978, 1979). Third, however, these methodological and multidisciplinary activities are undertaken primarily for conceptual reasons. If contextual influences were not seen as crucial for understanding individual development, then neither methods for their assessment in relation to the individual, nor information about the character of these levels of analysis would be necessary.

In sum, the development of life-span developmental psychology in the 1970s has been associated with renewed interest in a multidisciplinary view of human development, one suggesting that individual changes across life are both a product and a producer of the multiple levels of context within which the person is embedded; that is, this life-span view rests on a conception of development one may describe as developmental contextual: In so doing, it sees individuals as being marked by plastic processes and, as a consequence of this plasticity, as both products and producers of the context, which provides a basis of their development.

How can career development be conceptualized from this perspective? In the final section of this chapter an attempt is made to present an approach to career development that utilizes the developmental-contextual concept of development introduced in Chapter 2, and that incorporates the key features of the life-span developmental approach to human development discussed thus far in the present chapter. This allows us to illustrate the features of the person and of his or her context, which we believe to be important for understanding the place of career development in a person's development across life.

A GOODNESS-OF-FIT MODEL OF PERSON-CONTEXT RELATIONS

The developmental-contextual, life-span view leads to the idea that people, by interacting with their changing context, provide a basis of their own development. It is important to emphasize, however, that scholars who have argued for the role of the person as an agent in his or her own development (e.g., Lerner, 1982; Lerner & Busch-Rossnagel, 1981b; Scarr & McCartney, 1983; Thomas & Chess, 1977), do not view the characteristics of people, which promote their own development, as acting in a predetermined or fixed manner. Instead, the probabilistic character of such "person effects," and of development in general, is emphasized. This stress occurs because the reciprocal nature of all person effects is taken seriously. The context enveloping a person is composed of, for example, a specific physical ecology and the other individually different and developing people with whom the person interacts. This context is as unique and changing as is the person lawfully individually distinct, for example, as a consequence of his or her genotype and experiential history. One cannot say completely in advance what particular features of the context will exist at a specific time in a given person's life. As a consequence, we may only speak probabilistically of the effects a given person may have on his or her context, of the feedback the person is likely to receive from the context, and of the nature of the person's development that will therefore ensue.

Thus, "person effects" on development are not so simple as they may seem at first. Indeed, the probabilism of development represents a formidable challenge for theory and research. To understand how people may influence their own development it is necessary to have more than just a conceptualization of the nature of the individual characteristics or processes involved in such effects. It is also necessary to conceptualize and operationalize the features of the context, or of the ecology within which significant interactions occur for the person. We have attempted this task in Chapter 3 in spite of the fact that Bronfenbrenner (1979) has so eloquently reminded us that psychologists are neither readily prone nor typically adequately trained to do this. Doing justice to both the person and the context requires a special kind of model, one that accounts for the full complexity of person-context relations in the "real world." We propose such a model, which we have labeled the *goodness-of-fit model of person-context relations.*

Features of the Model

Both individuals and the world they inhabit are composed of multiple "levels of being" or, simply, multiple dimensions. These dimensions are thought to be interdependent and developing and/or changing over time. Various theorists and researchers have wrestled with the conceptual complexity of this framework, both from the perspective of life-span development and from that of career development. Thus, Schein (1971) speaks of the structure of the individual and the structure of the organization, suggesting that a career is fashioned as the individual moves through the organization. Clearly, this represents a complex person–context model. Super's (1980) concept of the life space and individual development within it represents another prominent example from the career development literature. In life-span development a number of authors have concerned themselves with complex person–context relationships (e.g., Baltes, Baltes, & Reinert, 1970; Belsky, 1984; Bronfenbrenner, 1979; Nesselroade & Baltes, 1974; Schneirla, 1957; Thomas & Chess, 1977; Tobach & Schneirla, 1968).

Figure 4.1, adapted from Lerner (1984), attempts to describe such person–context complexity with particular reference to career development. It must be emphasized that this figure is only descriptive of the relations that the various theorists and researchers have noted as being involved in person–context relations. Indeed, the bidirectional arrows in the figure correspond to relations identified in various segments of the human development and career development literature.

It should be stressed that we do not believe that it would be useful or even possible to do research testing the figure as a whole. Instead, the use of this or similar representations of person–context relations is to guide the selection of individual and ecological variables in one's research and to provide parameters about the generalizability of one's findings; that is, this representation should be a reminder that one needs to consider whether

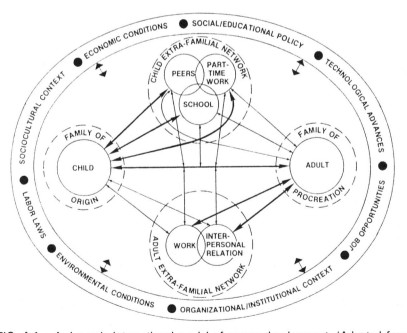

FIG. 4.1.   A dynamic interactional model of career development. (Adapted from Lerner, 1984)

the results of a given study may be generalized, beyond the particular individual and ecological variables that have been studied and applied to other community, societal, cultural, and historical contexts.

But it should also be emphasized that the representation is a useful guide to theory development. What is illustrated by this and other such figures is that there need to be three components of theory-guided research on person–context relations. First, one needs to have some conceptualization of the nature of the attributes of the person one is interested in studying. Second, one must have some conceptualizations of the features of the person's context one wishes to explore and a rationale for why this portion of the context is pertinent to the personological attribute(s) one is assessing. Third, and most important, one needs some conceptualization of the *relation* between the individual attribute(s) and the contextual feature(s).

This third point allows the features of the goodness-of-fit model to be introduced. The person and the context described in Fig. 4.1 are likely, indeed are surely, to be individually distinct as a consequence of the unique combination of genotypic and phenotypic features of the person and of the specific attributes of his or her context. The presence of such individuality is central to understanding the goodness-of-fit model. As a consequence of characteristics of physical individuality, for example, in regard to body type or facial attractiveness (Sorell & Nowak, 1981) and/or of psychological individuality, for instance, in regard to conceptual tempo or temperament (Kagan, 1966; Thomas & Chess, 1977), children promote differential reactions in their socializing others; these reactions may feed back to children, increase the individuality of their developmental milieu, and provide a basis for their further development. T. C. Schneirla (1957) termed these relations *circular functions.* Through the establishment of such functions in ontogeny people may be conceived of as producers of their own development (Lerner & Busch-Rossnagel, 1981b). However, this circular functions idea needs to be extended. In and of itself the notion is mute regarding the specific characteristics of the feedback (for example, its positive or negative valence) a child will receive as a consequence of its individuality. What may provide a basis of the feedback?

Just as an individual brings his or her characteristics of individuality to a particular social setting there are demands placed on the individual by virtue of the social and physical components of the setting. These demands may take the form of first, attitudes, values, or expectations held by others in the context regarding the individual's physical or behavioral characteristics. Second, demands exist as a consequence of the behavioral attributes of others in the context with whom the individual must coordinate, or fit, his or her behavioral attributes for adaptive interactions to exist. Third, the physical characteristics of a setting (such as the presence or absence of access ramps for the motorically handicapped), constitute contextual demands. Such physical presses require the individual to possess certain behavioral attributes for the most efficient interaction within the setting to occur.

The individual's individuality, in differentially meeting these demands, provides a basis for the feedback he or she gets from the socializing environment. For example, considering the demand "domain" of attitudes, values, or expectations, employers and spouses may have relatively individual and distinct expectations about behaviors desired of their employees and husband or wife, respectively. Employers (e.g., in the banking or mortgage and loan industry) may want certain employees to show little flexibility in regard to company rules and be rigid in terms of company policy and practice. Spouses however, might desire their husband or wife to be more flexible, for example, when decisions concerning the entire family need to be made. Individuals whose behavioral individuality was either generally rigid or flexible would thus differentially meet the demands of these two contexts. Problems in functioning at work or at home might thus develop as a consequence of an individual's lack of match, or "goodness-of-fit," in either or both settings.

Similarly, considering the second type of contextual demands that exist—those that arise as a consequence of the behavioral characteristics of others in the setting—problems of fit might occur when an individual who is highly irregular in such biological functions as eating and sleep–wake cycles, interacts in a work setting composed of highly regular and behaviorally scheduled superiors and co-workers. In turn, considering the third type of contextual demands that exist—those that arise as a consequence of the physical characteristics of a setting—an individual who has a low threshold for noise and who is also highly distractible might find it problematic to perform efficiently in a setting with high-noise levels: for instance, in a factory, or in a large, pool-like secretarial setting; such an individual might not perform well on tasks which necessitate concentration and/or attention.

Thomas and Chess (1977, 1980, 1981) and J. Lerner (1983) have argued that adaptive psychological and social functioning do not derive directly from either the nature of the person's characteristics of individuality per se or the nature of the demands of the contexts within which the person functions. Rather, if a person's characteristics of individuality match, or "fit," the demands of a particular setting adaptive outcomes in that setting will accrue. Those people whose characteristics match most of the settings within which they exist should receive supportive or positive feedback from the contexts and should show evidence of the most adaptive behavioral functioning. In turn, of course, mismatched people, whose characteristics are incongruent with one or most settings, should show alternative developmental outcomes.

The goodness-of-fit concept describes the status of the relation between an individual and his or her setting as it exists at one point in time. However, when one becomes concerned with "circular functions" between individuals and their contexts, it is clear that fit established at one time will have implications for the future history of feedback and of developmental outcomes. As such, to appraise the developmental import of goodness-of-fit we have to, in effect, take a longitudinal series of "snapshots" of the person–context relation. Changes in what is seen in the "snapshot" can be understood as a consequence of whether the feedback, derived as a consequence of the fit at one point in time, leads to changes in the person, the setting, or both.

CONCLUSIONS

We believe that the goodness-of-fit model, as an instance of the type of approach to development promoted by a developmental-contextual, life-span view is useful to the extent that it guides the study of theoretically selected features of the developing person in relation to his or her changing context. In addition, such models are useful in emphasizing that any one feature of a person's development—such as the focus of this book, vocational role and career development—should be viewed in the context of the other features of the person that are developing and in the context of the particular, history-bound features of the settings within which the person interacts.

Thus, the development of a vocational role, the progression of a career, should be conceptualized as one feature of a person's development—and as such must be understood as it both influences and is influenced by his or her cognitive, personality, physical, and social developments. In addition, the ways in which a person's changing context—family, school, friends, community, and culture, for instance—influence and are influenced by these individual developments must be understood as well. Accordingly, the study of development—and vocational development in particular—needs to be conceptualized as a focus that involves basic research in general psychology, in sociology, in anthropology, and in history.

In short, we call for a developmental and multidisciplinary approach to the study of vocational role or career development. This approach must emphasize the antecedents and the consequents of features of vocational development—it must look at features of vocational development as potentially involving all of the life-span—and it must emphasize too the context within which such development occurs, a context which itself has developmental features. In the remainder of this book we use the developmental-contextual, life-span perspective in our discussions of existing and to-be-conducted research and intervention efforts in vocational and career development.

5 Career Development: The Sample Case of Adolescence

In preceding chapters we have stressed that career development must be seen as a facet of the other developing characteristics of the person. The cognitive and behavioral developments associated with career behavior and development—for example, attitudes, values, preferences, orientations, etc.—are shaped by, and shapers of, the physical, cognitive and behavioral attributes, and behavioral changes occurring in domains of functioning other than those related to careers. For instance, the cognitive and behavioral attributes of an individual's career development may interact with his or her developing motivational and physical characteristics.

We have stressed too that these intraindividual relations between "cognitive/behavioral career" and "cognitive/behavioral-noncareer" domains are influenced by, and influences on, features of the context surrounding the person; that is, intraindividual development is related bidirectionally to a person's social and physical contexts—his or her familial, peer, educational, and vocational networks, physical ecology, and sociocultural settings. Finally, because all these intraindividual and individual-context relations may vary over time we have stressed the need for a developmental design for research aimed at understanding these relations.

Given these emphases, then, the developmental-contextual model that was developed in Chapters 1-4, and illustrated in Fig. 4.1, constitutes more than a codification of the set of ideas found in this approach to the study of career development. This model also serves as a means to integrate existing research; it allows us to summarize the sorts of intraindividual and individual-context relations that have been studied and to thereby note too which possible relations have not been investigated. Thus, the model also serves

85

as a vehicle for pointing to lacunae in the literature, to studies that need to be done.

There has been considerable within-age-level research pertinent to career development, and some across-age-level, cross-sectional or longitudinal research as well (cf. Crites, 1983). However, the application of the developmental-contextual model as a means to organize existing research and to point to uninvestigated or underinvestigated relations indicates that considerable gaps exist in our knowledge of career development. To illustrate these uses of the model and to thereby indicate how this perspective may be a generative one for furthering novel research, we review research on career development in adolescence. This is the period of life that has attracted the most intense empirical interest, partly because of the relatively ready availability of high school and college samples but also because of theoretical ideas linking this period of life to key career decisions (e.g., Erikson, 1959, 1963, 1968; Marcia, 1980; Super, 1957; Waterman, 1982). Thus, we focus on adolescence as a sample case. However, we should note that our interest in this review is not to provide an exhaustive summary of what has been done in this area; other published reviews have had such objectives (e.g., Jepsen, 1984; Tinsley & Heesacker, 1984). Rather our goal is to illustrate the integrative and generative potential of the developmental-contextual model.

THE STUDY OF
CAREER DEVELOPMENT IN ADOLESCENCE

Relative to other age periods, e.g., mid-life or retirement, there has been considerable research focused on adolescent career development. Nevertheless, organization of this research by means of the model depicted in Fig. 4.1 indicates several limitations: Most of the research clusters into a few areas of the model; a large proportion of the research is not developmental in design; and considerable further work—appraising more of the developing relations suggested in Fig. 4.1—needs to be done before we can assert with any confidence that we have an adequate understanding of career development in adolescence.

Studies of Intraindividual Relations

Studies of this type typically involve the interrelation of one personological variable with another. For instance, self-concepts and occupational concepts are often interrelated (e.g., Kidd, 1984; Super, 1957). If a third or fourth variable is considered in this genre of research they are usually sex and age, or grade (e.g., Gribbons & Lohnes, 1965; Kelso, 1977; Lokan,

Boss, & Patsula, 1982). The inclusion of the age variable usually occurs within the context of a cross-sectional design. As such, only age-group differences and not age changes are in actuality studied, and no direct statement may be made about developmental trajectories on the basis of such cross sectional data (Baltes, Reese, & Nesselroade, 1977).

To illustrate, Borgen and Young (1982) studied 544 students in grades 5 to 12. Students were asked to describe five common occupations: automotive mechanic, nurse, sales clerk, chef, and bookkeeper. There existed across the age-groups differences in descriptions. Among the younger groups the descriptions were more behavioral, whereas among the older ones the descriptions focused more on interests, career progress, and outcomes. However, we cannot conclude from these data on age-group differences that as fifth graders age (i.e., as they develop into high school) their descriptions will show a sequential change from behavioral orientation to interest orientation. Variables other than ones marked by age may moderate the association between group membership and type of description. For instance, the history of curricula differences between the groups may foster different descriptions.

Thus, because of limitations of their research designs many studies that are aimed at providing information about the development of careers in adolescence cannot actually do so. Data reported in studies by Kelso (1977), by Lokan et al. (1982), and by Tinsley, Kass, Moreland, and Harren (1983) are cases in point.

Kelso (1977) was interested in studying the relations among school grade, vocational maturity, vocational choice realism, and "stages of vocational development." A sample of 1,695 children and adolescents, in grades 5 to 12 of suburban Melbourne, Australia schools, were administered: (a) either the Otis Intermediate Test or the Otis Higher Test; (b) Crites' Vocational Development Inventory (which elicits attitudinal or dispositional response tendencies in regard to vocational maturity); and (c) a Student Survey designed to measure vocational choice realism. Kelso found that across grade groups there were increased mean scores in regard to vocational choice attitudes and vocational choice realism, group differences that remained significant even after the possible influences of intelligence were statistically controlled. These grade differences are of interest in that they do tell us how people who differ in at least one status attribute (age in this case) differ also in regard to selected vocational attitudes. However, these results do not tell us about whether, as one group ages, it will show at a subsequent point in time responses comparable with those shown by another group at an earlier point in time. As noted earlier, a cross-sectional design such as Kelso's (1977) does not assess changes, and it precludes discriminating between age effects and effects due to historical (or other unmatched) differences between groups. Simply, in such designs there is a confound between age and birth cohort (Baltes et al., 1977).

Moreover, in Kelso's (1977) study there is a conceptual problem with the use of the concept of "stage." Kelso says a "stage of vocational development" exists if there is a significant difference between the means of adjacent grades. As we explained in Chapter 2, however, such a use of the "stage" idea is quite inconsistent with the uses of the term found in the human development literature (e.g., Flavell, 1971; Lerner, 1976; Wohlwill, 1973). Given our previous discussion we need not reiterate here the thrust of this literature. Let it suffice here to note this conceptual incompatibility and to indicate further that Kelso's (1977) operationalization of the "stage" concept suffers from a host of methodological problems as well, for example, inferring an intraindividual sequence of change from interindividual difference data.

As we have pointed out, however, Kelso's research is not alone in having such methodological shortcomings. Lokan et al. (1982) studied over 700 students in Grades 9 and 11 from several Canadian high schools. The students were administered the Super et al. Career Development Inventory (CDI) and the Nowicki and Strickland Locus of Control (LOC) scale for children. Using the three CDI scales as dependent variables in a MANOVA, Lokan et al. reported significant main effects for LOC, grade level, and sex, and no significant interactions; however, after adjusting the F values only the main effects for LOC and grade level remained. Inspection of the means associated with these significant Fs indicated that the internal LOC group had higher ("more mature") CDI scores than did the external LOC group and that the Grade 11 group had higher ("more mature") CDI scores than did the Grade 9 group. However, because of the cross-sectional nature of the design used by Lokan et al. (1982) little appropriate inference about developmental change is possible. Cohort differences between the grade groups could as readily account for the group differences as could age associated differences. Put simply, groups that differ in age may differ also in a host of other variables.

Of course, even when intraindividual change is directly studied there is no necessary assurance that the research design is adequate. As explained by Baltes et al. (1977) and Nesselroade and Baltes (1979), design and measurement issues in the study of change are exceedingly complex and among the most difficult to address adequately. To illustrate, consider the research of Tinsley et al. (1983) who studied 174 college women in the fall of 1976 and again in the fall of 1977. The women were administered such measures as the Assessment of Career Decision Making, an index of their sex-role orientations, a scale to assess their attitudes toward females, and an index of cognitive differentiation. Tinsley et al. used cross-lagged panel analysis in an attempt to discern causality of influence among these variables across these two times of measurement.

Given the goals and assumptions of Tinsley et al., this study was executed quite well. Nevertheless, as they acknowledge, cross-lagged panel analysis is permissible only when the assumption of equal stability of the variables over the time of measurement is satisfied. Furthermore, using standardized coefficients (i.e., correlations) to represent cross-lagged relations is warranted only when equality of the variance is maintained over time (e.g., see Rogosa, 1979), a condition that apparently was not tested by Tinsley et al. In addition, cross-lagged panel analyses are problematic procedures for modeling developmental causality (Rogosa, 1979) and more appropriate structural equation modeling procedures are available (e.g., Huba & Harlow, 1986). Finally, simple, one cohort longitudinal designs have well-known problems of instrument decay, retest effects, and measurement equivalence (Baltes et al., 1977).

What these remarks about existing cross-sectional and longitudinal research suggest is that it is difficult to do adequate developmental research. In addition, although there may be quite a bit of information about career behavior and development in adolescence, much of the data is from studies, which have neglected to use research methodologies that are developmentally appropriate. Thus, few generalizations about career development change in adolescence are warranted on the basis of such information. Nevertheless, as we have implied earlier, there may be reasons for doing cross-sectional research other than for an interest in the developmental process. For instance, cross-sectional knowledge about the response patterns of different age-groups can help set educational policy or aid in the planning of curricula revisions or intervention needs.

The research by Grotevant and Durrett (1980) serves as an illustration of well-designed cross-sectional research in this area. These investigators studied 6,029 high school seniors (about 50% males) from 57 Texas public school districts and assessed the interrelations between occupational knowledge and career choice. Using the "High School Interest and Information Survey" in 1976, Grotevant and Durrett found that the correlations between educational plans and the educational requirements for the chosen profession were, at most, .41. Indeed, of the students who claimed to have at least considerable understanding of their first choice career, only about half planned to attain the amount of education needed to enter the occupation. Clearly, such research has important implications for the high school curriculum; more attention must be paid to instructing students about the educational levels requisite for their chosen careers.

Several studies of intraindividual relations involved in adolescent career development have not had a focus on potential age-related variation. Instead, links between personality and other intraindividual variables have been assessed. For instance, Grotevant and Thorbecke (1982) interviewed 41 male and 42 female high school juniors and seniors in regard to their identity status. In addition, assessments were made of the adolescents' achievement motivation, vocational identity, masculinity–femininity, and orientation to social desirability responding. Although Grotevant and Thorbecke did not find sex differences on the two identity measures, vocational identity among males was positively related to masculinity, to orientations toward mastery, and to a lack of concern about negative evaluations from others. Among females, vocational identity was positively related to masculinity and to an orientation toward hard work; it was negatively related to competitiveness.

Similar to the genre of research exemplified by Grotevant and Thorbecke (1982), there are a host of studies, which interrelate various personality measures with indices of vocational or career processes. For example, Lokan and Biggs (1982) used a national random sampling of 50 high schools in order to obtain a sample of 1,250 Grade 11 Australian students. Through administering a general information questionnaire, a word knowledge test, the CDI, and a learning process questionnaire (in order to assess motivational and strategy aspects of learning), Lokan and Biggs found that vocational maturity (CDI) scores were related to different approaches to career development; for instance, some students were intellective and deliberative; others were concerned and personally involved and had high aspirations; others were concerned and personally involved but had low aspirations; and still others were uncertain and confused. Similarly, Grimm and Nachmias (1977) found that among 1,000 Israeli high school students interrelations existed among measures of vocational interest, creativity, and anxiety; and Zagar, Arbit, Falconer, and Friedland (1983) reported that in a sample of 489 high school and college males, aged 15 to 34 years, and 137 females, aged 16 to 35 years, interrelations existed among scores from the MMPI, the Edwards PPS, and the Kuder Preference Record-C. In a corresponding vein, Jones, Hansen, and Putnam (1976) assessed 846 adolescents, in Grades 8 to 12, with the Tennessee Self-Concept Scale, Crites' Vocational Development Inventory, and the Holland Vocational Preference Inventory. As noted in greater detail later, subjects may be divided into six vocational categories on the basis of scores on the latter instrument, and Jones et al. (1976) reported that males and females within three of these categories differed in regard to their vocational maturity and self-concept. However, the relation between vocational maturity and self-concept was weak but significant in four of the six Holland groups.

In essence, then, the studies of the interrelation of personality variables with vocational and career development variables do indicate that some relationships exist between these two domains of intraindividual functioning. However, all relationships are in need of replication, and many of the relationships that have been found are of low magnitude and therefore are suggestive of little psychological significance. Moreover, because of problems of statistical analysis even these relatively simple interrelational research designs tell us much less about the links between personality and career variables than may, at first blush, seem to be the case. Thus, we may have even less knowledge about covariation between personality and career variables than we believe we have.

Two studies by Holland and his associates exemplify this unfortunate state of affairs. Holland and Nichols (1964) longitudinally studied a sample of 513 late adolescents (about 60% males). The adolescents were National Merit Finalists and therefore had quite high scholastic aptitude. In addition the students were from high SES backgrounds. The adolescents, assessed at the end of their senior year in high school and at the end of their freshman year in college, were asked to respond to a questionnaire about their choice of a major field and a vocation; in addition, they completed a personal history questionnaire and completed 17 measures of personality and originality.

The students indicated also their rank-order preference for six types of occupational titles: Realistic, Intellectual, Social, Conventional, Enterprising, and Artistic. If, at the second time of testing an adolescent had the identical occupational preference given at the first time of testing he or she was a *nonchanger*. If he/she changed major but still fell into the same type of occupation (e.g., if in the Artistic category he or she went from art education to music education) he or she was labeled an *intraclass changer*. Students who changed into a different type of occupation were *interclass changers*.

The key results of this research are presented in two tables, on pages 237 and 240, respectively, of the Holland and Nichols (1964) report. Table 2 summarizes the relation between change in major field and the personality variables measured in the study. The table presents a matrix of 153 correlations; this number is derived by the fact that there were: (a) nine (9) occupation by sex groups (i.e., a male Realistic category group, and a male and a female group for four of the remaining five categories—that is, for all remaining categories except Conventional); *crossed with* (b) 17 personality variables. Among these 153 correlations only 14 (9.1%) are significant, a proportion only slightly greater than chance. Moreover, only 4 of 68 correlations (5.8%) are significant for females and only 10 of 85 correlations (11.8%) are significant for males. None of the correlations for either sex group appear systematic. Furthermore, Holland and Nichols did not deal with the issue of multicolinearity among their measures, and the problem of capitalization on chance was not taken into account. For example, if two of the personality variables were highly correlated (i.e., a case of multicolinearity), then they may be tapping a similar dimension, which would render any significant correlations between these personality variables and the occupation by sex groups redundant. In addition, when several correlations are tested for significance independently, the chance of making a Type I error within the given experiment is increased, and unless this is taken into account (e.g., by adjusting the alpha level), then some of the correlations may be significant solely because of chance. Thus, the relatively few and unsystematic significant findings they report represent an *overestimate* of the true relations between personality and leaving (change in) a major field.

Identical statistical problems exist in regard to the data reported by Holland and Nichols (1964) in their Table 3. This table summarizes the relation between change in major field and student achievement, aptitude, vocational interests, etc. A matrix of 261 correlations is presented by crossing the previously described nine occupation X sex groups with 29 achievement, aptitude, etc. variables. Of the 261 correlations reported only 34 (13.0%) are significant—18 of 145 (12.4%) for males and 16 of 116 (13.8%) for females. However, as before, these relations appear unsystematic and, in any event, no corrections have been made in regard to problems of multicolinearity and capitalization on chance. Thus, as before, it is not possible to conclude that these data suggest any substantial link between personality and career development variables.

The research of Holland and Holland (1977) is similarly problematic. This study investigated the characteristics of students who are decided or undecided about a vocational goal. Samples of 1,005 high school juniors and 692 college juniors were administered the "Life Plans Inventory." This broad assessment device included in it: the Vocational Attitudes and Occupational Information Scales from Crites' (1973) Career Maturity Inventory (CMI); the Interpersonal Competency Scale; the Preconscious Activity Scale; the Anomy Scale; and the Identity Scale. Furthermore, a "Self-Directed Search" scale to which the students responded afforded several additional scores.

Holland and Holland (1977) compared Decided and Undecided students on all variables. Tables 1 and 2 of their report show that the groups are alike on most variables; there are few between group differences. Moreover, Table 1 involves within-sex, but between decision status group (i.e., Decided vs. Undecided) comparisons on 24 variables. However, there occurred no correction of alpha level (to control for experiment-wise error rate, to protect against capitalization on chance, and to begin to address problems of multicolinearity). Thus, the four differences of 24 comparisons (16.6%) found for males and the seven differences of 24 comparisons (29%) found for females represent overestimates of the number of actual differences that may exist. Similarly, in Table 2 the 6 of 18 differences (33.3%) reported for males, and the 5 of 18 differences

(27.8%) reported for females, also are overestimates for precisely the same reasons.

Table 5 of the Holland and Holland (1977) report presents correlations among undecided students only between the number of explanations (for being unsure, dissatisfied, or undecided about vocational choice) and the 24 assessment variables. For the high school males 3 of 24 correlations (12.5%) are significant, and for the high school females significance occurs in regard to 6 of the 24 correlations (25%). For the college males only one of 18 correlations (5%) is significant, whereas among the college females 5 of 18 (27.8%) are significant. Table 6 of the Holland and Holland (1977) report presents a matrix crossing the assessment variables with the number of explanations used by members of the unsure, the dissatisfied, and the undecided student groups. For the high school males 5 of 24 correlations (20.8%) reach significance, whereas for the high school females 10 of 24 correlations (41.6%) do so. For the college males 6 of 18 correlations (33.3%) are significant, whereas for the college females 4 correlations of 18 (22.2%) are significant. However, as before, the correlations reported in Tables 5 and 6 appear unsystematic, and, in any event, are presented without any correction of alpha level and with no steps taken to protect against the problems of multicolinearity and capitalization on chance. As such, Holland and Holland's (1977) assertion that their findings provide evidence for an "undecisive disposition" represents an egregious over-interpretation of their data.

In sum, the study of intraindividual relations among career developmental and organismic (e.g., age and sex) and/or personological variables has suffered in several respects. First, conceptually, of the several possible intraindividual interrelations that may be studied only a few have been investigated. An individual may be examined with regard to a multiplicity of organismic variables other than age or sex; rate of physical and physiological development in adolescence, race, handicapped or disabled status, health status, and disease history are just some of the variables that could have been, but as yet have not been, well studied. Indeed, it is particularly surprising that in the study of adolescent career development focused attention on organismic or biological variation has been so consistently lacking. The theoretical and empirical literatures of developmental psychology are replete with information about the marked physical and physiological changes spanning the early-to-late-adolescent period. These changes may quite reasonably moderate career development. For example, a male child with a lean and frail build may have to alter his plans regarding a career in contact sports when he fails to develop requisite height and muscle mass across the adolescent period. In turn, girls who aspire to enter such careers as modeling or ballet may have to alter their plans as a consequence of greater than desired breast development; in turn, such females may alter their dietary and exercise patterns, even to the point in some cases of becoming anorexic, in order to maintain their desired career plans (Brooks-Gunn & Ruble, 1983).

In addition to the omission of biological and organismic variables, numerous cognitive developmental, personality, and motivational variables have not been systematically assessed. For instance, do concrete operational adolescents have career interests and make career decisions in the same ways as do formal operational adolescents? Theory would lead us to expect that the answer is no (Inhelder & Piaget, 1958). However, we have little data pertinent to the issue.

Second, the design of research has been problematic. Cross-sectional research is too limited to reveal much of importance about age changes. The few longitudinal studies that have been done (e.g., Holland & Nichols, 1964; Tinsley et al., 1983) have typically included only two times of measurement and thus have been unable to discriminate between true (age) change and regression to the mean (e.g., see Cronbach & Furby, 1970; Nesselroade, Stigler, & Baltes, 1980). In addition, the studies have failed to include appropriate control groups (Baltes et al., 1977), and the issue of measurement equivalence has never been addressed. Furthermore, even when age changes have been appropriately studied there has been an omission of concern with the process by which age-associated variables influence career development. Simple interrelations among age, or other status variables, and career variables, or among personality and career variables tell us little about the bases of any significant covariations that may be found. Such research may provide some useful descriptive information but is often in and of itself of little value in explaining the process by which career development occurs.

This failure to assess process within one's research is not merely a problem found in regard to the study of adolescent career development. Although we have selected the adolescent age period for focused discussion in the present chapter, we should note that career development research in other age periods also suffers from an emphasis on description of covariation rather than concerning itself with explaining the process by which the observed variation occurs; this research suffers too from many of the design and data analytic problems we have identified in the adolescent literature.

To illustrate, in a study by Costa, McCrae, and Holland (1984) measures of vocational interests and personality were assessed in a sample that included a wide age range. Participants were members of the Augmented Baltimore Longitudinal Study of Aging; a group of 241 males, aged 25 to 89 years, and 153 females, aged 21 to 86 years, from this longitudinal study took part in the Costa et al. investigation. Participants were administered the Holland Self-Directed Search (SDS) measure, the instrument by which vocational interests are classified as fitting one of the earlier-described six groups. In addition, a personality measure of the participants' neuroticism (N), extraversion (E), and openness (O) was administered.

Little evidence for age and sex differences were found when sex X age group ANOVAs were performed with total interest scores as the dependent variable. In regard to the interrelation of personality and interest scores, however, several significant correlations were reported. Table 1 (page 395 of the Costa et al., 1984, report) presents a matrix composed of columns representing: first, 30 SDS scale scores, i.e., for each of the six SDS occupational categories there are four "part" scores and one "total" score—a score it should be noted that *must* share variation with the four part scores; second, N, E, and O scores for males; third, N, E, and O scores for females; and fourth, for the total group (males and females) "scores" for age and sex. Thus, for males there is a matrix of 30 SDS scores X three personality (N, E, and O) scores, or a matrix of 90 correlations; for females there is an identical 90 correlation matrix; and for the total group there is a 60 correlation matrix (30 SDS Scores X Age X Sex).

Among males, 42 of 90 correlations (46.7%) are significant whereas for females there are also 42 of 90 correlations (46.7%) significant. For the total group 40 of 60 correlations (66.7%) are significant. However, as was the case in regard to the other studies by Holland and his colleagues, the study by Costa et al. did not take into account the multicolinearity that existed among these scores; again, some of the correlations that are presented in Table 1 as if they were independently significant correlations are in actuality part–whole correlations. Moreover, there may of course be multicolinearity among the similar part scores for the six different SDS categories, e.g., the activities subscore for the Social category may covary with the activities subscore for the Enterprising category; however, no attempts to ascertain and correct for potential or existing multicolinearity were reported. Similarly, there was no correction of alpha level for capitalization on chance. If such a correction were made then the number of significant correlations would approximate a chance level. In short, given these data analytic problems the use of the Costa et al. data to support a link between vocational interests as measured by Holland's SDS and personality is severely constrained.

In another example, Vaitenas and Wiener (1977) studied 38 young and 27 older career changers and compared them to 45 young and 40 older vocationally stable "controls." Although no major age-group differences were found the career changers differed from the controls in regard to having higher emotional maladjustment and fear of failure and lower consistency of interest. These differences between the groups and the lack of an age-group difference are hard to explain, however, within the context of the data set provided by Vaitenas and Wiener (1977). There are no data that can be used to account for the direction of influence between such variables as (a) emotional maladjustment and consistency of interest, and

(b) career stability and change: Does "a" cause "b," does "b" cause "a," or are they reciprocally related? What led younger changers and nonchangers to be similar to older changers and nonchangers, especially given that their initial career development occurred in historically distinct eras? Questions such as these remain unanswered, and the data from the Vaitenas and Wiener study, although potentially provocative, are in the final analysis less than satisfying because of the absence of a concern with explanatory processes of influence.

Similar objections may be raised about the study by Dobson and Morrow (1984), who interrelated several demographic variables with measures of career orientation, retirement attitudes, intended age of retirement, and retirement preparation. Although Dobson and Morrow are able to report that career orientation variables are more strongly related than are demographic ones to retirement attitudes, their failure to be concerned with process obviates their ability to explain these distinct patterns of covariation. Moreover, they are similarly unable to account empirically for a reversed pattern of relations present in their data as well, that is, that demographic variables are more related to retirement age and level of preparation for retirement than are career orientation variables.

In short, in both the mid-life career change literature and the retirement literature there is—as is the case in the adolescent career development literature—an absence of concern with process. We return later to the issue of the need to deal empirically with the process of career development. However, at this point it should be noted that, third, the research we have reviewed has often suffered from inadequate and inappropriate data analysis. Problems of capitalization on chance and of multicolinearity have been all too common.

Finally, fourth, these intraindividual studies have been conducted "as if" findings could without question be generalized across time and space; that is, there is little if any appreciation of the possibility that features of the adolescents' contexts could moderate any intraindividual association found in a particular study. Indeed, a major problem we see in the study of career development in adolescence is that the investigation of intraindividual relations is often disassociated from the study of individual-context relations. Thus, it will be noted that as the study of intraindividual relations has been largely unconcerned with the appraisal of individual-context relations, the study of individual-context relations has not generally appreciated the possibility that these relations may be moderated by intraindividual ones.

Studies of Individual-Context Relations

As noted earlier it is often the case in regard to studies focusing on intraindividual functioning, and on how age-associated variables may covary with such functioning, that there is no direct concern with the processes by which this covariation occurs (e.g., Holland & Nichols, 1964; Tinsley et al., 1983); instead age is used to mark a largely unspecified process of influence. A similar state of affairs exists in regard to many—although not all—studies of individual-context relations. Here such variables as socioeconomic status (SES) are used to mark largely unspecified and unstudied processes by which the context influences individual career development.

For example, Bogie (1977) studied the occupational plans of 1,835 high school seniors from rural schools in three different regions of Kentucky. The regions differed in SES, and Bogie reported that males' expectations for entering high-status occupations were lowest in the lowest SES regions and increased with corresponding increases in SES. However, this pattern did not hold for females, who displayed an absence of systematic regional variation. Moreover, statistically controlling for IQ did not account for either the within-sex or the between-sex patterns. Furthermore, although statistically controlling for family SES virtually eliminated the regional differences among males, among females this control resulted in lower SES females having the highest expectations. Thus, a complex set of relations exists among region, family SES, gender, and occupational plans for the high school students studied by Bogie; however, this complexity cannot be unraveled given that Bogie's method did not allow a determination of how parents of a particular SES level and geographical area of residence interact with their sons or their daughters in manners that result in SES being positively related to high-occupational expectations for male children and being negatively related to high-occupational expectations for female children. Bogie's (1977) data are valuable in that they tell us that these patterns of covariation exist, but they reveal nothing about the causal processes linking the contextual and individual developmental variables.

A key reason for the importance of focusing on process is illustrated by the study by Super and Nevill (1984), which involved an assessment of several hundred New Jersey high school students. Here, no significant relations were found between SES and career maturity scores. However, given that process of influence was not assessed the authors are not in a position to speak to the issue of why SES did not relate to career maturity. The point is that research should not merely assess if a contextual variable is or is not related to individual functioning. Research should be aimed at specifying the conditions under which such relations do and do not obtain. Only by focusing on processes of influence may such specification be achieved.

The need to focus on the process of influence between contextual and individual variables is best seen in the most frequently studied instance of the literature pertinent to individual-context relations: Studies of the relation between the family context and career development. For instance, using a cross-sectional design Wijting, Arnold, and Conrad (1978) studied the work values of children in Grades 6, 9, 10, and 12 as well as the work values of the children's parents. Wijting et al. report that in the younger age-groups children were more like their same-sexed parents. However, in the older groups both males and females were most similar to their fathers. What is the process accounting for the age-group differences? Did parents of the younger children interact with their offspring in ways which differed from that shown by parents of the older children? Were there features of individual development (e.g., cognitive or identity developments) that interacted with parental characteristics to produce the group differences? Answers to these questions cannot be readily formulated because of the absence of study of processes linking the parents' behaviors to those of their children. Unless one studies the process of influence among family and child variables one cannot adequately understand the absence or presence of links between parental functioning and child development (Lerner & Galambos, 1985; Zaslow, Rabinovich, & Suwalsky, 1983).

Results of a study by Acock, Barker, and Bengtson (1982) illustrate the potential use of incorporating a concern with process into studies of person-context relations. Acock et al. assessed the relation of maternal employment on parent–youth similarity among 647 father–mother–youth triads. At the aggregate level children of mothers who had high-status work positions tended to be less traditional than children of mothers who worked in either low-status positions or who were housewives. However, although this study was well designed and executed the results do not indicate how the status and nature of the mothers' work were transduced into parent–child behavioral exchanges, which had as their outcome child traditionality or atraditionality. Thus, the group analyses of Acock et al. could be usefully supplemented by somewhat more molecular appraisals of specific parent–child relations, which may mediate between mother's roles and children's developments (Lerner & Galambos, 1985b).

Several other studies of the relation of the family context on youth career development could have profited from such additional analyses. Dillard and Campbell (1981) studied the relationship between parents' work (career) values and adolescents' career-choice attitude maturity among an ethnically diverse sample of adolescents and their parents. No assessment beyond this interrelation was made, however; thus, they could not ascertain the bases for the differential presence or absence of links between work values and attitude maturity in their different ethnic groups. Similarly, Ridgeway (1978), studying 457 college women, found that a career orientation among females who identified with their mothers was associated with greater levels of maternal employment and with less conventional sex-role ideology in mothers and fathers; in turn, a career orientation among females who identified with their fathers was associated with less distance between the female and her father, with lower levels of maternal employment, and with greater maternal sex-role traditionality. However, despite the provocative nature of these associations we do not know the process by which such variables as maternal employment status and degree of parental adherence to traditional sex-role ideology is differentially translated into parent–child interactions in females who are identified with either the same or with the opposite-sex parent. Indeed, the complexity of these interrelations cannot be understood without theory-guided, process-oriented research (Lerner & Galambos, 1985a).

The need to focus on processes of influence becomes even greater when researchers collect longitudinal data. Problems of unraveling causality within unitemporal patterns of covariation are compounded when cross-time variation is introduced. The research of Jackson and Meara (1981) is a case-in-point. Males (N = 99) from rural, economically deprived school districts were studied when they were high school seniors, 1 year after graduation, 5 years after graduation, and 10 years after graduation. The males were divided into those who had low identification with their fathers (the LI group) and those who had high identification with their fathers (the HI group). Although there were no differences between the groups in regard to optimism about the future, occupational satisfaction, personal satisfaction, satisfaction with status, or spouse's occupational achievements, the groups did differ in several other respects; that is, the HI group exceeded the LI group in respect to: occupational status, occupational aspirations, educational achievement, educational plans, and spouse's educational achievements. Moreover, Jackson and Meara report that these group similarities and differences are consistent across measurement occasions.

Why? What is the process by which level of identification with one's father becomes transduced into a male's psychological status (e.g., in regard to life satisfaction), behavioral attainments (e.g., occupational and educational achievements), and social relationships (e.g., marriage to a woman having particular educational achievements)? What leads to the presence of particular associations and the absence of others? Moreover, what is the means by which the absence or presence of these associations is maintained across a decade of adult life? What do the HI males do and/or what do the LI males not do to promote the continuation of these group differences? Unfortunately, valuable as it may be in other respects, the research of Jackson and Meara (1981) does not allow any of these questions to be adequately addressed.

How might a concern with process begin to be incorporated into person-context research? One quite interesting direction is suggested in a study by Grotevant (1979). Indeed, this study is quite unique in that it considers the role of biological variation in adolescent career development, a focus for which we called earlier in this chapter. Concerned with family influences on adolescent vocational interest development, Grotevant studied a group of 844 parents and adolescents from 114 biologically related and 101 adoptive families. The parental and adolescent groups completed the Strong–Campbell Interest Inventory. Family environment variance was found to contribute to the variance in vocational interests in both the biological and the adoptive families. In addition, however, genetic variance was implicated in the vocational interests of the adolescents in the biological families. This finding suggests that biogenetic variation may mediate some of the features of adolescent career development, and that biometrical techniques may be used in trying to uncover at least some of the processes linking family (parental) variables and offspring development (Plomin & Fulker, in press). In other words, by drawing on variables from levels of analysis other than social contextual and individual psychological it is possible to account for potentially causal variation in the process of career development.

Another means by which insight may be gained into the process of career development is to interrelate behavior in one context with that shown in another setting. In this way a structural pathway of direction of influence may be modeled, given the implicitly time-ordered character of behavior in one versus another context. Longitudinal data reported by Steinberg, Greenberger, Garduque, and McAuliffe (1982) shows the potential utility of such an approach. These investigators studied more than 200 high school students from four high schools in Orange County, California. The effects of working versus nonworking on personal and nonworking context behaviors were ascertained. Steinberg et al. report that working facilitates the development of personal responsibility (self-management) but not social responsibility (concern for others). Moreover, working diminished involvement in such nonworking contexts as the school, the family, and the peer group. Finally, working leads to the development of cynical attitudes toward work, to the acceptance of unethical work attitudes, and to increased use of cigarettes and marijuana.

The antecedent-consequent relations among contextual and individual and social variables, which can be inferred from the findings of Steinberg et al. (1982), derive from several desirable features of their research design: Repeated longitudinal assessments of adolescents in multiple contexts were made and comparison groups of working versus nonworking students were appraised. Given the time ordered nature of the several assessments, cross-time relations found within one group could be compared with those seen in the other group in order to gain insight about processes of influence linking experiences/outcomes of work with personal and nonwork-related social behavior.

In sum, research on individual-context relations has, on the whole, been limited by a lack of attention to processes of influence. Except for a few notable exceptions (e.g., Grotevant, 1979; Steinberg et al., 1982) research designs have not included assessments that allow statements to be made about the conditions under which a given contextual feature will or will not be linked to a given feature of individual development. Only one study, to our knowledge, has attempted to gain insight into variation contributed by processes linked to biological as well as social contextual and individual psychological levels of analysis (Grotevant, 1979). In turn, with few exceptions (e.g., Steinberg et al., 1982) studies have not considered cross-context influences and/or the social ecology of career development (Bronfenbrenner, 1979). This latter shortcoming is particularly distressing given that both our own analysis (see Chapter 3), and that of other reviewers (Crouter, Belsky, & Spanier, 1984; Smith, 1981; Young, 1983), indicate that Bronfenbrenner's (1979) system can usefully integrate existing information about social context-career development relations as well as suggest directions for future research.

CONCLUSIONS

Our review in this chapter does not allow us to be especially positive about the quality and extensiveness of extant knowledge about career development in adolescence. We have seen that most research is adevelopmental, and that problems of design, method, and analysis plague even much of the research that has the minimal requirements of a study of intraindividual change, i.e., two times of measurement. Moreover, there have been few studies that have gone beyond the description of covariation among some marker variables (e.g., age, sex, SES) and career development-related variables. Little knowledge about process of influence in career development can be gleaned from this literature. Moreover, it is unfortunately the case that the status of the literature in regard to adolescent career development is better than that, which exists in regard to other age levels, e.g., mid-life and retirement—if only because of the simple reason that there have been many more studies done in regard to adolescence than in regard to the other two age levels combined.

This negative view of the extant literature derived from use of the model depicted in Fig. 4.1 as a means to organize and critique research. However, at the same time the use of this model, by allowing us to point to problems in the literature, facilitated our specification of methodological "remedies" derived from the developmental, contextual, and relational perspective we have developed in Chapters 1–4. In other words, we believe that in addition to being critical we have been constructive; we have implied throughout our review what sort of methods should be applied to study intraindividual change, interindividual differences in such change, and the person-context relational processes, which may account for these changes. In Chapter 6 we turn directly to a discussion of the methodological strategies we see as being necessary in the study of career development and, in addition, we propose a conceptually based research agenda consistent with these strategies. We illustrate our approach with examples drawn from our own laboratory.

6
Toward A Methodological Agenda for the Study of Vocational Behavior and Career Development

The major emphasis of the presentation in this book has been conceptual. Throughout we have stressed a developmental-contextual perspective (Lerner, 1984; Lerner & Kauffman, 1985), wherein we emphasized the reasons for conceptualizing vocational and career behaviors and careers: as part of developmental processes encompassing the entire life-span; as involving relations both within the person—among his/her biological and psychological processes, and between the person and his or her immediate interpersonal and broader societal and cultural setting; and therefore as being textured by the context of life, a context involving levels of analysis ranging from the bioevolutionary to the social historical. However, across the presentation of this perspective we have pointed out that specific methodological strategies are prescribed by our conceptual stance. For instance, in reviewing adolescent vocational development in Chapter 5, we pointed out that a stress on a developmental and relational perspective requires longitudinal research—to appraise intraindividual, or developmental, change—of a multivariate nature—to encompass the intraindividual and interindividual variables whose interrelations comprise the developmental process.

The specification in previous chapters of the methodological implications of our developmental-contextual perspective has been important in at least two respects. First, this specification suggests not only that our perspective can be translated into scientifically testable ideas, but also that there are particular empirical procedures that are appropriate, indeed requisite, for performing these tests. Second, this specification shows what we regard as the appropriate direction of influence between theory and research; that is, methodological strategies and options (should) derive from theory; one should not let one's methodological preferences dictate the questions one investigates. Rather, theory should guide the formulation of the questions one asks, which, in turn, should lead to the use of a particular methodology.

Both of these reasons for the importance of specifying the methodological implications of our perspective shape our presentation in this chapter. Moreover, we agree with Crites (1983) who has recently observed that "although the field of vocational psychology has been dominated by the developmental point of view for the past 30 years . . . , sophistication in developmental data designs has lagged far behind conceptualization" (p. 339). Thus, we expand here on the methodological prescriptions that were only briefly presented in other chapters because of their more substantive foci. Specifically, we describe in some detail the methodological issues and options associated with our developmental, relational, and contextual perspectives. In addition, we illustrate our views by presenting one concrete research example derived from our conceptual position, that is, the study of patterns of short-term changes in people's work values through the use of P-technique factor analyses of intraindividual variability. We turn first to a discussion of the methodological implications associated with each of the three components of our developmental-contextual perspective.

THE DEVELOPMENTAL COMPONENT: METHODOLOGICAL ISSUES AND OPTIONS

Unless one were to contend that career and vocational behaviors arise from preformations in the genome and that they therefore exist in an immutable form across the life-span, one must consider that such behaviors undergo change across life. Such changes may or may not be developmental ones, either totally or in part (see Chapter 2), but the presence of change requires that people be studied at two or more times. Indeed, the only way in which to detect intraindividual change is through the application of a repeated measurement, longitudinal, design. And because of problems of discriminating true change from the effects of regression to the mean more than two occasions of measurement are needed within such a design; that is, regression effects may become increasingly negligible as occasions of measurement increase to three and beyond (Nesselroade, Stigler, & Baltes, 1980).

Longitudinal designs are not, of course, without problems, most of which center around issues of internal and external validity, e.g., testing effects, instrumentation, selection, experimental mortality, interaction effects of testing (Campbell & Stanley, 1963; see also Baltes, Reese, & Nesselroade, 1977). A potential problem of particular interest from a developmental-contextual perspective is the problem of cohort effects. Specifically, when only one birth cohort is involved in a longitudinal study ontogenetic effects are confounded with historical effects on development (e.g., Baltes, Cornelius, & Nesselroade, 1979). For example, because of technological advances and sociocultural changes, the timing, sequence of "stages," and outcomes of vocational developmental processes may be different for those born in the 1940s than for those born in the 1960s. In short, in longitudinal designs, unless more than one birth cohort is followed over time, the unique interaction of individual lives and historical time cannot be uncovered.

The advent of sequential designs (e.g., Baltes, 1968; Schaie, 1965) has made it possible to identify cohort effects. Essentially, sequential designs involve the observation of at least two birth cohorts over time in either a succession of longitudinal studies (longitudinal sequences) or of cross-sectional studies (cross-sectional sequences) (e.g., Baltes et al., 1979). In the former case, the same individuals are measured repeatedly at different ages (thus involving the problems associated with repeated measurement), and in the later case, independent observations with respect to age and cohort are gathered (thus circumventing problems associated with repeated measurement but creating problems associated with the inference of intraindividual change). These two forms of sequential strategies can be exploited in various ways, combined or repeatedly, to describe and explain cohort effects on development. It should be noted, however, that disagreement exists over methods of estimation and the utility of such designs in *explaining* cohort effects (see Baltes, 1968; Schaie, 1965; Schaie & Baltes, 1975). This controversy underscores the need to embed one's methodology within theory; that is, explanation comes from theory and not from the data one collects through particular methodologies.

To illustrate the sequential approach, let us consider the following example, which could be a study of vocational interest development. The design could involve varying age, sex, and cohort membership in a coordinated series of short-term longitudinal sequences, each requiring three times of measurement. Several birth cohorts (let us assume four) could take a vocational test battery in three successive years, thus enabling the study to cover a 6-year age span in subjects: Birth cohort 1972 would be 13 years old at the first time of measurement (1985), 14 years old at the second time of measurement (1986), and 15 years old at the third occasion of measurement (1987). Birth cohort 1969, on the other hand, would be 16 years old at the first time of measurement (1985), 17 years old at the second time of measurement (1986), and 18 years at the third time of measurement (1987). Comparable longitudinal sequences would take place for the intermediate birth cohorts 1970 and 1971.

The two major limitations to be guarded against in this type of design are: (a) selective dropout or attrition of the longitudinal sample; and

(b) retest effects that can result in the longitudinal subjects showing apparent increases or decreases in level over time, which are unrelated to normative ontogenetic change. Unless steps are taken either to randomize, or estimate and correct for such effects, the conclusions and generalizations one makes are problematic. With regard to retest effects a number of control groups are necessary. Thus, in addition to the core longitudinal sample an additional sample of males and females, drawn randomly from each cohort, should be tested for the first time at the second occasion of measurement; still another independent sample should be tested for the first time at the third occasion of measurement. Thus, at each occasion of measurement for which the longitudinal core sample will be repeatedly measured, there will be an independent sample, which will be equivalent to the longitudinal sample except for one characteristic—they will not have had prior exposure to the measurement battery. Comparisons of the resulting several data sets will then permit analysis of the effects of repeated testing as well as the introduction of appropriate corrections (Labouvie, Bartsch, Nesselroade, & Baltes, 1974).

The Use of Change Sensitive Measures and the Measurement of Change

The most elaborately designed longitudinal study will not allow development to be appraised adequately if the measures used to assess development are not sensitive to change. If our measure of the temperature of the air was the placement of our hand outside our kitchen window, then despite our repeated (longitudinal) application of this measure across a summer afternoon we would be able to discriminate only the widest possible variation in temperatures. Our measure would not be sensitive to the variations of just a few degrees that other measures—designed explicitly to be sensitive to such variation—would detect.

Similarly, if, in the longitudinal study of career and vocational behaviors one relies on measures, which were explicitly devised to be insensitive to age-associated or contextually associated variation, then one is not conducting an adequate or unbiased investigation of development. Thus, when trait-like measures of vocational and career behaviors are used in such research (e.g., as in Costa, McCrae, & Holland, 1984), such research is biased in the direction of finding a lack of change—at least to the extent that the measures have been developed adequately to fit the theoretical conception of a trait as a stable and enduring organizational characteristic of behavior (e.g., Buss & Plomin, 1984; Hall & Lindzey, 1978).

Of course, the use of a change-sensitive measure, i.e., a measure capable of detecting intraindividual variation, does not guarantee that change will be found. The presence or absence of change in a given study should be an empirical question. But, the point is that when one uses a change-insensitive measure to study change, one is in actuality taking steps to preclude finding what one is purportedly subjecting to empirical scrutiny. The findings of such research are, therefore, of little value to a balanced assessment of the presence or absence of change and any theory built or relying on the use of data from such research would most likely be egregiously flawed.

But, how does one construct measures that can fairly appraise change? There are a host of issues and problems associated with designing and implementing instruments for the measurement of change. Essentially, these issues and problems refer to the isolation of the construct to be measured and then measuring it in such a manner that observed changes reflect changes in and only in the given construct. Although any number of topics could be discussed here, ranging from the various problems of internal validity and reliability to the dangers of using change scores (e.g., Cronbach & Furby, 1970; but see Nesselroade et al., 1980; Rogosa, Brandt, & Zimowski, 1982), we focus our attention here on the problems associated with measurement equivalence and construct lability—two topics which have not been given adequate attention in either the developmental literature in general or the literature on career and vocational development in particular.

Measurement Equivalence.   For purposes here, measurement equivalence refers to the problem of determining whether observed change on a given instrument is due to change in the individual, change in what the instrument is actually measuring, or some of both (e.g., Baltes, Reese, & Nesselroade, 1977; Labouvie, 1980). For example, suppose that in a group of students, measured with the same instrument prior to and after their college careers, the importance assigned to the work value of economic returns increases over time. Unless measurement equivalence is established, it is not possible to conclude that these students have become more economically oriented, for it may be the case that the instrument measures qualitatively different aspects of economic returns at the two times of measurement. Several methods exist for establishing or assessing measurement equivalence (e.g., Cattell, 1970; Labouvie, 1980; Labouvie, Frohring, Baltes, & Goulet, 1973; see Eckensberger, 1973, for a review), none of which are best or appropriate for all cases. The point is that measurement equivalence, which can be examined at the level of observed variables and latent variables, is a matter that vocational development researchers must recognize and deal with.

Stability Versus Lability.   The stability or the lability of a given construct is also an issue that researchers need to address when attempting to measure change. Whether a construct is stable across time or whether it shows change (lability) should be an empirical issue. Neither stability nor lability should be merely assumed to exist. However, an overarching assumption in the vocational literature has been that vocationally relevant outcomes reflect stable constructs akin to personality traits. For example, differential researchers have taken individual differences found at one point in time to represent stable individual differences over time. In addition, in long-term longitudinal studies, mean changes in the given construct have been viewed as indicating long-term change or maturation. It is entirely possible that the constructs under consideration encompass some component of lability (steady-state variability), akin to state dimensions (e.g., mood). If, for example, vocational interests demonstrate day-to-day variability (*not* representing measurement error), then a one time measurement could misrepresent interindividual differences, and long term longitudinal measurement could distort intraindividual change. The point is that just because vocational constructs are labeled as stable, they are not necessarily stable. This is especially important when determining the reliability of an instrument. For example, test-retest correlations over periods of even a few days are only good indicators of reliability when the construct is known to be exceedingly stable (e.g., Nesselroade, 1983). If the construct is given to some lability, then the reliability estimates based on test-retest data will be attenuated. One can only wonder about the number of good, reliable measures of vocational phenomena that have been discarded because of low test-retest correlations.

Longitudinal Data Analysis

Once change sensitive longitudinal data have been obtained they must be appropriately analyzed. Numerous useful data analytic strategies exist. Indeed, several recent advances have been made in such techniques as repeated measures ANOVA, multivariate analysis of variance, time series analysis, confirmatory factor analysis, and causal modeling (for related discussions, see Horn & McArdle, 1980; Nesselroade & Baltes, 1979; Nesselroade & von Eye, 1985). It is not the purpose of this presentation to provide the detailed statistical characteristics of these advances. Instead, we highlight two types of analytic procedures, which appear to hold much promise specifically for the analysis of longitudinal vocational data.

Causal Modeling. The first comes under the generic label of causal modeling with latent variables. In essence, causal models permit the testing of hypotheses and the construction of causal chains without experimental manipulation. There are two parts to a causal model—the measurement model (i.e., constructing latent variables from observed variables via confirmatory factor analysis, thus circumventing problems due to measurement error), and the structural equation model (i.e., setting up and solving systems of structural regression equations). The perhaps more familiar technique of path analysis is a special case of structural equation models, which does not include a measurement model (e.g., Rogosa, 1979). The successful construction of causal models depends on explicit specifications of causal links, which ideally are theoretically based. Although causal models have had only limited use to date in the study of career development (e.g., Kohn & Schooler, 1983; Mortimer & Kumka, 1982), the possibilities for future research efforts are endless *if* the field moves to more theoretically guided longitudinal tests of developmental change.

Analyzing Lability Versus Stability. The second analytic procedure that we want to highlight is P-technique factor analysis (Cattell, 1963), which, when coupled with a research design involving intense, repeated measurement of an individual, allows one to address empirically the idea that vocational phenomena may not be as stable as they are often assumed to be. To explain the use of this procedure let us ask what is assumed when, in order to formulate a recommendation to a person about his/her career development, one administers to that person a test of vocational interests on a single occasion? The implicit theoretical, or at least operational, assumption is that vocational interests as measured on that single occasion provide an index of the person's enduring interests. Indeed, if we believed that interests did not show such trait-like stability but instead showed day-to-day fluctuations, there would be little sense to measuring interests on one (conveniently or arbitrarily chosen) day. In other words, when we use a single occasion of measurement to index a person's vocational interests, attitudes, etc. we are implicitly excluding as relevant any state-like variation, or lability. Simply, our assumption is one of trait stability and not one of state lability.

But is such an assumption warranted? To best answer such a question should we not put our stability assumption to an empirical test? If our answer to this question is "yes," how can the assumption be tested? One possible procedure to use involves intensive repeated measurement of a subject and analysis of the resulting data through use of what is termed P-technique factor analysis (Nesselroade & Ford, 1985). Although a presentation of the details of this type of factor analysis is beyond the purposes of this chapter (but see Cattell, 1952a, 1952b; Nesselroade & Bartsch, 1977), its conceptual features are fairly straight forward.

If we believe that it is possible that a person's vocational interests may change from day to day, and that these changes may be systematic, we need to do at least two things. First, we need to measure the person repeatedly, say every day for 100 or so days, in order to obtain a sufficient number of observation points to statistically test for systematicity of change. This first requirement is analogous to what is needed in more conventional approaches to observing people in order to obtain data useful for factor analysis; that is, in what is termed R-technique factor analysis, wherein one wants to see how items covary within a single occasion of measurement, one needs a large number of subjects; this is because people, in our analogue to measurement occasions, constitute observation points (e.g., in such R-technique analyses one may want a ratio of subjects-to-items of 3:1, 5:1, 10:1, etc.). The point is, then, that in all types of factor analytic procedures one wants to have sufficient observations of that "entity" one wishes to generalize across—people in R-technique factor analysis and occasions in P-technique factor analysis. In short, because we want to test the possibility that our vocational variable may be labile and may therefore show variation from day to day, we need a sufficient number of days in our "sample" to perform this test. Accordingly, our study must involve a period of intensive measurement, which we have noted is conventionally about 100 days in the P-technique literature.

Of course, the second thing we must do to test the possibility of lability in vocational variables is to analyze the data derived from our intensive measurement design. Here the computational procedures of P-technique factor analysis are employed; although the technical details of these procedures need not, as noted, be presented here, the essential idea of the procedures is quite simple. The procedures allow one to determine if change occurs from day-to-day and if that change is systematic. Day-to-day change is, of course, variation, and unless variation occurs no correlations among variables across occasions can exist; in such a case the result of the P-technique factor analysis would lead one to reject the idea of lability within a person over time. However, variation may occur and the results of the P-technique analyses might still be negative. This would occur if there was no covariation across days within and across items. However, if significant patterns of covariation were found this would indicate systematic change within a person over time. Such systematicity would indicate that the person did change from day to day but that the change was not random. Indeed, the change could be grouped into a factor or factors—statistical constructs that describe, in this case, a given person's state-like day-to-day fluctuations in vocational interests, attitudes, etc.

The discovery of such factors would not be a point of minor methodological interest. Such a finding would constitute a serious challenge to approaches that seek to make generalizations about vocational phenomena on the basis of a single occasion of measurement. Just as we know that for many, if not all, people moods fluctuate from day to day, and that we would not therefore want to make a trait-like attribution about a person's emotional status (e.g., as "she is a sad person," or "he is a fearful person") on the basis of a sample from a single day, we might not want to make a trait-like characterization of, or a long-term recommendation about, vocational phenomena if we have only a sample from a single measurement occasion.

Indeed, our reluctance to rely on single occasion information would be bolstered if we included a highly desirable, but not essential, component in our intensive measurement, P-technique study. Simply, if we replicated our procedures with several individuals and, then, found comparable results, we would be in a stronger position to argue for the existence of state-like factors. For this reason, as well as because such replication allows one to determine not only possible similarities among people in within-person change but also interindividual differences as well, replication across individuals is virtually a standard feature of P-technique studies (Cattell, 1966; Nesselroade, 1983). Thus, by focusing on changes within individuals, and also on the extent of similarities across individual change patterns, the P-technique is a powerful strategy with which to ascertain intraindividual change in vocational phenomena as well as to address differences and similarities across individuals with respect to such changes.

Two further points regarding the P-technique need to be emphasized. First, its use is not limited to studying intraindividual variability over time. For example, instead of studying individuals, one could study organizations, and ascertain intraorganizational variability over time. In addition, instead of varying occasions according to *time,* one could vary occasions according to *situations;* that is, if a sufficient number of different situations (say, several various work-related situations) could be obtained, one could ascertain intraindividual variability across situations. The second point regarding P-technique is that it is not without limitations. There is some controversy in the literature regarding the possible time-series nature of P-technique data (e.g., Holtzman, 1962). Specifically, there may be some dependencies among the observations (because many observations are gathered from the same source, e.g., from the same individual, institution, etc.). These dependencies could reflect time-series or "lagged" relationships (e.g., how one feels today may have *some* impact on how one may feel tomorrow or next week). Traditional P-technique factor analysis (as described earlier), however, does not attempt to exploit time-series relationships; that is, the analysis only considers the *simultaneous* relations among the variables across the several occasions (e.g., it assumes that how one feels today has nothing to do with how one may feel tomorrow). Unfortunately, currently there is no easy statistical means to evaluate both possible time-series dependencies and ascertain simultaneous (cross-time) relations. However, statistical work continues to address this limitation, and some of it appears quite promising (Molenaar, 1985). In sum, although it has limitations, as does any other statistical technique, the sensitivity to change that P-technique provides is an asset that outweights its potential limits.

Our discussion of the features of P-technique factor analysis and the potential implications of its use in the study of vocational phenomena is not based on totally empirically unsupported opinions. Results from some initial P-technique research on work values, which was conducted in the laboratory of the first author, indicate that single occasion studies of such values may not be adequate and that the assumption of trait-like stability may not be warranted. Although we have reason to discuss this research in greater detail later in the chapter, we should note that systematic, day-to-day lability in work values was found (Schulenberg, Vondracek, & Nesselroade, 1985). Moreover, this research involved conducting simultaneous P-technique factor analyses on seven subjects, and the results of these replications indicated that there are very likely some similarities in intraindividual change patterns in work values across subjects. Such findings raise the idea that other vocationally relevant variables that have been considered by others to be quite stable, trait like, and therefore useful to examine outside of a longitudinal, repeated measures design—for example, variables such as vocational interests (Costa et al., 1984)—may be more profitably and appropriately examined using P-technique factor analysis.

In sum, our developmental-contextual perspective leads us to prescribe the use of particular types of longitudinal designs, particular types of measures (i.e., change sensitive ones equivalent across developmental epochs), and particular types of strategies for data analysis. These recommendations are in the service of studying developing people in relation to their changing contexts. Thus, our prescriptions implicitly pertain to the second component of our conceptual perspective—the relational one. We turn now to a consideration of the implications of this component for methodology.

THE RELATIONAL COMPONENT: METHODOLOGICAL ISSUES AND OPTIONS

Our concept of relationism (see also Looft, 1973) stresses that any target behavior or behaviors, e.g., career or vocational ones, exist along and interact with: (a) other intraindividual characteristics of the person; and (b) interindividual and broader contextual features of a person's milieu. At least three features of research derive from relationism.

The Need for Multivariate Measures. If any given variable exists in relation to others than a univariate study can provide only a very narrow view of behavior. In our view, measures of any target variable must be assessed in relation to the other intraindividual and interindividual variables for which theory predicts there may be covariation. Hence, multiple variables should be assessed in any given study.

The Need for Multidimensional Assessment. Although any given construct can be assessed in a multivariate manner—and, given our preference for causal modeling techniques, such multiple indicator assessment should be the rule—relationism implies that multiple individual and/or contextual constructs be assessed. In other words, in any one study more than one dimension of individual functioning and/or of the context should be included. For instance, in addition to measures of vocational and career behaviors measures should be included of other dimensions of individuality, e.g., biological, personality, and motivational constructs should be included. Furthermore, measures of dimensions of the context, e.g., the family, the school, and the work setting, should be part of any study informed by our concept of relationism.

The Need for Multilevel Research.   The multiple dimensions of person and context to be included in the prototypic developmental-contextual study indicate that such research should be more than individual-psychological in character. Variables from multiple levels of analysis need to be assessed in such endeavors. Thus, in addition to psychological dimensions of functioning, biological, sociological, cultural, and historical constructs need to be measured.

Such multilevel research is particularly important in the study of career and vocational behavior because the array of possible careers available to a person changes historically in the face of alterations in such phenomena as: technology (e.g., 50 years ago the role of computer programmer did not exist); values and mores (e.g., consider the changing proportion of women, particularly of mothers, in the work force over the last 40 years); social policy and laws (e.g., regarding equal opportunity employment laws); and the physical ecology (e.g., increasing urbanization has led to the diminution of farm and grazing land and, accompanied by increasing technological advances in agriculture, many roles have disappeared from the agricultural scene; for instance, how many people become shepherds nowadays?).

Relationism's promotion of multilevel research is obviously quite related to the third component of our conceptual perspective—the contextual one. We now consider the implications of this component for methodology.

THE CONTEXTUAL COMPONENT: METHODOLOGICAL ISSUES AND OPTIONS

It is the context to which the individual is dynamically related in our developmental-contextual perspective. Hence, it is our view that measures of the context must be interrelated with assessments of the individual in any study derived from this perspective. Moreover, we want to point out once again that this interrelation should be theory guided. We have illustrated such work in our discussion of the person-context goodness-of-fit model (Lerner & Lerner, 1983) in Chapter 4.

The need to take a contextual perspective raises the same multivariate, multidimensional, and especially and most obviously multilevel issues raised in respect to relationism. But the contextual component is not just redundant with relationism. Contextualism implies rather directly that it is more than the individual's relation to the context, which must be considered in research. In addition, the context must be considered in its own right. The family, the society, and history may not then be merely reduced to individual-psychological terms, thereby for instance making the relationism we call for nothing more than a consideration of stimulus–response relations (e.g., see Bijou, 1976). Instead, each level of the context must be studied with respect to its own units of analysis.

For instance, the family and the socialization experiences that occur within it should not be reduced to a set of learning regimens impinging on the individual. The family is more than a setting within which a person's vocational and career preferences and interests unfold. It is itself a dynamic entity responsive to and influencing the community and broader social context within which it is embedded.

Given the need to study the context in a nonreductionistic manner, then, the multilevel research promoted by contextualism must be multidisciplinary in character. Such collaboration is especially important for psychologists to engage in because, as noted in Chapter 3, psychology as a discipline is not particularly skilled either theoretically or methodologically in measuring the context. Accordingly, the methods of physical and behavioral ecologists, of urban planners, of sociologists, and of historians are of particular salience. Moreover, the data analytic techniques of these other disciplines are often of special use. For instance, the techniques of cohort analysis (e.g., Riley, Johnson, & Foner, 1972) and of log linear analysis (e.g., Clogg, 1981), found in sociology, and the quantitative historiography methods of historians (e.g., Vinovskis, in press) are excellent cases in point.

THE COMBINED IMPORT OF THE COMPONENTS
OF OUR MODEL FOR METHODOLOGY

We believe it is fair to characterize the methodological prescriptions derived from our developmental-contextual perspective as involving procedures, which are both rigorous and complex. However, anything short of our approach leads readily to the prospect of ending up with narrow, overly restricted, biased, and all too often adevelopmental studies of career and vocational development. Admittedly, our conceptual approach is a comprehensive one that calls for the study of developmental phenomena in their full complexity. This position leaves our position open to the criticism that it is trying to do too much (Gottfredson, 1983). However, in regard to the conceptual features of our position, we may note that Scarr (1984), commenting on the developmental-contextual perspective in her recent presidential address to the Division of Developmental Psychology of the American Psychological Association, stated that the developmental-contextual view is "discrepant from the prevailing psychology-of-main-effects, in which everyone is affected in the same way by the same, observable events. I predict that . . . [this view] . . . will become the dominant psychological lens of the 1980s. Psychological studies will focus on person–situation interactions and invent new 'facts' about the differential effects of environments on individuals" (p. 33).

Of course, to achieve the promise of our conceptual position the research for which we call has to extend over a period of time. Not only is development complex, especially when viewed from a developmental-contextual perspective, but so too are the vocational and career behaviors we wish to assess in relation to the other developing and/or changing individual and contextual features of life. As such, by necessity, research must be programmatic: No one study can include assessments of all potential sources of individual and contextual variation, which may impact career and vocational development. Accordingly, the scope of the variables needed to be included in research derived from our perspective needs to be tempered by the need to conduct a feasible study with precision. It is through a program of research involving the methodological considerations we have detailed in this chapter, that the potential of the developmental-contextual perspective can be realized.

It is useful, then, to provide an empirical illustration of the sort of programmatic developmental-contextual research for which we call. As noted earlier in this chapter, the empirical illustration involves some initial research in our laboratory, which used an intensive measurement design and a P-technique factor analysis to test whether a specific vocational construct— work values—showed state lability or trait stability.

AN EMPIRICAL ILLUSTRATION:
PATTERNS OF SHORT-TERM CHANGES IN
INDIVIDUALS' WORK VALUES—P-TECHNIQUE
FACTOR ANALYSES OF
INTRAINDIVIDUAL VARIABILITY

Work values are considered by some vocational psychologists to be of central importance in the career decision process (e.g., Katz, 1963; Rosenberg, 1957; Super, 1970). However, work values are generally assumed to be traits and, as such, to show trait-like stability. Indeed, in discussing the work values literature, Pryor (1980) asserted that "the discussion of the concept of 'stability' as a concept and its methodological implications have been virtually ignored" (p. 147). Most work values studies have been, in fact, concerned with structuring interindividual differences at one point in time. Of those relatively few studies that have attempted to assess, rather than assume, the stability of work values (for reviews see Jepsen, 1984; Kapes & Strickler, 1975; Zytowski, 1970) most have either approximated change by mean differences between age-groups in cross-sectional designs, or by correlations of scores or mean changes in scores over at least a 1-year period in longitudinal designs (see Pryor, 1980, for a notable exception). All have been concerned with average change at the group level. No attention has been accorded to the short-term changes that can occur within individuals (i.e., intraindividual variability). Thus, it appears that work values are assumed to be either trait like and static (in the interindividual differences studies), or given only to long-term change or maturation effects (in the developmental studies). In both cases work values are assumed to be stable or trait like over short periods of time.

The illustrative study we discuss represents a major departure from traditional conceptual and empirical work on the stability of work values in two important ways. First, no assumption is made regarding the short-term stability of individual's work values. Rather, it is the subject matter of investigation. Secondly, because the first concern is with possible changes *within* individuals, multiple single-case designs for data collection and analysis are utilized. Although this idiographic focus may appear to run counter to the prevailing nomothetic approach in the social and behavioral sciences, it does not. Rather, idiography can be viewed as complementary to, and indeed necessary for, the nomothetic purpose (Lamiell, 1981; Marx, 1956; Nesselroade, 1983; Zevon & Tellegen, 1982); that is, because the goal of the nomothetic approach is to establish the general laws of behavior, it may fall short in describing or explaining the behavior of a given individual (Hoyer, 1974). By first identifying idiographic patterns, and then ascertaining the extent of interindividual similarities and differences in intraindividual patterns (as is done in the presently discussed study), it may be possible to provide a more powerful and adequate identification of the laws governing behavior (Nesselroade, 1983; Zevon & Tellegen, 1982).

An essential feature of our illustrative study is the utilization of multivariate, replicated, single-subject designs (Nesselroade & Ford, 1985), the data from which are analyzed by P-technique factor analyses (Cattell, 1963, 1966). Because the P-technique was more fully described earlier (for detailed discussions of the P-technique, see, e.g., Lebo & Nesselroade, 1978; Roberts & Nesselroade, 1983; Zevon & Tellegen, 1982), we need only reiterate here some of its essential components. In a typical P-technique study, one subject is measured on several variables on many (preferably at least 100) occasions (Cattell & Scheier, 1961). The responses are intercorrelated over the several occasions and the resulting correlation matrix is factor analyzed. In contrast to the more familiar R-technique factor analysis, the P-technique combines the sampling of variables and occasions for one subject, rather than the sampling of variables and subjects on one occasion. Furthermore, whereas the R-technique yields factors that describe interindividual differences at the time of measurement, the factors derived from P-technique describe the structure of intraindividual variation or change over the times of measurement (Nesselroade, 1983). The resulting factors are clearly states or state dimensions (Cattell & Scheier, 1961; Nesselroade & Bartsch, 1977). Thus, the P-technique emphasizes the examination of systematic, occasion to occasion covariation among variables for the single case. Matters of generalizability across persons can be examined by comparing the factors that result from several P-technique analyses to ascertain the extent of interindividual similarities in short-term intraindividual change (e.g., Lebo & Nesselroade, 1978; Roberts & Nesselroade, 1983; Zevon & Tellegen, 1982).

By means of concurrent replications of the P-technique design, our study sought to answer two questions regarding the short-term change in work values: (a) Do work values scores manifest sufficient intraindividual variability that they can be reasonably portrayed as having a significant state component?; and (b) Assuming work values scores manifest coherent intraindividual variability for at least two study participants, to what extent are the dimensions of that variability similar across participants?

To address these issues seven college students were given Super's (1970) Work Values Inventory (WVI) for 100 consecutive days with standard instructions, except for an added admonition to respond to all items definitely based only on how they felt about each item *at the time,* without regard for whether they had answered the items the same way the previous day. This was done, essentially, to minimize practice effects. Informal feedback from the subjects confirmed that this strategy worked reasonably well.

For each subject, those scales that showed sufficient response variability over time were intercorrelated and factor analyzed. Results indicated that work values could, indeed, be characterized as state dimensions. In other words, response variability (in effect, intraindividual variability) was found, and it was determined that it was not due solely to measurement error, but rather to systematic changes in the subject's responding from one occasion to another. Furthermore, it was found that although each subject had rather unique factor structures, some of the factors, or states, were common across subjects (particularly those states encompassing the work values of "variety" and "creativity"). In sum, the results suggest that work values, long assumed to be trait like, also have state-like dimensions.

Schulenberg et al. (1985) made the following conclusions:

> Our findings do not offer evidence of simplicity in the work values domain. For those interested in making broad generalizations at the group level, the results offer reason to be concerned about the validity of those generalizations. For those interested in acknowledging and examining the complexities of vocational behavior and development, the results and their implications offer some indication of work that needs to be done. Indeed, the findings here lend empirical support to recent conceptual efforts aimed at breaking out of the predominant individual differences or organismic developmental paradigms, and considering vocational development as a dynamic process characterized by multivariate and multidirectional change (e.g., Markham, 1983; Super, 1980; Vondracek & Lerner, 1982; Vondracek, Lerner, & Schulenberg, 1983a). Finally, the study points toward the utility of combining the idiographic and nomothetic approaches in an effort to discover at what level generality resides among possibly idiosyncratic patterns of observable change. To be sure, we expect that there are commonalities across individuals in vocational behavior and development; however, the search for these commonalities should not preclude the possibility of divergence at some levels of observation and analysis. We join with others (e.g., Zevon & Tellegen, 1982) in the belief that progress is more apt to occur if idiographic and nomothetic searches are conducted in a complementary manner. (pp. 21–22)

Of course, the aforementioned study was clearly exploratory, and further research would be needed to bolster its conclusions. In addition, future efforts of this type should be tailored to delineating the causes of systematic fluctuations in work values, causal determinants that reside within the individual (e.g., moods), within the context (e.g., an organization in which the person intended to work shuts down), and within the individual-context interaction (e.g., negotiation with parents regarding future course of study).

Furthermore, we suspect that similar results might be obtained in studies of other vocational development variables, such as vocational interests. Considering the fact that the one-time testing of vocational interests is a multimillion-dollar industry in the field of vocational guidance, one can easily see the potential implications of recognizing that the trait scores do not tell the whole story. Interventions based on a one-time measurement of vocational interests or work values would very likely have to be conducted with greater caution. Equally important, however, are the implications for theory and research. As we have noted in other chapters, theory must be able to accommodate two changing targets, namely, the individual and his/her context. This means that theory must account for and be sensitive to changes of all kinds, including the kind of intraindividual change patterns discovered in the study of work values we have just discussed. It also means that attempts must be made in the design of measuring instruments to tap both the static (trait) as well as the fluctuating (state) components of the constructs to be measured.

As we have stressed, such requirements for research makes the study of vocational and career development quite complex—certainly more complex than found in other approaches. Nevertheless, if the phenomena we hope to understand are complex and dynamic ones, can we dare to use methods not capable of capturing that complexity?

7 The Career Development of Women

The occupational experience of women is very different from that of men. Women's participation in the work force, at least in Western industrialized societies, has always differed from that of men in significant ways, ways that have typically resulted in lower level, lower paid, lower power work. Fox and Hesse-Biber (1984) report that in 1979, 77% of all employed women worked in "white-collar" occupations (typists, secretaries, book-keepers, and clerks), and in "blue-collar" occupations (machine operators, assemblers, etc.). Most of these occupations represent "dead-end" jobs that offer only limited opportunities for advancement within the occupational category and almost none provide opportunities to move up into more promising career tracks. In summarizing the current state of women's career experiences, Fox and Hesse-Biber (1984) state that:

> In spite of . . . high and growing rates of participation in the labor force, women continue to face tremendous occupational barriers. Their work capacity is still funneled into a few sex-typed jobs in which their pay is low, their influence is limited, and their mobility and options are restricted. Even though social norms and values are changing, and even though the women's movement has helped set the pace for further changes, the labor force status of women continues to be depressed. Much remains to be done if women are to enjoy a fuller range of work opportunities and a greater share of work rewards. (p. 39)

The negative situation described by Fox and Hesse-Biber (1984) is also reflected in a recent review by Fitzgerald and Betz (1983). Thus, there is some concensus about the current status of women's careers. However, other than for its decidedly negative depiction of this status, current data are difficult to use to predict much about the long-term consequences of a women's embeddedness in a given career. This deficit exists because there is a lack of comprehensive conceptualizations or of theories that are capable of producing meaningful, testable hypotheses regarding the *development* of women's careers (Fitzgerald & Betz, 1983; Fitzgerald & Crites, 1980). In this regard Perun and Del Vento Bielby (1981) call for a human development perspective in studying the career development of women. They note that:

> The task of explicating the work cycle of women clearly rests with social scientists of the life course, human developmentalists, whose perspective is uniquely suited to integrating and interpreting... changes in patterns of female labor force participation with changes in the development of the work cycle in women. However, in spite of the overwhelming evidence of life course changes in women's lives, little has been done to explain such changes in developmental terms or incorporate them into theories of development of occupational behavior. (p. 235)

Similarly, Mednick (1982) argues that in the study of (women's) achievement and work "to a large extent we are dealing with a psychological problem, that of personal change" (p. 49). She notes too that this psychological change needs to be understood in relation to contextual changes reflected, for example, by current labor market statistics. Mednick (1982) points out that "theorists such as Lewin, Murray, Murphy, and Brunswick argued that behavior was embedded in an inextricably linked, interdependent field of internal and external determinants" (p. 50), and she concludes that any approach that does not treat the person and the environment in such mutually interconnected terms is doomed to failure. Mednick thus calls for an approach to the study of women's career development that is quite consonant with the developmental-contextual view we have taken: Psychological changes (*development*) need to be understood in *relation* to the changing sociocultural *context*.

Although the views of Perun and Del Vento Bielby (1981) and of Mednick (1982) thus support our own appeals for a developmental and contextual theory of careers, it is premature at this point in time to propose such a formulation, especially in respect to the elements of research that would need to be integrated in order to understand the historical and contemporary processes affecting the career development of women in particular. The data sets pertinent to women's career development have, in our view, either been: (a) developmental but insufficiently contextual (and in some respects insufficiently developmental as well in that little long-term longitudinal data exist in respect to life course changes in women's careers); or (b) contextual but insufficiently developmental, i.e., historical and socio-logical research has not paid sufficient attention to intraindividual changes, especially as they influence and are influenced by the context in which they are embedded.

Accordingly, our goal in this chapter is not to propose a theory of women's career development. Instead, our purpose is to note some of the major trends in theory and research that fall within each of the three dimensions of our perspective, that is, the developmental, the contextual, and the relational one. This integration is not designed to represent literature reviews of research related to each dimension. Rather, we note the major features of extant research and use our developmental-contextual perspective as a framework for suggesting important conceptual and empiri-cal issues that need to be addressed, especially if future scholarship is intended to lead to the sort of theoretical model called for by Perun and Del Vento Bielby (1981) and Mednick (1982).

Much of our current knowledge of women's careers is related to sociological and demographic analyses of the contemporary social con-text. Consequently, we focus first on the contextual dimension of our developmental-contextual model.

THE CONTEXTUAL DIMENSION
OF WOMAN'S CAREERS

The context of women's career development is a multilevel one, comprised of the immediate family setting (and including the family of origin and of procreation), the women's social support network, and their community, societal, and cultural milieus, along with their associated institutions (e.g., schools, the military, corporate entities). Of course these elements of the context are not static; they change over time. Hence, the historical dimen-sion is perhaps the superordinate element of the context. There exists considerable scholarship about historical changes in women's careers.

Smuts (1971) observes that the key historical difference between women now and women prior to World War II is that today's woman is much more likely to work for pay, a trend that began very likely around the time of the Civil War. Women have always more than carried their share of the burden of work, especially black, lower class women (Brookins, 1984), but often it was the case that the true contribution of women to the productivity of society was obscured by the fact that it took place mostly in the home or on the farm, or was discounted or ignored because of the race of the woman. Moreover, the prevailing views of society were alarm and concern over the increasing proportion of women in the paid labor force. Smuts (1971) summarized the situation as follows:

> A great deal of concern was expressed in 1890 over the presence in the labor force of some four million women, most of them single. Since World War II, however, the decisions of millions of middle-aged, middle-class wives and mothers to go to work has caused little alarm. It is now permissible for any woman to work. She may not have the full approval of her church, her neighbors, or her family, especially if she has young children. But neither will she meet with general opprobrium, even if she has young children, as long as she provides adequate substitute care. To understand this contrast it is helpful to recall again that the opposition to women's employment in 1890 stemmed largely from the fear that it constituted one among several dangerous threats to the stability of the family and the well-being of society. Today's acceptance of married working women suggests that such fears have long since been alleviated. (p. 147)

Fox and Hesse-Biber (1984) also point out that historical changes have altered the degree to which women who have family roles (e.g., spouse, parent) also have extrafamilial careers. They note that although across this and the preceding century women's opportunities to engage in extrafamilial careers would often change dramatically during wars or other periods of economic and political upheaval—thus giving women access to occupations usually reserved for men—the changes made during periods of national emergency were often reversed quickly thereafter. However, World War II may have marked the beginning of the end of this pattern. Fox and Hesse-Biber point out that extrafamilial labor force participation of women approximately doubled from roughly 25% in 1940 to 51% in 1980. Furthermore, a shift took place in the composition of this rapidly expanding female work force: the percentage of married women more than tripled as a percentage of total women's labor force participation.

In this regard Hoffman (1974a) notes that after World War II two opposing trends occurred; the increase in family size and the employment of women with children. Although they seemingly opposed one another, Hoffman (1974a) infers that they both may have been responses to the same social changes: economic events (i.e., an expanding economy) and technological advances (i.e., labor saving devices). Both changed the role of the housewife and opened up job opportunities for women; that is, by this era the job of housewife had changed dramatically; what remained in the role were repetitive, dull tasks, and the full-time housewife with no children was viewed as playing a luxury role. In addition, the availability of jobs made women feel that by remaining a full-time housewife in the face of all the labor saving devices, availability of commercial food products, etc. she was not making a serious contribution to the household.

Thus, as might be expected from the post-World War II changes, perhaps the most dramatic instance of this historical change in married women's labor force participation occurred in respect to women with children. Table 7.1 summarizes the labor force participation rates of mothers with children under 18 years of age from 1940 to 1984. A more than seven fold increase occurred between these two points in time. A small minority of mothers with children were in the labor force in 1940. By 1984 the majority of all mothers with children of these ages worked.

What were the lives like of the women whose careers developed within this historical range? How did the early socialization experiences of women with children who worked in 1940 differ from the experiences of working mothers in 1984? What stresses and/or supports existed for 1940 working mothers as compared to 1984 working mothers? What long-term, personal, social, and vocational consequences occurred for 1940 working mothers? How will these consequences compare to those that will occur for contemporary working mothers? What differences exist in the way these two groups of working mothers socialize their offspring?

TABLE 7.1
Labor Force Participation Rates of Mothers
with Children Under 18, 1940–1984

Year	% of Mothers
1984	60.5
1982	58.5
1980	56.6
1978	53.0
1976	48.8
1974	45.7
1972	42.9
1970	42.0
1968	39.4
1966	35.8
1964	34.5
1962	32.9
1960	30.4
1958	29.5
1956	27.5
1954	25.6
1952	23.8
1950	21.6
1948	20.2
1946	18.2
1940	8.6

Note: Source: L. W. Hoffman (1985).

Hoffman (1974a) has speculated about these issues. Although an expanding economy resulted in increased job opportunities for women after World War II, women faced numerous career barriers such as discriminatory policies, restrictions due to family commitments (Hoffman, 1974a), and psychological barriers such as anxiety resulting from a fear that achieving and being successful would result in a loss of femininity and rejection by men (Horner, 1972). Although stereotypes about career women prevailed into the 1970s (Epstein, 1970) the woman who pursues a career in the 1980s may find more support than her postwar counterparts. Increases in high-quality daycare and beliefs that a mother does not have to be the sole caregiver of her child may have relieved many of the stresses normally placed on women who decide to take on the dual roles of mother and professional career woman. Although these changes are well documented, many questions remain about the long-term effects on women's lives.

Such questions—despite their provocative nature and their potential importance for understanding the meaning of a woman's employment for herself and her social network—remain unanswerable given current lacunae in the research literature. As just noted, extant historical/contextual analyses are not typically integrated with analyses of the ontogenetic changes involved in the life courses of working women. Historical/contextual research that includes an individual-developmental focus is, therefore, needed. Such research may use the idiographic, P-technique longitudinal methods described in Chapter 6, as well as more conventional nomothetic longitudinal procedures and/or qualitative, biographical analyses of the life course. The intent of any of these methods would be to ascertain the nature of the work experience for women of a particular historical era, to understand the antecedents and consequences of this experience, and to thereby understand the processes by which a set of contextual conditions influence—for better or worse—the lives of working women.

Some historians have attempted to depict these relations. Tilly (1985), for instance, traced the historical relationships between family, gender, and occupation in France. She argues that both before and after industrialization it was employers who "were the chief agents of . . . segregation and discrimination of the characteristics of workers in a given occupation" (p. 209). Tilly (1985) notes, however, that:

the motives [of employers] make sense only when individuals are put into relationship with households. . . . Households also made discriminatory decisions about male and female children's education and first jobs and how a wife and mother should spend her time. Neither employers nor households were interested in an infinite expansion of women's low-waged employment. Both preferred its containment: Employers because of added flexibility in any commitments for workers and the greater reliability of male workers, with their domestic needs serviced by wives and mothers: households because of the wages of unmarried daughters and the housework of wives. . . . Employers and households . . . shared one strategy, . . . that of preventing women's full commitment to waged labor in the expectation that as childbearer, she would also do child care and housework. The gender of occupations, designated as they were by employers . . . both shaped and were shaped by the division of labor in workers' households. (p. 210)

Although Tilly's (1985) description of how women were kept at the lower range of the occupational spectrum refers to conditions in France, the conditions do not appear farfetched when applied to relatively recent conditions in the United States (Albrecht, Bahr, & Chadwick, 1977; Birk, Tanney, & Cooper, 1979). Nevertheless, despite the aptness and potential generalizability of these historical accounts of the social context of working women's life experiences, these descriptions do not meet our requirements either for a full account of the life course of working women or for a basis of insight into the explanatory processes linking the social context with women's career development.

Because of a corresponding absence of concern with developmental processes, similar shortcomings exist in respect to other contextual research. Current demographic analyses usefully depict the current work climate for today's woman but, as we argue, do not have similar utility for allowing us to understand the developmental importance of this climate. For example, as implied by Table 7-1, working outside the home is statistically normative for today's woman, despite whether she is the mother of a young child. The data presented in Table 7-2 indicate that this trend exists for a majority of mothers of children 3 years or older regardless of their marital status; moreover, even for mothers of children younger than 3 years of age, 45% or more work regardless of marital status. Furthermore, independent of their parental status, most American women are employed. Waldman (1985) indicates that 54% of all women are employed. This is a marked increase from 1950, when only 34% of American women worked. (The corresponding percentages of working men in 1985 and 1950 are 78% and 86%, respectively.)

This shift in women's employment is unprecedented in modern history, and it has had a significant impact on families; for example, it has changed the familial roles men and women play. For example, Pleck (1984) reports that a substantial change in the allocation of work and family roles between men and women has taken place, but that inequalities persist because of "asymmetrically permeable boundaries" between work and family roles for both men and women. In particular, Pleck indicates that the increased employment of married women has caused a reduction in women's family role, without, however, a corresponding increase in the husband's family role.

TABLE 7.2
Percentage of Mothers in the Labor Force
by Marital Status and Age of Child 1984

Marital Status of Mother and Age of Child	Percentage
Mothers with children 6–17 only	
Married, husband present	65.4[a]
Widowed, divorced, separated	76.5[b]
Mothers with children under 6	
Married, husband present	51.8[c]
Widowed, divorced, separated	53.2
Mothers with children under 3	
Married, husband present	48.3[d]
Widowed, divorced, separated	45.0

[a]Of these 65.8% were full time, 29.2% were part time, and 5.0% were "unemployed but looking."

[b]Of these 73.4% were full time, 14.7% were part time, and 11.9% were "unemployed but looking."

[c]Of these 58.9% were full time, 32.2% were part time, and 8.9% were "unemployed but looking."

[d]Of these 57.8% were full time, 32.8% were part time, and 9.4% were "unemployed but looking."

Note: Source: L. W. Hoffman (1985).

Another major demographic feature of the contemporary American family that is having a major impact on women's employment is the increase in single parent households. Waldman (1985) reports that women who have never married constitute 25% of the female labor force, and that the particularly notable increase among the 25- to 34-year-old singles indicates a trend toward postponing marriage. Still, divorced women with children aged 6–17 are more likely to be employed than any other group of women classified by marital status (Waite, 1981). In fact, women in that category were reported to be fully twice as likely to be active members of the labor force than women who lived with their husbands and who had children under 3 years of age. Clearly, it is appropriate to conclude that the joint consideration of economic and parenting factors made a difference in determining whether women held employment.

Yet another change in families is defined by the very fact that both spouses are employed outside of the home: the dual-provider family. According to Mortimer and London (1984) "the dual-provider family is rapidly becoming the most prevalent family pattern" (p. 27). At the same time Mortimer and London make an important distinction between "blue-collar dual-provider" families and "dual-career" families. Women in the former hold more traditional values and are drawn into the labor market often to keep their families above the poverty line. Women in dual-career families pursue demanding professional or managerial careers that may result in special stresses on her as well as on the family as a whole. This is due in part to the excessive time demands of their careers on both spouses and the persistent asymmetry reported by Pleck (1984) with regard to household chores and childcare responsibilities. Although this asymmetry is less pronounced in the middle-class families of dual-career couples than in the lower socioeconomic status families of blue-collar workers, women tend to carry a disproportionate share of the total work burden. Moreover, in middle-class families, whether the wife works or not tends to be determined more by her choice than by adherence to traditional role definitions. In working-class families, on the other hand, because of economic necessity women work in spite of traditional role definitions (Rainwater, 1984).

Kohn (1984) has also studied the relation between social class and work. He finds that parents' social class positions "profoundly" influence their values (preferences) and child-rearing practices. The higher the parent's social class position (defined primarily by education and occupational position) the more likely he/she is to value self-direction in his or her children. Conversely, lower social class position tends to be strongly related to valuing conformity. In the same vein, Ogbu (1981) notes that the values and beliefs held by parents lead to socialization practices whereby parents teach their children the kinds of competencies they anticipate their child will need later in life. These parental preferences, according to Kohn, hold regardless of the age or sex of the children. Self-directedness, in turn, has been found to be important and necessary in high levels of career salience and career orientation in women (Spence & Helmreich, 1980).

The demographic analyses indicate that whereas a women's employment outside the home is currently statistically normative there exist social class differences in the sorts of careers in which women engage, and in the attitudes women have towards their work. Moreover, data reported by Waldman (1985) indicate that despite social class variation women in general are likely to be embedded in lower paying, lower status jobs, a contextual condition that we have noted earlier has been described by Perun and Del Vento Bielby (1981), and Fox and Hesse-Biber (1984). Thus, Waldman (1985) notes that the percentage of employed women in professional and managerial occupations has increased from roughly 17.5% in 1973 to 22% in 1983 (Waldman, 1985). At the same time, however, Waldman reports that women are much more likely than men to work part time and that they have less seniority. Those factors may at least provide a partial explanation of why women continue to earn considerably less than men. How does the modern working woman deal with the normative reality of working and yet the widespread presence of constraints on her career development? If the recent history of federal legislation can be used as one indication of the political pressures imposed by American women as a consequence of their reaction to this situation, we can speculate that dissatisfaction is one outcome of the discrepancy between having the opportunity to work and working with limited opportunities. Fox and Hesse-Biber (1984) indicate how, until the early 1960s, so-called "protective legislation" essentially designed to improve working conditions for women, actually went beyond their intent in creating "unnecessary constraints on women who sought a better and larger role in the labor force" (pp. 86–90). Such constraints were dismantled to some extent, starting with the Equal Pay Act of 1963 and the equal employment provisions of Title VII of the Civil Rights Act of 1964. The culmination of efforts to provide for equality for women via legislative means was the passage by both houses of Congress of the Equal Rights Amendment to the constitution in 1972. Although the ERA has not been passed by the requisite number of states to make it part of the U.S. Constitution, many believe that its mere proposal has, nevertheless, signaled the beginning of the end of officially and legally sanctioned differential treatment of men and women (workers) in the United States.

Current efforts to have the "equal" pay for "equal work" provision of the Equal Pay Act of 1963 interpreted as referring to "comparable work" represent the latest attempt to not only obtain equality narrowly defined, but to redress structural inequalities, such as lower pay for women due to the sex segregation of occupations (for a review of this issue, see Beatty & Beatty, 1982). Slowly but surely, legislation in the United States is likely to produce what Ruggie (1984) has called the "universalization" of the category of worker. Ruggie explains that "this means that the distinctions among workers based on class, occupation, and sex, are breaking down and becoming less determinant of worker's opportunities and rewards" (p. 340).

Thus, one reaction to the difference between the frequency with which contemporary American women work and the range of opportunities open for their career development has been the enactment of legislation. However, as the brief account of the history and status of this legislation indicates, the statutory support for women's equal opportunity is far from perfect at this writing, and it has not been demonstrated that this legal situation in any way mollifies or moderates women's reactions to the contemporary status of women's careers in general. Indeed, we know selectively little about how women feel about their career situations and trajectories, Kohn's (1984) work not withstanding. Other than the social class variation, we know little about the sources of interindividual differences in career *development* and we know even less about the ontogenetic bases of intraindividual changes in careers.

In sum, the demographic data about the contemporary features of women's careers is relatively mute about the individual-psychological antecedents or consequences of women's work lives. In our view unless contextual analyses are combined with assessments of the consequences of work for individual's lives, little understanding of the meaning of employment for the woman and/or her social context may be gained. Little understanding will be achieved in respect to both the immediate and later life complications of working in a particular career within a given historical era. However, as we noted earlier, not only can contextual research be enhanced by integration with individual-development analyses but, in turn, research on ontogenetic change can be significantly furthered by embedding it in studies of the context of individual development. This point is evidenced as we turn to an analysis of the developmental dimension of women's careers.

THE DEVELOPMENTAL DIMENSION
OF WOMEN'S CAREERS

It is clear that no child—female or male—is born with a set of career aspirations, expectations, values, etc. It also is clear that the adult woman or man possesses such perspectives and that these orientations are often linked behaviorally to a specific vocational role and/or career. As such, a seemingly obvious conclusion to draw from these two sets of observations is that career development has occurred. Such a conclusion has, in fact, been made by developmental psychologists who have considered these phenomena. However, although there is agreement that careers do develop, there is no unanimity about the source of this development.

As explained in Chapter 2, developmental psychologists divide in regard to the nature of the variables and processes they believe govern development. Within the study of women's career development, in particular, there have been efforts to propose explanations based on processes associated with nature, with nurture, or with interactions between these two sources (Lerner & Spanier, 1980; Maccoby & Jacklin, 1974). For example, McCandless (1970) proposed a theory that accounted for sex differences in vocational roles on the basis of drive reduction through social learning. Freud (1923), in turn, proposed a theory of role development stressing that anatomy is destiny and indicating that sex differences in personality and social behavior arose as a consequence of this biological difference between the sexes.

Today, the theoretical differences among developmentalists who study career development among women are not as sharply differentiated as might have been the case in previous eras. Certainly, neither the social learning-behaviorism of McCandless (1970) nor the extreme nativism of Freud (1923) are popularly used theoretical orientations in the design and conduct of such research. Today, either explicitly or, more often, implicitly the theoretical slant of most researchers in this area is interactionism. Although differences exist in the interpretation of the concept of interactionism (Lerner, 1985, 1986), most researchers would agree that characteristics of both person and setting need to be understood in accounting for career development.

There are many distinct research traditions that can be associated with this general interactionist view. However, in our view, the two most promising and empirically productive research traditions can be termed *identity development research* and *maternal employment research*. As we shall see, however, although both research traditions acknowledge person-context interactions, the conceptualization of the context and its differentiated study have not been hallmarks in either literature.

The Development of Vocational Identity

The field of identity development research has been most influenced by the theory of Erikson (1950, 1959, 1963, 1968). According to Erikson, there are sex differences in identity development, and these differences are due most basically to differences in anatomy. For the "outer space" oriented male, being agentic (Bakan, 1966), instrumental, and hence finding an independent role is a major issue in formulating an identity. For the female, however, who is oriented towards "inner space," being warm, expressive, communion oriented (Bakan, 1966), finding a suitable mate and having children are essential components of identity formation: Erikson (1968) states: "something in the young woman's identity must keep itself open for the peculiarities of the man to be joined and of the children to be brought up" (p. 283).

The notions that males center their identity primarily around individual, agentic concerns—which are often manifested in their attempts to establish nonfamilial roles, or careers—and that females center their identities around interpersonal, communication concerns have been popular among some personality and vocational psychologists (e.g., Douvan & Adelson, 1966; Erikson, 1968, 1975; Ginzberg & Yohalem, 1966; Josselson, Greenberger, & McConochie, 1977a, 1977b; Marcia, 1980; Osipow, 1975; Stein & Bailey, 1973). Although it may follow from this notion that males and females differ in the development of their vocational identities, most of the empirical evidence points toward the lack of sex differences (e.g., for reviews see Archer & Waterman, 1983; Grotevant & Thorbecke, 1982; Lerner & Spanier, 1980; Marcia, 1980; Waterman, 1982). For example, Waterman (1982) reports that of ten studies that investigated the distribution of males and females in the four identity statuses described by Marcia (1980) (i.e., identity achievement, moratorium, foreclosure, and identity diffusion—see

Chapter 8 for a detailed discussion of these identity statuses) from adolescence through adulthood, all but one (Hodgson & Fisher, 1979) reported no sex differences in vocational identity statuses. This is not to deny that important differences exist between males and females in regard to the concerns associated with identity development. As Archer (1985) stated: "If females are primarily interpersonal and males occupational in their orientations . . . then the findings of gender similarity with respect to occupational identity requires an explanation. Perhaps the real issue for females is the potential conflict that may arise because they desire both roles" (p. 294).

The last statement by Archer (1985) appears to be at the heart of the matter of potential sex differences in vocational identity development. Although males and females may be similar in terms of the chances of being in one of the (vocational) identity statuses, forging a vocational identity may be more difficult or complex for females because of potentially greater concerns regarding conflicts between work and family (e.g., Dellas & Gaier, 1975; Zytowski, 1969). To empirically consider this possibility, Archer (1985) investigated the "seriousness" of female career plans and the barriers that may make vocational identity formation in females more difficult. She interviewed 96 high school students (12 females and 12 males in each of four grade levels: sixth, eighth, tenth, twelfth), and collected information on identity statuses with regard to occupational choice, sex-role preference, and family-career priorities, as well as on orientations toward societal expectations (traditional, liberated, or transitional). With regard to gender differences in the identity statuses, differences were not found in the domains of occupational choice or sex-role preferences, but they were found in the family-career priorities, with females generally questioning their family roles more than males, suggesting, as stated by Archer (1985), "that females may have a more complex identity to develop. They may be attempting to define themselves in more domains at this point in their lives" (p. 302). Furthermore, it was found that females were far less likely to be traditional in their views about what their roles should be than were males. Assuming that traditional notions regarding the roles of females are predominant, then females may once again find it more difficult to implement their identities. In short, the females were quite concerned with how their vocational and family (of procreation) identities may fit together in the future, whereas males gave little thought to how the two roles may mesh. As such, the females studied by Archer (1985) were concerned with balancing or integrating extrafamilial, agentic career orientations with sex-traditional familial, communion orientations. However, among her male subjects, such an integrative orientation was generally not seen.

The males' felt need to combine what may be traditional familial roles with mostly traditional career orientations may limit the career aspirations or expectations of females. In this regard, Block (1973) notes that the traditional socialization process narrows the sex-role definitions and behavior options of women although it widens these definitions and options for men. Indeed, Block's (1973) research led her to conclude that it is more difficult for women to achieve higher levels of ego functioning because this involves conflict with prevailing cultural norms. As a consequence, few women of the cohort she studied had sex-role definitions that combined agency and communion orientations. Block (1973) concludes that "it was simply too difficult and too lonely to oppose the cultural tide" (p. 26). Yet, she notes that some balance of agency and communion was apparently necessary for advanced ego functioning. Highly socialized men had this adaptive status, but because of restricted socialization, highly socialized women did not (Block, 1973).

However, although the data of Archer (1985) and of Block (1973) converge in suggesting that women, more than men, are oriented to integrating agentic and communion orientations, we do not know if the cost of such integration for women found by Block exists for the sample studied by Archer. Have socialization practices changed historically to eliminate the implications for advanced ego functioning that Block (1973) found for women? We do not know, and unless historically sensitive longitudinal research, e.g., a cohort sequential study, is undertaken it will be difficult to uncover such information. What is needed, therefore, is a contextualization of identity development research, a contextualization that is aimed at finding historical, cultural, and societal variables that may be linked to interindividual differences in vocational identity development and/or to intraindividual change in such development. Although exploring the import of historical changes in socialization practices is one key example of the sort of contextual research for which we call, it is not the only one. For instance, several reports (Hoffman & Nye, 1974; Nye, 1974; Shappell, Hall, & Tarrier, 1971) indicate that socioeconomic status moderates the relation between the employment status of women and their life satisfaction; more strongly at higher socioeconomic levels than at lower ones, employed women have been found to be more satisfied with their lives than are housewives.

However, a feature of the context more proximate than socioeconomic status may moderate vocational identity development. This element of the context is the family and, particularly, the role models and social relationships occurring therein. This example of a contextual moderator leads us to a discussion of the second research tradition noted earlier, that of maternal employment research.

The Effects of Maternal Employment

A major instance of developmental concern with the bases of career development derives from the literature assessing the effects of maternal employment on children. Although the major concern in this literature has been on whether maternal employment has a positive or negative influence on children, a sufficient number of studies have used female vocational role orientation and/or career interests, values, etc. as dependent variables to make this literature pertinent to our purposes. Traditionally, however, and somewhat paradoxically, this research has not been especially contextual. As explained by J. Lerner and Galambos (1985a, 1985b) a rather simplistic "causal model" has been the traditional guiding perspective underlying this research; that is, researchers were concerned with whether maternal employment per se had a detrimental effect on children.

In this "direct effects" model the view of the context was a rather simplistic one: Did the mother work or not? Little, if any, attention was paid to her reasons for employment, her satisfaction with her role, or better, roles (worker, mother, and often spouse), her work situation (e.g., her job status, her salary, her hours), or her social support. Moreover, the type of family in which the mother lived (e.g., nuclear, divorced, reconstituted) was not typically considered, and social class, cultural, and historical variation was also neglected (J. Lerner & Galambos, 1985a; 1985b).

As J. Lerner and Galambos (1985b) explain, this neglect of contextual factors left the maternal employment literature in a confused state (see also Hoffman, 1974b, 1979); that is, some studies indicated an influence of maternal employment on variables such as female vocational development and other studies did not. Testing only the "direct effects" model left much variation difficult to explain. However, when the earlier-noted contextual factors began to be studied, for example, in tests of the "mediated effects" model of J. Lerner and Galambos (1985a), the conditions under which maternal employment did or did not have an effect began to be uncovered. Thus, it was not until the maternal employment literature became more inclined to consider the context, and the interaction between person and context (J. Lerner & Galambos, 1985a, 1985b), that the process by which maternal employment influences females vocational development began to be understood.

What generalizations and/or reliable findings may, therefore, be derived from the maternal employment literature as it is now conceptualized? Findings of the effects of maternal employment on children are, at best, inconsistent. Some trends have emerged, however. In general, there are about as many studies that find no differences in child outcomes between the children of employed versus nonemployed mothers as there are studies that *do* report group differences; in some cases these studies show positive effects for children of employed mothers, whereas others show negative effects. In addition, these effects tend to differ across age, sex, and social class. Whatever effects have been found in the early years seem to diminish as children get older (Dellas, Gaier, & Emihovich, 1979; Powell & Steelman, 1982).

One relatively consistent finding is that school-aged sons of employed middle-class women perform more poorly academically than do girls, but this finding is not seen in male adolescents of employed mothers (see Bronfenbrenner & Crouter, 1982 for a review). In addition, the mother's employment is associated with fewer sex stereotypes—beliefs that particular behaviors or attributes are characteristic of one sex group as opposed to another (Lerner & Hultsch, 1983)—held by daughters and sons. This has been found to be true in adolescents (Chandler, Sawicki, & Stryffeler, 1981; Gold & Andres, 1978), and college students (Vogel, Broverman, Broverman, Clarkson, & Rosenkrantz, 1970). Moreover, adolescent and college-age children of employed mothers tend to be more achievement oriented than the children of homemaker mothers (Powell, 1963; Stein, 1973), suggesting a relationship between maternal employment and masculine personality dimensions.

Several findings suggest that maternal employment has beneficial effects for the career development of female children. The most common conceptualization in this area is that working mothers represent positive role models that are likely to be imitated by their female offspring. Thus, Banducci (1967) found that daughters of working mothers planned to combine family and work roles more often than daughters of nonworking mothers. In general, daughters of employed mothers had less stereotypic ideas about the "proper" roles for men and women (Almquist & Angrist, 1970; Bacon & Lerner, 1975; Baruch, 1972) resulting in more frequent aspirations toward male-dominated (nontraditional) occupations (Ginzberg, Berg, Brown, Herma, Yohalem, & Gorelick, 1966; Kutner & Brogan, 1979; Tangri, 1972).

Although most of these studies agree on the general impact of mothers' employment on women's aspirations toward and actual choice of nontraditional careers, Auster and Auster (1981) remind us of the complex interactions of women with their environments in producing different career outcomes. Specifically, they point out that women who enter nontraditional (usually higher level) careers tend to have the following family background features in common:

1. The mother works, probably in a high-level, nontraditional occupation.
2. The father is an achievement role model and source of occupational identification for the daughter's career orientation. 3. Both parents are sup-

portive of their daughters' career orientation, sometimes in different ways and with varying importance at different stages of their daughter's life. 4. Family socioeconomic status is high. 5. Family size is small and she is the firstborn or an "early born" among female siblings. (p. 260)

In sum, research on the effects of maternal employment provides a key example of the use of considering development within a contextual framework. When maternal employment effects are studied acontextually little can be said about when or why maternal employment may influence the development of females' vocational or career orientations. However, when this development is considered in relation to contextual variables such specification is more readily attained (cf. J. Lerner & Galambos, 1985a, 1985b). As such, because this literature highlights the need to study development in relation to the context in which it occurs, it allows us to point also to the third dimension of our developmental contextual model.

THE RELATIONAL DIMENSION
OF WOMEN'S CAREERS

Given that most extant contextual research has not been adequately related to individual-developmental assessments and that, in turn, major research traditions within developmental psychology have been incomplete (at best) in their consideration of the context of development, there is a great paucity of information about relations between developing individuals and their changing contexts. However, at the least, much of what we have said in the preceding sections of this chapter has, we believe, suggested the utility of studying person-context relations.

The potential of such research may be illustrated by considering the potential of *reciprocal* intergenerational influence between children and adolescents on the one hand and their social context (including parents) on the other. Earlier, we noted that since World War II the number of married women in the workforce has increased greatly. This, in connection with a divorce rate that has recently approached 50%, has led to an increasing proportion of children and adolescents who experience their families of origin either as single-parent or reconstituted families. Moreover, more and more children experience caregiving in nonhome settings, such as day-care centers. All these changes in the social context are likely to have an impact on parents, on their interactions with their children (i.e., the socialization behavior), and thus on the individual (career and sex-role) developments of the children or adolescents themselves.

For instance, what will be the career orientations of women who develop in nontraditional households? It has been repeatedly found that the daughters of working mothers are more likely to aspire to nontraditional careers than is the case of daughters of nonworking mothers (Hoffman, 1979). However, this relation does not speak to the issue of the nature of the career trajectory of females whose mothers work, or work in nontraditional roles, or are single parents, or place their child in day care etc. Will such offspring have careers over the course of their lives that differ from females whose mothers do not work, or are traditional in their work roles, or are in intact families, or do not use day care? More interestingly, perhaps, how will these two groups of offspring socialize their own children? What sorts of role models will they provide?

CONCLUSIONS

Only by studying the development of multiple generations over the course of history, and in a manner that is sensitive to the relations between developing people and their changing worlds will answers to questions such as the aforementioned be attained. This is an ambitious goal. Certainly, no one study will answer all questions, and probably no one scientist in her or his career may be able to collect enough information to adequately address all relevant issues.

Nevertheless, it is not one study we wish to promote or one scientist we wish to influence. Our goal is to redirect the nature of research in our field. We believe that only through the sorts of studies for which we call will knowledge of career development be achieved that is sufficient for the development of useful theory. In turn, such research and theoretical advances may facilitate the development of successful means to optimize the careers of women and men across their life-spans.

8 Career Development and Health

It is generally accepted that work may, under certain circumstances, have a significant impact upon the worker's health. It is also clear that the relationships between work and health are complex, involving once again the interaction between the individual's characteristics of individuality and the particular characteristics of his or her environment. Moreover, although much of the research in this area has focused on the deleterious aspects of work-related stress on health, there is also evidence to suggest that work and satisfying careers can have salutory effects on the worker's health and thus be health enhancing. In addition, there is evidence indicating that not working (unemployment) can have negative health consequences.

A related area that has received considerably less attention is concerned with the health implications of career decision making. Career decisions are made across most of the life-span: In childhood and early adolescence preferences emerge and choices are gradually narrowed, leading to an initial career decision; subsequently, many careers require periodic decisions, culminating, for some, in the much discussed mid-life or mid-career crisis; in mature adulthood decisions must be made regarding disengagement from work, retirement, or career continuation. Obviously, the decisions themselves may have health consequences. More important, perhaps, are the health consequences of the decision-making process itself, such as anxiety and self-doubt. Conversely, the decision-making process may result in increased self-confidence, a sense of competence, and improved self-esteem and self-concept.

Examining the diversity of perspectives and viewpoints in this area reveals that it has been addressed by researchers from a number of different disciplines, such as sociology, economics, organizational behavior, management, human relations, industrial psychology, medicine, vocational psychology, and social work. What is needed is a conceptual framework that permits the integration of findings from these diverse disciplines, a framework that can be applied to the entire life-span and that attends not only to the person and his/her family and interpersonal situation but also to the broader socioeconomic, environmental, and organizational context.

In our view the most satisfactory framework for this purpose is the developmental-contextual life-span model developed in the first section of this book. In this chapter we show how use of this model may facilitate understanding of the complex ways in which illness and health may be related to career development across the life-span. To illustrate the links between career development and health, we have selected the following health-related topics for discussion: (a) vocational identity development in adolescence; (b) adult career transitions (especially mid-life career change and retirement); and (c) the interactions among individuals and their work contexts. Of course, several other topics could be addressed here, including, for example, the health consequences of job loss (e.g., see Brenner, 1973; Feather & Davenport, 1981; Kahn, 1981; Liem & Rayman, 1982) or job-related "burnout" (e.g., see Cherniss, 1980; Freudenberger & Richelson, 1980; Maslach, 1976); however, it was necessary to be selective, and the applicability of the developmental-contextual perspective to other health-related topics should be apparent in the following discussion. Although we recognize that there are both physical and mental health implications for, and consequences of, various career development paths, our focus is primarily on mental health (except when discussing retirement). We have purposely taken a broad view of mental health, or to follow A.S. Waterman's (personal communication, April, 1985) suggestion, psychological well-being, and include such matters as adjustment, coping, and adaptation in our discussion.

Health and Career Development in Adolescence

Preadolescent children may develop their ideas about occupations and careers on the basis of increasing cognitive skills (Nelson, 1978), exposure to vocational role models (Weeks, Thornburg, & Little, 1977), and gender, ethnic, and socioeconomic background variables (Frost & Diamond, 1979; MacKay & Miller, 1982; Vondracek & Kirchner, 1974). Very likely, however, they are not in a position to consider or make actual vocational choices. That is a task that is usually not taken seriously by others and by the individual until adolescence, and thus it is unlikely to have any identifiable health consequences until then. This is not to say that events and processes that occur before adolescence are not indicative of functioning during later years. Indeed, as Waterman (1982) suggests, in line with Erikson's (1968) epigenetic principle, successful vocational identity development may depend in part on successful resolution of earlier developmental tasks (see also Munley, 1975, 1977).

Erikson (1959, 1963, 1968) has been the developmental theorist who has been most explicit about vocational development in adolescence. He sees vocational development as a component of the larger task of identity development: Erikson (1968) states:

> The young person, in order to experience wholeness, must feel a progressive continuity between that which he has come to be during the long years of childhood and that which he promises to become in the anticipated future; between that which he conceives himself to be and that which he perceives others to see in him and to expect of him. (p. 87)

The conflicts that are clearly implicit in this description of the process of identity development culminate in what Erikson has called the identity crisis. The crisis has been defined by Erikson as a bipolar continuum, ranging from the achievement of identity to role confusion. Individuals can be located anywhere along this continuum, based on how well they resolve a number of developmental issues, including the choosing of a religious and/or political ideology and of a sexual orientation. Equally important, the adaptive adolescent must make a choice of an occupation that is socially acceptable as well as personally suitable.

Erikson originally introduced the construct of identity for the purpose of clinical analysis and thus did not see any need to operationally define it. As Waterman (1982) has observed, this has proven to be a problem for researchers wishing to investigate the identity construct. Partly to resolve this problem and partly to extend and refine Erikson's original formulations, Marcia (1966, 1980) developed his concept of "identity statuses." Identity statuses are operationally defined by means of a semistructured interview. They represent four distinctive modes of dealing with the issue of identity formation in adolescence. Marcia (1980) states:

> Those classified by these modes are defined in terms of the presence or absence of a decision-making period (crisis) and the extent of personal investment (commitment) in two areas: occupations and ideology. *Identity Achievements* are individuals who have experienced a decision-making period and are pursuing a self-chosen occupation and ideological goals. *Foreclosures* are persons who are also committed to occupational and ideological positions, but these have been parentally chosen rather than self-chosen. They show little or no evidence of 'crisis.' *Identity Diffusions* are young people who have no set occupational or ideological direction, regardless of whether or not they may have experienced a decision-making period. *Moratoriums* are indi-

viduals who are currently struggling with occupational and/or ideological issues; they are *in* an identity crisis. (p. 161)

Marcia goes on to point out that there are both healthy and pathological aspects to each of these statuses, with the possible exception of the identity achievement status, which identifies individuals who are strong, self-directed, and highly adaptive (Marcia notes, however, that early identity achievement may limit one's future adaptiveness). Individuals who are classified as foreclosures, although committed and thus not in an identity crisis, may be viewed as conforming or rigid; those classified as identity diffusions have not made a commitment, may or may not be in crisis, and could be viewed as unconcerned or irresponsible; those identified as moratoriums are very likely to be in an identity crisis and often are viewed as anxious and vascillating.

Several studies have provided evidence concerning the implications of one's identity status for well-being and adaptive functioning (see Marcia, 1980, for a review). For example, adolescents in the moratorium status have been found to be more anxious than those in the other identity statuses, especially those in the foreclosure status (e.g., Marcia, 1967; Podd, Marcia, & Rubin, 1970; Stark & Traxler, 1974). In addition, compared to foreclosures and diffusions, moratoriums and achievements have been found to have a more stable self-esteem (e.g., Marcia, 1967), and to be more autonomous (e.g., Matteson, 1975; Orlofsky, Marcia, & Lesser, 1973). It has also been found that state anxiety is negatively correlated with both occupational commitment (e.g., Berger-Gross, Kahn, & Weare, 1983) and vocational decisiveness (e.g., Hawkins, Bradley, & White, 1977). In regard to the literature on sex differences, Marcia (1980) and Waterman (1982) report that although some specific sex differences have been found, the basic process of identity development has been found to be quite similar for males and females (see also Archer, 1985; Grotevant & Thorbecke, 1982). The greatest similarity is found in the identity achievement status, which is associated with well-developed adaptive capacities, and in the identity diffusion status, which for both sexes is associated with difficulties in adaptation and coping. The health implications of the moratorium and foreclosure statuses appear to differ somewhat for males and females, although more research on women is needed (Marcia, 1980) (see Chapter 7 for a more detailed discussion of sex differences in identity development).

To understand more fully how a given vocational identity status may influence psychological well-being, it is important to place the identity statuses in a developmental and contextual framework. Waterman (1982) has provided a descriptive model of alternative pathways of identity development. To illustrate the various pathways that are possible, consider an adolescent girl who has chosen to follow her father's profession as a lawyer without considering alternatives or undergoing an identity crisis, and thus is in an identity foreclosure status. She may enter the moratorium status (e.g., if her commitment to law is challenged by the emergence of other career interests and she enters an identity crisis), the identity diffusion status (e.g., a waning of commitment without a replacement by other interests), or she may remain in a foreclosure status and continue with her commitment to law. Likewise, an adolescent boy who is undergoing a vocational identity crisis (e.g., in a moratorium status), in attempting to decide between a career in acting or one in auto mechanics, may enter either an achievement status (i.e., making a strong commitment to one or the other career), or a diffusion status (i.e., giving up both careers without considering others) (note that by definition, he could not achieve foreclosure status because he has undergone a crisis, and that he probably would not remain in a moratorium status for a long period of time). As Waterman (1982; Archer & Waterman, 1983; see also Marcia, 1980) points out, the normative pathway of identity status formation is characterized by *progressive* developmental shifts (i.e., from diffusion to foreclosure or moratorium, from foreclosure to moratorium, from moratorium to achievement); however, *regressive* developmental shifts are possible. In the aforementioned examples, regressive developmental shifts would occur if the adolescent girl moved from foreclosure to diffusion, or if the adolescent boy moved from moratorium to diffusion. It is also possible for an adolescent in an achievement status to enter either a diffusion or a moratorium status. Thus, as was just implied, the identity statuses are not necessarily static, nor do they necessarily follow a unidirectional progression, which stops once identity is achieved. Indeed, Grotevant and Thorbecke (1982) suggest that "the identity formation process be viewed instead as a continually evolving self-structure . . . that is, a spiral of cycles of exploration and commitment" (p. 403).

Insofar as a commitment to a career is associated with psychological well-being, foreclosure and achievement would be the preferred identity statuses. Nevertheless, when viewed within a developmental and contextual framework, each of the identity statuses could have positive or negative consequences for psychological well-being. For instance, in the earlier example of the adolescent boy in the moratorium status, although any anxiety associated with the identity crisis may represent a lack of psychological well-being in the present, the anxiety may serve as a motivating factor to resolve the crisis and make a meaningful and informed commitment (Waterman, personal communication, April, 1985), thus increasing the possibility of long-term psychological well-being. Furthermore, the amount of anxiety that he experiences during the crisis, as well as his chances of successfully resolving the crisis may depend in part on (a) what is occurring in his context (e.g., are his parents or other significant persons pressuring him to make a decision? is he given time and assistance to work through the crisis?); (b) what has occurred previously in his attempts to formulate an identity (e.g., has he been in an identity crisis before and how did he resolve it?); (c) how the vocational identity crisis interacts with the statuses in other areas of identity formation (e.g., is he currently also in a crisis regarding a religious or political identity?); and (d) the extent to which he has been active in bringing about the crisis, in the circumstances surrounding the crisis, and in resolving the crisis (e.g., was the crisis anticipated? is he awaiting "divine intervention" to resolve the crisis?).

The earlier illustration should make it apparent that the links between psychological well-being and vocational identity formation in adolescence are best understood, in our view, when considered within a developmental-contextual framework that emphasizes mutual embeddedness and dynamic interactions. Given that the course of career development is probabilistic, there are no predetermined consequences of a given pathway of identity formation for future psychological well-being. For example, making a firm commitment to a career during adolescence is no guarantee that future crises will be avoided. As Grotevant and Thorbecke (1982) suggest, "adolescent identity formation is ... one round in a life-long series of developmental challenges regarding occupational choice" (p. 403). Optimal career development is marked by the successful coping with, and adaptation to, the everchanging context in which the individual is embedded (e.g., see Vondracek & Lerner, 1982), and the implications of vocational identity formation in adolescence for psychological well-being depend in part on how well a given pathway reflects adaptive functioning in the current context, as well as how well the pathway serves to encourage adaptive functioning in future contexts.

Empirical evidence regarding the links between vocational identity formation and psychological well-being that illustrates the developmental-contextual perspective is lacking. Nevertheless, Waterman (1982) has proposed a number of hypotheses regarding the antecedent and concurrent conditions of alternative courses of identity development, which we review as exemplifying the research that is needed.

These hypotheses pertain to identity development in general, including but not limited to vocational identity. The following is an attempt to restate Waterman's (1982, p. 345) hypotheses with particular emphasis given to vocational identity development:

1. Strong identification with parents before or during adolescence increases the likelihood of making a commitment to the parent(s) occupation or line of work. Foreclosure is the most likely vocational identity outcome.

2. Permissive, neglecting, or rejecting parenting styles will most likely

produce conflict and difficulty in adolescents trying to make vocational choices. The result will be vocational identity diffusion, i.e., vascillation or an inability to make any commitment to a vocational choice. Democratic, or authoritative, parenting may be the most likely parental strategy to produce consideration of a number of vocational alternatives, followed by a sound commitment to one, and thus vocational identity achievement.

3. The chance of undergoing a vocational identity crisis increases with the number of vocational identity alternatives the individual encounters.

4. The availability of occupationally successful models facilitates the process of making a vocational commitment.

5. Social expectations regarding vocational choices, which arise within the contexts of the family, the school, or the peer group will have an effect upon the pathway employed to achieve a vocational identity.

6. Vocational identity will be established more successfully in those individuals in whom preadolescent personality provides a suitable foundation, such as sufficient levels of autonomy, initiative, and industry.

Clearly, some liberties have been taken to highlight vocational developmental concerns apart from other identity components that are considered part and parcel of the identity development process by such writers as Erikson, Grotevant, Marcia, and Waterman. What the earlier discussion was designed to illustrate, nevertheless, was that the first important health consequences of career development can be observed within the context of adolescent identity formation. Furthermore, it was shown, at least hypothetically, that identity formation and its implications for psychological well-being need to be understood in terms of individual development-context interactions previously discussed in Chapter 4. Finally, it should be apparent that understanding antecedent and concurrent conditions such as those suggested earlier could serve to foster the design of truly developmental interventions that could be applied in guiding adolescents into vocational developmental pathways that lead to optimal career development.

Health and Adult Career Transitions

The career decision-making process does not end when the adolescent or young adult makes an initial commitment to a career or work role. The days when an initial choice routinely turned into a lifelong career or commitment to one company are gone for most members of today's work force. Unprecedented mobility and prosperity following World War II have provided previously unknown degrees of freedom of choice and freedom to change jobs or careers to most workers. The changes produced by exercising this freedom of choice are not always those originally envisioned, and even if they are, such changes are almost always accompanied by substantial stress. Although much has been written in recent years about the mid-life crisis and mid-life career changes (e.g., Levinson, Darrow, Klein, Levinson, & McKee, 1974; Lynch, 1980; Robbins, 1978) and about retirement planning and decision making (e.g., Buchmann, 1983; Parnes, 1981), relatively little attention has been given to the many transitions, both large and small, that have become commonplace in contemporary career development.

Before examining in more detail the health implications of some of the more extensively described career transitions it may be useful to note that Louis (1980) has attempted to describe and develop a typology of career transitions in general. Louis defines career transitions as a "period during which an individual is either changing role (taking on a different role) or changing an orientation to a role already held" (p. 202). Included here are both objective (observable) and subjective (experienced) components of career transitions. Louis (1980) proceeds to indicate what individuals must cope with when they proceed through career transitions. She proposes:

> that during CTs (career transitions) individuals are faced with a variety of differences between old and new roles, role orientations, and role settings; that the more elements that are different in the new role, or situation, and the more different they are from previous roles, the more the transitioner potentially has to cope with (regardless of the extent to which differences were anticipated and/or were seen as desirable by the transitioner); that the type of the transition undertaken is a rough indicator of the nature and magnitude of differences to be coped with; that there is a general coping process by which individuals manage or respond to differences experienced during transitions of all types; and that an understanding of the coping process can be used to facilitate individuals in transition. (p. 203)

Louis suggests that the aforementioned generalizations are appropriately applied to all career transitions. The simplest common denominator can thus be reduced to the observation that all career transitions involve "something to cope with." This, of course, is consistent with the early work of Holmes and Rahe (1967) who considered all changes (in this case career transitions) as stressors, whether they are positive or negative, sought or imposed. In sum, change creates stress and thus the potential for deleterious health consequences.

It goes without saying that, in fact, not all career transitions result in negative health consequences. As a matter of fact, there is at least ample anecdotal evidence that many career transitions result in an enhancement of "well-being" and of health. However, given the relative paucity of sound empirical evidence, a question remains as to what determines whether a career transition has a negative, positive, or neutral impact on a given individual's health and well-being. The answer, most certainly, is not to be found in the individual alone, nor in the life and career circumstances surrounding his/her transition. In our view, the key to understanding the health impact of career transitions lies in understanding the dynamic interaction of individual and context. In order to gain a better understanding of the issues involved, we next examine some of the evidence that has been accumulated on two major career transitions: mid-life career change and the transition to retirement.

Mid-life Career Change and Health.   There are many reasons for the current interest in mid-life career change. The work of Levinson and his associates (Levinson, Darrow, Klein, Levinson, & McKee, 1978), resulting in a bestseller, has popularized the notion that individuals must make a mid-life transition during which they complete a number of tasks including a reappraisal of the past, a restructuring of negative aspects of their current life situation, and a resolution of important unresolved conflicts or "polarities." Another reason for the interest in mid-life career change has been the fundamental change in mature industrial societies, like the United States, that has resulted from technological advances. Automation and technological innovations have eliminated millions of jobs in heavy industry and manufacturing, although creating new opportunities in high technology and service industries. As a result, an unprecedented number of individuals have been forced to contemplate a mid-life career change. Finally, mid-life career change has been viewed increasingly as a legitimate vehicle for enhancing self-fulfillment and career satisfaction (Neapolitan, 1980; Thomas, 1980). The realization that an initial career choice—even if it has resulted in a well-established career—does not have to be a life-long choice has been a liberating revelation to an increasing number of individuals in many different types of career.

It thus appears that mid-life career change is an increasingly common phenomenon. One pertinent question in the present context is whether mid-life career change is synonymous with mid-life crisis or whether it is just sometimes accompanied by a mid-life crisis. Clearly, if the mid-life career transition is frequently accompanied by a mid-life crisis, substantial health consequences would be expected. Most writers (e.g., Levinson et al., 1974, 1978; Louis, 1980; Robbins, 1977) agree that a crisis is not inevitable, but that it frequently occurs. Levinson et al. (1974) define any developmental transition as a point or region "between two periods of greater stability." They go on to note that whether an actual crisis occurs does not depend entirely on whether an individual achieves his goals or not: some may experience their success as empty or hollow. The critical issue is the "goodness of fit between the life structure and the self" (p. 254). This notion is, of course, entirely consonant with our position described in

Chapter 4, although we should note that there are substantial differences between Levinson's general theoretical position and ours, particularly regarding his deterministic conceptualization of development.

While the theoretical positions referred to earlier are unanimous in that they see substantial potential for stress and consequent health problems inherent in mid-life career changes, the empirical evidence in this area is limited. What has been found is that career changers tend to show lower emotional stability and higher fear of failure (Vaitenas & Wiener, 1977), and that they report lower congruence between vocational interests and actual jobs than do nonchangers (Gottfredson, 1977; Vaitenas & Wiener, 1977; Warren, Winer, & Dailey, 1981). This lack of congruence could be postulated to be a major contributor to job dissatisfaction, leading not only (ultimately) to career change, but very likely, in the meantime, to depression, anxiety, and stress-related disorders. Levinson and his associates (1978) reported that among the 40 men they studied 7 had to cope with serious failure or decline as part of their mid-life transition whereas 3 had such an unstable life structure that their chances of successfully "becoming their own man" seemed slim.

Nevertheless, we do not think that a mid-life career change necessarily always involves negative or pathological reactions (see also Brim, 1976; Herr & Cramer, 1984; Levinson et al., 1978). Rather, the desire to seek out a greater congruency between one's personal orientations and the particular demands of the job may ultimately be quite adaptive and lead to greater psychological well-being. For example, Thomas (1980) found that the two most frequent reasons given for mid-life career changes were to find work that was more meaningful and to obtain a closer fit between one's work values and the job characteristics. Likewise, Neapolitan (1980) found that the primary reason for a major job change was to find a better fit between personal needs and desires and the rewards of the job. In both cases, the striving for congruency is apparent, and although there may be substantial risks and stress involved in undergoing a career change, the result of finding better fit between one's orientations and characteristics on the one hand and the job's requirements and rewards on the other is most likely quite beneficial. Of course, not all mid-life career changers fare well. Although mid-life career change can result in greater personal and career satisfaction, as Levinson et al. have shown, individuals must often pay a substantial price for attempting to advance successfully through the mid-life transition. All available evidence suggests that the magnitude of the price depends on the personal strengths and weaknesses the individual brings to his life situation and how those strengths and weaknesses match up with the demands of that situation.

Transition to Retirement and Health.   As people get older they become more concerned about their health. This is quite natural and would lead one to suspect that a great deal is known about the health implications of an event that almost exclusively affects older individuals, namely, retirement. Unfortunately, the scientific evidence on this subject is relatively meager. Moreover, as Eisdorfer and Cohen (1983) have observed, "it is important to recognize that health changes may be a cause as well as a result of retirement, that age of retirement is more flexible than often suspected, and that beliefs about health may be more important to functioning than are objective indices of health" (p. 57).

Fairly conclusive evidence exists that shows that health affects retirement, particularly early retirement. Although it is true that there has been a trend toward earlier retirement regardless of health concerns, Kingson (1981) has reported that among white male retirees aged 45 to 59 only 15% reported no work-limiting health conditions. Thirty-four percent reported that health conditions prevented them from working or limited their ability to work, but that they were not receiving Social Security disability benefits, and 51% had disabilities that resulted in their receiving Social Security disability benefits. A sample of black males of the same age showed very similar distributions. Clearly, declining health is a determining factor in most cases of early retirement (for recent discussions see also Morrison, 1983 and Parnes, 1983), although as Kingson points out other factors, such as job satisfaction, age discrimination, inflation, occupation, industry, skill level, marital status, and preference for leisure are also important in the retirement decision (1982, p. 105).

There is another perspective on the impact of health on retirement. As Eisdorfer and Cohen (1983) point out, some occupations have very stringent health requirements that obligate individuals to periodically demonstrate proficiencies that may be compromised by a variety of health problems. In particular, they note that a number of occupations, such as airline pilot, flight officer, and FBI agent affect public safety, and that retirement may be mandated for medical reasons. It should be noted, also, that in some physically demanding occupations, such as construction work, mining, and professional athletics, voluntary decisions to retire may be made as a result of physical limitations that would not generally be classified under "health" reasons.

The decision to retire often results in the most dramatic life-style change in decades for the retiree. We observed previously that any major change may be a stressor with the potential for a deleterious health consequence. It should thus not be surprising that just as health affects the decision to retire, retirement itself may affect health. If retirement is a significant stressful life event, health should decline significantly immediately after retirement. Of course, anecdotal evidence abounds about men dying almost immediately after retiring. Coach Paul "Bear" Bryant's death within weeks of coaching his last game only seemed to confirm this commonly held belief that retirement often kills. However, Minkler (1981) has pointed out that research findings to date are inconclusive regarding this issue.

Adams and Lefebvre (1981) investigated the association between retirement and mortality in a cohort of 15,260 men and 5,632 women who retired at age 65 in Canada. They found differences not only between the mortality patterns of men and women but also between the mortality patterns in the entire sample when compared to the corresponding specific death rates in the Canadian population in general. Most notably, among men they found relatively low mortality in the first year after retirement and "elevated" mortality in the second year after retirement. They attribute this elevation to a possible delayed stress reaction. In the third and fourth year after retirement mortality in the male cohort was increasing at a higher rate than in the general population. Adams and Lefevbre interpret these findings as offering support for Atchley's (1976) proposal that retirees experience a "honeymoon" phase immediately following retirement, which is later followed by a "disenchantment" phase. Interestingly, for women retirees mortality is highest in the first year after retirement, followed by a decline in the death rate in the second and third years and a slight upturn in the fourth year. Throughout the four postretirement years studied by Adams and Lefevbre the death rate for female retirees was lower than the corresponding death rates for women in the general population. The authors conclude that because women retiring at age 65 are such a small percentage of 65-year-old women in the population in general they must constitute a specially select group having some advantage with respect to mortality. They urge further research on this group.

Mortality is, of course, only one indicator of health (or illness) after retirement. As a matter of fact, some researchers have focused on the psychological well-being of retirees to determine the effect of retirement. For example, Gore (1978) has documented the critical importance of supportive family members in major work transitions, such as loss of job or retirement, and Greenblatt, Becerra, and Serafetinides (1982) have pointed out the importance of the entire social network in the maintenance of mental health. In another report Turner (1981) describes four studies that demonstrate the importance of social support for psychological well-being. Moreover, he emphasizes that social support appears to be most important in terms of buffering stressful life events (see also Holahan & Moos, 1981).

Liebow (1983) has summarized succinctly the problems involved in examining the relationship between retirement and health:

> A major problem is that it is not simply the relationship itself that is complex; the central constructs, especially 'retirement,' are also complex. Retirement—whether viewed as an event, a status, or a process—involves different kinds of

people in radically different circumstances, with different personal, social, and health histories, and equally different futures. The profound social, psychological, and economic changes often occasioned by retirement argue strongly for a powerful connection between retirement and health. But these powerful connections—good for Jones' health but bad for Smiths'—will probably continue to wash out into ambiguity until we take a much closer look at Jones and Smith through the progressive disaggregation and specification of populations, occupations, circumstances, and histories. (p. 95)

Liebow's characterization of the complexity of the relationship between retirement and health could easily be recast to apply to the relationships between other work-related transitions, such as entering an occupation in early adulthood or changing occupations at mid-life. In each case we return to our premise that a thorough understanding of the complex features of career development can be achieved only by examining the interaction of a given person with unique characteristics of individuality with his/her given, specific context. Moreover, as Liebow implies and as we have stressed, this examination must take place within a developmental framework. A projection about the unique features of individuals can be had only if we understand their unique pasts and presents.

WORK AND HEALTH

Career transitions represent one important aspect of careers that may, as we have seen, affect the individual's health and sense of well-being. There is a second aspect of career development that also has a profound effect on the health of individuals and on the quality of their lives: work and the circumstances of work. Recent years have witnessed increased concern about the quality of work life (e.g., Gardell & Johansson, 1981). This concern has focused not only on removing health hazards from the workplace but also on maximizing the satisfaction that workers can get from their work (e.g., Akabas & Kurzman, 1982).

There are a number of research areas that have addressed the relationship between work and health from different perspectives. Two particularly important areas have focused on stress in the work or organizational context (e.g., Dohrenwend & Dohrenwend, 1981; Frankenhaeuser, 1981; Frankenhaeuser & Gardell, 1976; Kahn, Hein, House, Kasl, & McLean, 1982; Levi, Frankenhaeuser, & Gardell, 1982), and on mental health and work (e.g., Ling, 1955; Osipow, 1979, 1983; Weiner, Vardi, & Muczyk, 1981). A third area with obvious implications for health is the area concerned with the physical aspects of the work environment. Clearly, concerns about the physical well-being of workers through mine safety regulations, standards for the handling of toxic materials, and many other regulations speak to the well-recognized hazards to the worker's health from such sources. It is beyond the purposes of this chapter to examine this particular area, although this should not be interpreted as implying that this is a less important area than those on which we do focus.

A number of recent publications (Caplan, Cobb, French, Harrison, & Pinneau, 1980; Cooper & Payne, 1978; Corlett & Richardson, 1981; French, Caplan, & Harrison, 1982) have addressed themselves to issues of work and health from a perspective that is very closely compatible with the features of the "goodness-of-fit" perspective described in Chapter 4. For example, Caplan et al., (1980) examined

> occupational differences in psychological stresses in the job environment and the impact of stress on affective and physiological strains and on illnesses reported by the worker. Four hypotheses were tested: (1) job stresses will produce strains in the worker; (2) traits, needs, and abilities of the worker will also affect strain; (3) the goodness of fit between the job stresses and the characteristics of the worker will have an even stronger impact on strain; and (4) these strains, in turn, will raise the rates of illness. (p. i)

By collecting questionnaire data from 2,010 workers in 23 different job categories, Caplan and his associates were able to show very strong support for the hypothesis that job stresses produce strain in the worker; they found very little evidence for the notion that personality variables directly influence psychological or physiological strains experienced by the worker. Regarding Hypothesis 3 Caplan et al., (1980) reported that "poor fit between the stresses on the job and the needs of the worker with respect to these stresses . . . was strongly associated with dissatisfaction. The goodness of fit accounted for more variance than either the stresses in the environment or the needs of the worker" (p. i).

The gist of these findings confirms our own view that it is the dynamic interaction of the person's characteristics of individuality with the unique characteristics of the environment that determines whether a "good fit" exists. Moreover, because both person and environment are constantly changing, this determination involves more than a simple, one-time matching of individual and environment (career, occupation, job). French, Caplan, and Harrison (1982), explain that "the utility of P–E (person–environment) fit theory is based on the assumption that people vary in their needs and abilities just as jobs vary in their incentives and demands. When there is a poor fit between the characteristics of the person and related characteristics of the job, P–E fit theory predicts that employee well-being will be reduced" (p. 27). The authors recognize, however, that person–environment fit can take a number of different forms, involving, in one case "the discrepancy between the motives of the person and the supplies in the job and environment to meet the goals and preferences induced by those motives" (p. 28). The other form of P-E fit recognized by the authors concerns the relationship between job demands and the ability of the person to meet those demands. In further recognition of the complexities involved, French, Caplan, and Harrison demonstrate that poor fit between person and job can result in a variety of strains depending on a variety of specific individual and situational dimensions.

The methodological problems of a goodness-of-fit model can be quite challenging and must be considered in addition to the conceptual complexities of the model. As Harrison (1978) points out, the justification for using the more complicated P-E discrepancy measures rest on the demonstration that they are more predictive (of strain, for example), than the P and E measures themselves. In addition, Harrison emphasizes that his P-E fit theory is capable of predicting both linear and curvilinear relationships between fit and strain, which is superior to simply predicting a linear (or monotonic) relationship between some environmental characteristic and strain on the one hand or some personal characteristic and strain on the other.

The entire subject of work and health is obviously important, but just as obviously it is an exceedingly complex area. Apart from the more straightforward biochemical and physical threats to workers' health, most researchers postulate some form of stress as a mediating variable between the properties and characteristics of work and the health of the worker. Unfortunately, as Beehr and Newman (1978) and Elliott and Eisdorfer (1982) have observed, there is not agreement among scientists as to the meaning or definition of stress. Moreover, Beehr and Newman (1978) suggest, as part of their "facet analysis" of stress, that time plays an important role in understanding stress and the relationship between job stress and health. They note, in particular, that the inclusion of a time variable calls attention to the necessity for longitudinal research designs in ascertaining the direction of causality in the relationship between job stress and health. We wholeheartedly agree with this position and would add that the inclusion of a time dimension also satisfies our concern with viewing these domains from a developmental perspective.

9 Intervention in Vocational Behavior and Career Development

This chapter represents an effort to examine concepts and issues in vocational and career intervention that, more or less, arise out of our conceptualization of career development as a life-span process resulting from the dynamic interaction between the developing individual and his/her changing context. The fields of vocational counseling and career intervention are so large and consist of so many diverse approaches (Super, 1977a) that a single chapter could never claim to adequately represent them. Rather, we try to highlight interventions that are particularly germane to the issues raised in previous chapters. Thus, interventions in vocational behavior and career development are discussed as constituting a subclass of interventions that could be described, collectively, as *human development intervention* (Urban & Looft, 1973).

HUMAN DEVELOPMENT INTERVENTION

Human development intervention may be defined as constituting efforts to intervene into ongoing human developmental processes in a planned and deliberate fashion. Moreover, such interventions should be conceptualized as taking place, potentially, at any point in the entire life-span of the person, and involving intrusions into any or all of the subsystems of the person (i.e., cognitive, affective, physiological, biochemical) or of his/her environment. This, of course, poses substantial challenges for the human development interventionist. As Urban and Looft (1973) observe, interventions into one facet of the person's functioning cannot effectively take place without affecting other facets as well. Hence, they argue that any single discipline of study represents an unsatisfactory basis for conceptualizing human development intervention; a multidisciplinary and team approach is needed (see, also Lerner, 1984).

A further consequence of this perspective is the recognition that human development intervention requires a knowledge base far broader than any knowledge base typically associated with the more specialized and traditional human services. This, of course, has interesting implications for the training of human services personnel. Just as we believed that the conceptualization of human development intervention requires a multidisciplinary team effort, we must conclude too that the training of individuals in human development intervention methods also requires a multidisciplinary approach.

Baltes and Danish (1980) underscore these points by emphasizing the complex multicausality of development: "influences that covary systematically with chronological age are labeled *age-graded*, those that covary systematically with biocultural change are labeled *evolutionary history-graded*, and those that do not occur in any general or universal fashion (in terms of frequency, patterning, and timing) are labeled *non-normative*" (p. 52). Examples of non-normative life events of particular relevance to career development would be such events as getting fired from a job or getting unexpectedly promoted, an economic depression or a regional or national recession, a bankruptcy of employer, a relocation, debilitating accidents or illnesses, and a divorce. Baltes and Danish go on to note that because of the multicausality of development various facets of it can vary markedly from one person to another in terms of direction, rate of change, onset, and variability. Thus, life-span human development cannot be adequately represented as consisting of simple, unitary, cumulative developmental processes. As may be recognized, this view of life-span human development is entirely consistent with our views of a dynamic interactional perspective, detailed in previous chapters.

The implications of these conceptualizations for vocational and career interventions are substantial. First of all, interventions must be viewed as efforts to change something (systematically and deliberately) *that is already changing* without these special efforts—albeit not necessarily in the direction desired. This holds true whether the intervention is focused on the developing individual or the changing family, community, or cultural context. To design effective strategies of intervention from this perspective is much more likely if something is known about the developmental trajectory of the individual on the one hand and the environmental or situational change processes on the other. Thus, in the case of individuals it is necessary not only to know their developmental history but also their goals, aspirations, and objectives that may, in fact, be important determinants of current behavior. Concerning social and environmental conditions it is essential to understand the current influences, the history, and the *trends* (i.e., the change trajectories) that influence and help forecast social and environmental changes.

The following example may illustrate these points. Take, for example, an adolescent girl who has excelled in mathematics and science in school (developmental history), who aspires to be an astronaut (goals and aspirations), and who is actively engaged in information gathering activities regarding an astronaut career (current behavior). Even though this information would be very important, an interventionist would need additional information to make professionally sound decisions about the proper course of career interventions in this case. Thus, information regarding her family's ability and/or desire to assist her in going to college (environmental conditions) may be important. The status and outlook of funding for the astronaut training program (social conditions) may also play a role in determining the most effective career intervention in this situation. Because all these pieces of information are important in the design of intervention strategies, and because they are all subject to change (without prior notice), it underscores and illustrates our contention that a dynamic interactional perspective is necessary to implement a truly developmental approach to career intervention. If, for example, NASA were to decide that no more female astronauts were needed in the foreseeable future, all career plans would have to be changed. Thus, a social–environmental condition could effectively alter her career plans, requiring an intervention focus on *alternative* career plans. In any situation, a focus on the *interaction* between the developing individual and the changing environment is essential for effective intervention.

As Baltes and Danish (1980) have noted, it is precisely this focus on developmental change processes, which are at least in part predictable and sequential (Lerner & Kauffman, 1985), that allow the interventionist to focus on what some have called *early intervention.* In picking up on our earlier example of the astronaut aspirant, preventative intervention might focus on exploring related alternatives to the astronaut profession because selection and entry must be considered a low-probability event. Thus, if a process is reasonably well understood in terms of the timing and sequence of its constituent components, one could plan intervention early in the sequence to alter subsequent outcomes. As can be easily recognized, this, then, represents the basis for preventive intervention. (Parenthetically, it should be noted that non-normative influences on development, due to the fact that they are events with a low probability of occurrence, simply complicate the prediction of developmental trajectories, a prediction that is already difficult because of the probabilistic (rather than predetermined) nature of developmental change.) Moreover, it may be assumed that techniques of intervention could be chosen or developed that are most responsive to the particular points of development at which they are to be applied.

Implicit in such a view is the understanding that interventions may be designed to impact not just at single points in the developmental course, but that they may focus on sequential change (Danish, Smyer, & Nowak, 1980; Schaie, 1982). Thus, human development intervention, when seen from a life-span, dynamic interactional perspective, means that one intervenes not to influence a static point in life; rather one intervenes to affect a change trajectory—one potentially encompassing the individual's entire life course. Moreover, because the system (the person and his/her context) remains open to change we need to reassess if the person remains on his/her trajectory; and we may need to intervene again (and again) across life. Thus, intervention itself is a life-span process.

The most distinctive feature of human development intervention, however, is its concern with optimization rather than remediation. The underlying assumption is that there are certain ways in which human development can unfold that are more desirable than others. Thus, as in other conceptualizations of development (e.g., see Kaplan, 1983) and of career development and behavior (e.g., see, Herr & Cramer, 1984; Katz, 1963), the issue of values is a central one in our perspective. There are many ways in which optimization can be conceptualized. Some view it as a reduction in the discrepancy between actual and ideal self. Others prefer to think about it in terms of the fullest possible redirection of a person's potential, within a given context. Still others view optimization as narrowing the gap between a person's actual status and his/her goals and aspirations. In the case of the aspiring astronaut, optimization would involve encouragement of her aspiration, because her abilities, interests, and current behaviors point to a reasonable chance of success. At the same time, and as observed previously, optimization would also involve assisting her in seriously considering career alternatives, because being chosen to be an astronaut is not very likely in view of the small number of people needed in this profession. Clearly, a developmental approach, which assumes that any given individual can follow a number of different possible developmental trajectories, lends itself to a conceptualization of intervention, which presumes that individuals can be assisted in chosing one trajectory over another. Moreover, from this perspective it is possible on the basis of developmental theory and research (but within the limits imposed by the probabilistic character of development) to forecast the most likely consequences or outcomes that will be produced depending on whether one or the other developmental path is chosen.

The choice of one or another developmental path requires, nevertheless, a judgment about the goals or objectives to be pursued. If the individual is capable of making informed judgments, which are neither illegal nor impractical, the intervenor/facilitator can readily proceed to assist the individual as needed. If, however, the individual is too young or unable for another reason to make a reasoned or appropriate judgment, the intervenor may have to rely on his/her understanding of normative development in deciding whether intervention is warranted and if so, what its objectives should be. A thorough understanding of both the continuities and potential discontinuities of development over the entire life-span will place the intervenor in a position not only to assist the individual in chosing ways and means to achieve his/her chosen objectives but also to assist in the definition of objectives to be accomplished in the pursuit of an enriched or "optimal" existence.

In summary, the aforementioned conceptualization of human development intervention incorporates many features that make it, both on a conceptual and an applied level, a most appropriate framework for understanding intervention in vocational and career development: It requires a *comprehensive knowledge base* that fosters an integrated view of the *whole person,* operating in complex sociocultural and physical *contexts;* it views both the person and the context as changing over time and as *dynamically interactive;* and because it applies across the entire life-span of the person it can be said to be *life-span developmental* in focus. Moreover, the concern with the probabilism of developmental change, as for instance induced by the experience of nonnormative life events, fosters a longitudinal, "repeated measures" approach to intervention. People may be moved off a particular developmental trajectory by unanticipated perturbances. As we have noted, this requires the intervenor to repeatedly appraise whether the person is on his/her desired path and to be ready to institute corrective procedures if a deviation has occurred. Just as a succession of course corrections may be required to place a space satellite on its desired trajectory, a succession or sequence of interventions may be used to produce the desired course of human development.

VOCATIONAL AND CAREER INTERVENTION AS HUMAN DEVELOPMENT INTERVENTION

The foregoing conceptualization of human development intervention suggests not only the complexity but also the comprehensive nature of such interventions. A recently published glossary of terms, prepared by a panel of the National Vocational Guidance Association (Sears, 1982) appears to confirm that this complexity and comprehensiveness is part and parcel of accepted definitions of vocational and career counseling. For example, career counseling is defined as "a one-to-one or small group relationship between a client and a counselor with the goal of helping the client(s) integrate and apply an understanding of self and the environment to make the most appropriate career decisions and adjustments;" career guidance is

defined as "those activities and programs that assist individuals to assimi-
late and integrate knowledge, experience, and appreciations related to:

(1)   self-understanding, which includes a person's relationship to his/her
own characteristics and perceptions, and his/her relationship to others and
the environment;

(2)   Understanding of the work of society and those factors that affect
its constant change, including worker attitudes and discipline;

(3)   Awareness of the part leisure time may play in a person's life;

(4)   Understanding of the necessity for and the multitude of factors to
be considered in career planning;

(5)   Understanding of the information and skills necessary to achieve
self-fulfillment in work and leisure;

(6)   Learning and applying the career decision-making process" (p. 39).

The final relevant NVGA definition, that of vocational guidance, is adopted
from Super (1951): "The process of helping a person to develop and accept
an integrated and adequate picture of him/herself and of his/her role in the
world of work, to test this concept against reality, and to convert it into a
reality, with satisfaction to him/herself and benefit to society" (p. 141). The
NVGA definition then proceeds to elaborate that "this resulting current
view of vocational guidance is self-concept oriented and focuses primarily
on self-understanding and self-acceptance, to which can be related the
occupational and educational alternatives available to the individual" (p. 141).

These definitions, pertaining to career counseling and to career and
vocational guidance, are certainly not contrary to our conceptualization of
vocational and career intervention within a human development perspective.
They do not, however, reflect the unifying conceptual framework that we
believe to be essential for the proper design, implementation, and evaluation of efforts to intervene into ongoing (vocational and career) developmental processes in a planned and deliberate fashion across the life-span.
They also do not explicitly recognize the possibility of intervening at levels
other than at the individual level (e.g., at the family, organizational, or
cultural-economic level). Moreover, a cursory perusal of the vocational
and career guidance literature reveals that intervention services have evolved
in such a way as to be concentrated in the high school and college senior
years, when young people presumably most frequently "make" their vocational decisions. This is not unreasonable, of course, because intervention
resources are limited and thus need to be applied when they count the
most. It is inconsistent, however, with the comprehensive and longitudinal
developmental framework we have proposed. What, then, are the processes and events of concern to the vocational and career interventionist

who accepts our life-span developmental view of vocational and career development?

Jepsen (1984) has recently conducted a comprehensive review of research on the developmental perspective in vocational behavior. He concluded that "some vocational behaviors, when observed over time, show patterns that approximate developmental changes" (p. 210). Vocational behavior trends that were consistent with a developmental perspective were found, not surprisingly, most consistently in studies of adolescents and young adults. Jepsen found fewer studies providing replicated evidence of "developmental" changes in vocational behavior in later age periods, partly because there is a general dearth of research in these age periods. Of course, a review of the empirical research like that performed by Jepsen, is only one—albeit very important—means of identifying the processes and events of concern to the developmentally oriented vocational counselor. Another would be to recall the earlier-noted differentiation between three influences on the course of human development: (a) normative, age-graded influences; (b) normative, history-graded influences; and (c) nonnormative, life-event influences (Baltes, Cornelius, & Nesselroade, 1978). As applied to vocational and career development, normative, age-graded influences consist of vocational and career determinants (both biological and environmental), which correlate with chronological age. They include early vocational socialization experiences, the development of a vocational identity, physical and intellectual maturation, and retirement. They also include, for women, childbirth, and, according to Levinson et al. (1978), a mid-life crisis for men.

Normative, history-graded influences may also consist of both biological and environmental determinants. They, however, correlate with historical time rather than chronological age, and they may thus be described as cohort-specific. In other words, they are normative for individuals of a given age living in a given historical time period, and they thus define part of the context for a given cohort. As we discussed in Chapter 3, Elder's (1974) study of the effects of the Great Depression on individuals clearly is an example of a historical event that had an enormous impact on the vocational development of the cohort of individuals who happened to be in a position to make important vocational choices during this period. World War II and the Vietnam war constituted other historical events that very likely influenced the vocational development of other cohorts.

Nonnormative influences on vocational and career development represent life events, both positive and negative, which are only weakly related to either the individual's age or to historical time. They include such events as getting fired or laid off, winning the lottery, having a disabling accident, or getting divorced. Danish, D'Augelli, and Ginzberg (1984) have recently argued that the concept of life events is essential because it enables the researcher to more comprehensively represent both the expected and unexpected events in the individual's life course (for a more extensive discussion of nonnormative life events see Callahan & McCluskey, 1983).

Normative age-graded, and normative history-graded influences, as well as nonnormative events all impact the vocational and career development of individuals. In principle, it is possible to either modify these influences, or to modify their impact on a given individual or groups of individuals. The former type of modification will almost always require intervention into the context (except for altering the biological or genetic makeup of a person, which is unlikely to be part of vocational or career intervention), whereas the latter usually involves modifying the individual's capability or his or her competency.

UNDERSTANDING NORMATIVE AND NONNORMATIVE INFLUENCES ON VOCATIONAL AND CAREER DEVELOPMENT

Successful intervention into the vocational and career development of individuals is dependent, in part, on the counselor's understanding of the age-graded, cohort-specific, and nonnormative influences upon such developments. In Western society the normative course focuses upon the adolescent period as being critical for the successful initial milestone— with the first career choice—of the vocational development process. Vondracek and Lerner, 1982 state: This may well be the case of a "coincidence of adolescent developments and societal demands . . . [which require] an adaptive synthesis of what are individual and societal changes currently prototypic of American society" (p. 604). Clearly, an approach focused on normative, age-graded influences would focus interventions primarily in the adolescent years, with perhaps a secondary emphasis emerging in mid-life, and another one in the retirement period, between the ages of 60 and 65. This approach encompasses the vocational guidance efforts in the high schools and it probably accounts for a very substantial portion of the resources expended for vocational and career development. Due to the fact that significant differences exist in the normal developmental course of individuals, in the cohort-specific (history-graded) influences they encounter, and in the nonnormative life events they may face, this may not be the best way to utilize resources. In short, the timing and thus the significance of specific vocational decisions varies widely from one individual to another.

There is ample evidence to support this view. The number of individuals who are satisfied with their initial vocational choice is small. Even in their first two years of college, many individuals are unable to make a definitive decision regarding their career choice (e.g., Crites, 1969; Greenhaus & Simon, 1977). Experienced vocational or career guidance counselors will confirm that they have encountered 12-year-olds who not only had a clear idea of what they wanted to be but who actually went on to implement their vision of a career. By the same token, other individuals are encountered who did not find "their niche" in the world of work until they reached the age of 40. Such differences, we would assert, are part of the normal variation involved in such development.

Even if the intervenor is knowledgeable regarding normative, age-graded influences on vocational and career development, it is essential that he or she also understand that different cohort membership is capable of producing great divergences in the course of vocational development. In turn, there is also the need to understand *intra*cohort variations. For example, the sociocultural influences that shape vocational development in the inner city ghetto are significantly different from those that influence youth in a rural village in Pennsylvania or Mississippi. The vocational guidance or career counselor must understand these differences in order to effectively serve individuals who are faced with important vocational or career choices (e.g., Herr & Cramer, 1984). Finally, every guidance counselor has encountered "special circumstances" produced by nonnormative life events. For example, take a young man planning to enter college, whose father is killed in an accident, thus leaving the family without its breadwinner. Under such circumstances even the best laid vocational plans may be abandoned because of a need to respond to unexpected events. The young man may be forced to search for a job that pays enough to support him and his family, regardless of whether the job meets any of his other criteria, previously thought to be important in choosing a career. It should be observed, in this context, that strictly speaking, picking a job for such external reasons is not at all the same as making a relatively unimpeded career choice.

What emerges from the foregoing is that the intervenor in vocational and career development cannot be effective unless his/her understanding of developmental processes includes an understanding of normative development, of historical or cohort influences on development, and of the impact of nonnormative life events on development. Simply stated, the significance of vocational and career decisions is altered by these influences, and the intervenor may need different strategies of intervention in light of the overall developmental status of the individual. Osipow (1982), for example, has addressed this issue in relation to the criteria to be used in evaluating career interventions:

Should vocational maturity be a criterion to seek in counseling adolescents, but productivity a suitable criterion for adults? Should information seeking behavior be a criterion to be used when a client appears to be naive, as opposed to decision-making skills for the client who apparently has all the information needed to make a decision? (p. 28)

These comments clearly illustrate that selection of intervention strategies based on the age of the client alone makes no sense at all. Nor does it make any sense to select intervention strategies based solely on the cohort membership or historical context of the individual. As Osipow (1982) points out, career counseling has many facets.

It can be individually oriented, group oriented, and programmatic in effort. It can focus on skills development such as decision-making; processes which focus on life span development, for example, or have an outcome focus such as job seeking and obtaining. It can also stress adjustment and satisfaction in work. (p. 29)

Fretz (1981), in a recent monograph on evaluating the effectiveness of career interventions, points out that career interventions should not be evaluated—and, by implication, should not be designed—without recognizing the unique characteristics of the individual and of his/her context as they interact with the intervention parameters in influencing the myriad of variables that currently serve as career intervention outcome measures. Stated in terms consistent with a life-span developmental approach we would observe that career intervention must be based on a thorough assessment of the individual and his/her context; how else would one hope to recognize the unique attributes of individuals and their contexts?

Developmental and Contextual Assessment in Vocational and Career Development

Thus far we have concluded that vocational and career development, being part and parcel of human developmental processes, is subject to a variety of influences both from within and from outside the individual. We have also concluded that, as a result, significant individual differences occur with regard to the timing and significance of important vocational and career decisions. Finally, we have concluded that as a consequence of pursuing a developmental conception of career development a focus on "early" intervention and on optimization is possible. Such a focus, in our view, requires a thorough assessment of the individual's developmental status and of the context within which the development is occurring. We attempt to briefly outline the essential features of such assessment, first from an individual and then from a contextual perspective.

Three obvious time perspectives describe the essential features of the individual's developmental status: the past, the present, and the future. Regarding the past, vocational and career interventions must be designed in such a way as to build upon the prior relevant experiences of the person. Of particular importance in this part of the assessment would be a review of the individual's history with regard to the amount of occupational information he/she has, the prior work experience he/she has acquired, the decision-making skills he/she has learned, and the occupational skills and abilities at his/her disposal. For those already in the workplace, one would also want to know what, if any, problems were encountered in work entry or in other career transitions, and how the individual adjusted to the transition (e.g., see Crites, 1969, 1976).

In assessing the current (present) status of the individual, particular attention would be given to ascertaining his/her vocational interests, aptitudes, and values. In addition to these relatively standard features of vocational assessment, it is imperative to ascertain the developmental status of the individual. Such questions as "is the individual ready to make a career choice?" and "what type of career decisions is the individual prepared to make?" need to be asked. The concept of career (or vocational) maturity has been invoked to bring attention to the individual's readiness to make career decisions, and there is ample evidence regarding the usefulness of this concept and its salience in guidance and prediction (e.g., Crites, 1965, 1971; Gribbons & Lohnes, 1964; Herr, Good, McCloskey, & Weitz, 1982; Jordaan & Heyde, 1979; Super, 1955, 1977b, 1983; Super & Overstreet, 1960). As Super (1983) has recently emphasized, if truly developmental counseling is to take place, a person's "readiness for career decisions" must be ascertained. "This means that in planning the vocational assessment of students for career education or career counseling, one can now ask whether one is mature enough for his or her interest and value scores to have real meaning. If one is, one must then ask whether one is planful enough to benefit from the review of aptitude, interest, and value data for educational and vocational planning" (Super, 1983, p. 557). Another approach to ascertaining vocational developmental status is based on Erikson's (e.g., 1968) concept of identity, and has been concerned with the operationalization and measurement of vocational identity statuses (e.g., Grotevant & Thorbecke, 1982; Marcia, 1980; Waterman, 1982; Waterman & Goldman, 1976) (see Chapters 7 and 8 for a further discussion of this approach). If the individual has already established a career, this part of the assessment would also include a review of the development of his or her career, as well as his or her "career adaptability" (e.g., see Super, 1983). Such questions as whether career satisfaction and productivity is adequate, whether there is an appropriate fit between work values and affordances in the work context, whether promotions have been timely, and whether opportunities for further development exist would all be relevant.

The final part of the individual assessment would be focused on the future. Such a focus is relatively unique to *developmental* perspectives (e.g., Crites, 1969; Ginzberg, Ginsburg, Axelrad, & Herma, 1951; Katz, 1963). It tends to be neglected by most other approaches, in spite of the fact that it is widely accepted, even on a common sense basis, that goals and aspirations for the future represent important career development data. As Crites (1969) stated:

> In making a vocational choice, an individual is, in effect, making a prediction of his (her) future vocational adjustment. When he (she) expresses his (her) intention of entering a particular occupation, he (she) is estimating that, of the occupations which are known to him (her), this is the one he (she) thinks will bring him (her) the greatest happiness, wealth, recognition, or whatever it is he (she) is seeking. (p. 325)

In addition, however, it may be important to help individuals to understand and articulate what it is they want to become, not just vocationally, but as total human beings (e.g., Katz, 1963).

The assessment of contexts within which vocational and career development takes place could also follow the three time perspectives outlined earlier; in order to fully understand the individual's behavioral history, the context within which such history transpired must be understood. To appreciate fully the significance of the individual's current behavior, his/her current life context must be ascertained, and to completely understand the significance of goals and aspirations, their description must incorporate statements about the contexts in which the individual hopes to achieve them.

The principal distinction of utilizing such a temporally discriminated view of vocational and career development is that it places these processes squarely within the main stream of human development where, in our view, they belong. A second important feature of a comprehensive assessment approach is that it places in proper perspective such useful and widely used instruments as Holland's (1971) Self-Directed Search or the Strong–Campbell Interest Inventory (Campbell, 1974). Although they represent useful tools that can assist individuals in vocational decision making, they do not represent, in and of themselves, a basis for thoughtful vocational or career intervention. Clinical psychologists long ago overcame their initial enthusiasm for using the Minnesota Multiphasic Personality Inventory (MMPI) in lieu of careful clinical assessment.

Similarly, vocational guidance counselors and career counselors will resist the urge to oversimplify by assuming that a one-time measurement of an individual's interests, values, or preferences provides an adequate basis for decision making or for professional intervention. This suggests, of course, that a repeated measurements approach may often be the assessment approach of choice in vocational guidance and career development intervention. In fact, recent evidence suggests that interindividual differences in intraindividual change patterns on many career-relevant dimensions may have been underestimated (see, for example, Berzonsky, 1982; Schulenberg, 1984; Schulenberg, Vondracek, & Nesselroade, 1985), thus underscoring the need for the type of longitudinal, multidimensional, and temporally discriminated developmental/contextual assessment we are proposing.

Osipow (1982) appears to have reached similar conclusions, as he states that "an interactionist approach clearly seems to represent current thinking in the use of measurement in career counseling. Traits are not important alone, since context seems to be a significant moderator of individual behavior" (p. 32). In short, to base prediction and guidance practices solely on a one-time assessment of vocationally relevant traits followed by a matching of test scores to actuarial data is to assume that both individuals and contexts are static (e.g., Katz, 1963), an assumption that is clearly inconsistent with a developmental-contextual approach.

It should be clear at this point that the developmental and contextual approach we are advocating is incompatible with what Osipow (1983, p. 286) has called the "test them and tell them" approaches. On the other hand, we understand that not every conceivable intervention requires exhaustive prior assessment. Nevertheless, the recent work by Campbell and Cellini (1981) points to the fact that career development problems can be identified and classified in fairly reliable fashion; the importance of this task for meaningful intervention cannot be overestimated. Moreover, as Prediger (1974) has observed, assessment in career guidance can serve to stimulate, broaden, and provide a focus for career exploration and exploration of self in relation to career. In addition, he aptly observed that ultimately, the person him/herself makes the important decisions regarding his/her career, such decisions are not made by the test, the assessment procedure, or the intervenor. Following a developmental-contextual framework, the intervenor can, however, facilitate the attainment of optimal vocational and career development: development that promotes an optimal fit between the capabilities, interests, and needs of the individual on the one hand and the contexts within which he/she lives and works on the other hand.

INTERVENING IN VOCATIONAL
AND CAREER DEVELOPMENT

As we noted earlier, an attempt could not be made, within the scope of this chapter, to do justice to the multitude of vocational and career interventions currently practiced. The following should thus be viewed as only one of a number of possible ways to conceptualize developmental intervention in this field.

In a recently published article, Campbell and Cellini (1981) presented a carefully developed taxonomy of career problems, derived in part from a search of the literature and from a descriptive analysis of adult career problems. Reviewing and synthesizing various career development theories, they defined four stages of adult career development, namely, preparation, establishment, maintenance, and retirement, and they formulated a comprehensive list of career development tasks associated with each stage. For example, Campbell and Cellini (1981) state that:

> an individual in the preparation stage must: (1) assess personal attributes and the world of work in anticipation of work entry/reentry; (2) engage in decision making for work entry/reentry; (3) implement plans to prepare for work entry/reentry; (4) perform adequately in and adapt to the demands of the organizational/institutional environment during preparation; and (5) obtain a position in the chosen occupation. (p. 176)

Most interesting from our perspective is Campbell and Cellini's identification of four common tasks recurring *across* their four stages of career development. Thus, individuals gather information about themselves and their environments in order to make choices from among alternatives: they engage in *decision making;* based upon their decisions they engage in activities "over a period of time spanning the present and future" (p. 177): they *implement plans;* next, they must *reach an acceptable level of organizational/institutional performance,* and finally, they *adapt to the organizational/institutional environment.* (In Campbell and Cellini's terminology the term *organizational* refers to employment setting, whereas the term *institutional* refers to educational or training setting.)

Although Campbell and Cellini focus on adult careers, they do indicate, nevertheless, that the four major career tasks they define extend into adolescence and the career preparation stage as well. Moreover, it should be noted that they identify numerous subtasks, 80 to be precise, across the (career) life-span. Problems, as defined by Campbell and Cellini (1981) in their taxonomy of career development problems, occur "when an individual experiences difficulty in coping with a career development task, when a task is only partially mastered, or when a task is not even attempted" (p. 177).

The relevance of this innovative work for our conceptualization of developmental intervention can be demonstrated. First of all, the four general career tasks identified by Campbell and Cellini deal with both the individual and with the context within which he/she is operating. For example, when discussing problems in implementing career plans they note that such problems can arise because of certain characteristics of the individual or because of characteristics external to the individual, i.e., characteristics that we would call contextual. In the previously mentioned example of the young girl wishing to be an astronaut, problems in the implementation of her career plans could arise because she failed to maintain her outstanding performance in mathematics and science, or because she decided that she wanted to become a nun. Thus individual characteristics would have changed to foil the originally planned implementation. On the other hand, a decision by NASA to have a moratorium on the selection of new astronauts, or a family emergency requiring abandonment of college plans would be examples of contextual changes that would impede the implementation of career plans.

In another example Campbell and Cellini describe problems in organizational/institutional performance as difficulties that can arise either because personal standards or because institutional/organizational standards are not met. Thus, if the girl in the previous example, in spite of persistent efforts, was unable to perform at the highest level required by her school, she would be considered to have problems in her institutional performance that would adversely affect her career plans. Finally, Campbell and Cellini (1981) observe that one whole subclass of career development problems focuses on "the degree of adaptation of the individual to the total organizational environment" (p. 186) during the initial entry into an institutional/organizational setting, in dealing with changes over time, and in dealing with interpersonal relationships. Such a focus is clearly consistent with our concern with the goodness-of-fit between the developing individual and his/her context. To illustrate, let us assume that our aspiring astronaut actually succeeded in getting into the astronaut training program. She could still encounter a career development problem if the program turned out to be very different from what she expected and if she failed to adapt to the total institutional environment represented by the astronaut training program.

In sum, Campbell and Cellini provide, with their work, a taxonomy of career development problems that confirms and reinforces our belief in the importance of aiming toward the achievement of an optimal person/environment match in the interest of successful career development across the life-span of the person. Perhaps more important than Campbell and Cellini's identification of *career development problems* across the life-span is their identification of the four major, generic *career development tasks* (and associated subtasks) that recur across the various career development stages and that are defined by them as a composite of stages found in the most prominent theories of career development. This is of particular interest because of the previously discussed emphasis of a life-span developmental approach on optimizing human development. If individuals repeatedly, throughout their vocational and career development, face the tasks of decision making, of putting plans into action, and of performing adequately in and adapting to organizational/institutional environments, then it is only reasonable that interventions should be focused on assisting individuals in accomplishing these tasks in optimal fashion.

Vocational Decision Making: An Illustration

Taking the task of vocational decision making as an example, it is clear that a developmental intervention approach would favor intervention early rather than later in the life-span. This is the case because, as we discussed in Chapter 4, the prior, developmental organization of a system constrains the potential of a later influence to as easily lead to a change in the system as would have been the case if that same influence acted earlier in development (see, for example, Baltes & Baltes, 1980; Lerner, 1984 for discussions on the limits of plasticity in the later years of life). In other words, there is reason to believe that early training in decision-making skills could be more effective than later training. Note, however, that because the person maintains considerable plasticity across life, all is not lost if early intervention does not occur. Early training, focused on optimizing current decision-making skills, could also serve a preventive function by working against the acquisition of faulty decision-making behaviors and against the making of poor decisions that could have negative consequences. These faulty decision-making behaviors and poor decisions themselves could eventually serve as barriers or constraints against effective intervention. Although these considerations favor intervention as early as practical in the life-span, our previous discussion of plasticity across the life-span (in Chapter 4) should leave no doubt about the fact that the potential for successful intervention exists into old age.

At this point objections may be raised to an early intervention focus because a certain degree of maturity may be considered requisite to any career decision-making training. Although this may be true, we have previously also observed that the embeddedness of any target of intervention means that one may approach the same intervention target by focusing on variables from any one of several levels of analysis. Thus, children too young to be concerned directly with vocational decision making could, nevertheless, receive training in the component skills eventually necessary for effective vocational decision making. This could include, for example, training in what Krumboltz and Baker (1973) have called task approach skills in their discussion of vocational decision making: value clarifying, goal setting, predicting future events, alternative generating, information seeking, estimating, reinterpreting past events, eliminating and selecting alternatives, planning, and generalizing. Early training in these skills could, in effect, have salutory consequences in a much later developmental period such as middle age when important career decisions are faced by many.

Intervention into vocational decision making could also be viewed from other levels of analysis. For example, Krumboltz (1981) points out that environmental conditions and events (contextual and history-graded influences on development) also influence the nature of vocational decision making because of their impact on career preferences, skills, plans, and the activities of the individual. Examples given by Krumboltz include the number and nature of job and training opportunities, social policies, labor laws, technological development, changes in social organization, family background, and influences by the educational system, the neighborhood, and the community. Thus, the vocational decision-making process for an entire cohort can be significantly changed by technological developments, such as the introduction of the microprocessor. Today, few vocational decisions can be made without being cognizant of this major technological development. Although the technological breakthrough of the microprocessor was relatively "unplanned," other environmental conditions and events can, in fact, be planned, manipulated, and changed, so as to produce significant cohort-specific impacts on vocational decision making across the entire life-span, and on career development in general.

It may be timely at this point to recall our discussion of the concept of dynamic interactionism from Chapter 4. We observed that change on multiple, interrelated levels of analysis characterizes the human life-span, and that intervention into any level may, in fact, produce changes in all other levels. Consider, for example, the equal opportunity employment legislation, as well as the legislation aimed at increasing the availability of federally subsidized educational and training grants and loans that were enacted in the 1960s in an effort to counteract direct and indirect discriminatory practices in the workplace. This legislation represents an intervention at the macrosystem level that clearly influenced changes, for example, at the work organizational level (e.g., changes in hiring and promotion practices), at the educational institutional level (e.g., changes in college admission requirements and practices, changes in college enrollment), at the family level (e.g., lessening of financial burdens related to children's college attendance), and ultimately at the level of individuals' career development (e.g., lessening of financial or minority status barriers to training, entry, and advancement).

Thus, because intervention at any of numerous levels of analysis is, at least theoretically, possible in order to produce desired changes (see, for example, Krausz, 1982), one further issue to be considered is that of chosing the best target level(s) for intervention. For example, if a 16-year-old boy is not performing adequately in school one could intervene in his family (microsystem), his school situation (microsystem), or one could intervene to alter the relationship between family and school (mesosystem) as it exists for this boy. One could also, of course, intervene directly into the boy's cognitive system (by assisting him to learn more effectively or to think differently) or one could intervene at all of the aforementioned levels. Multiple considerations usually guide the choice of level of intervention. If the intervention is targeted on a given individual, then the specific level of intervention is usually selected as a result of a thorough evaluation/analysis of the situation/behaviors to be affected by the intervention and consultation with the individual him/herself about his or her preferences. Questions of "what will work best" (efficacy) and "what will require the least effort and resources" (efficiency) are usually paramount in such decisions. If, however, the intervention is targeted on a given cohort of individuals the level of intervention is almost always at the exosystem or the macrosystem level for efficiency reasons. Depending on the definition of a given cohort and the specification of the changes to be effected, intervention into individual development may also be feasible through media such as television or books, or through large group procedures.

In addition to deciding about the specific level(s) at which an intervention is targeted, decisions must be made about the timing of the intervention. The issue of timing is particularly important in intervention that is guided by a conceptual framework that is characterized by a life-span, developmental-contextual emphasis. This is true because: (a) a developmental focus makes possible the design of intervention strategies and techniques that produce sequential changes; (b) interventions may be designed to occur at various points or periods in the life-span so as to coincide with normative developmental and/or expected contextual changes; and (c) interventions may be designed to occur prior to the birth of a target cohort or target individual to have their impact through the mechanisms of intergenerational transmission (Bengtson & Troll, 1978; Spenner, 1981). Thus, the system is different at different times, and so the outcome of a given intervention will be altered. This is the essence of the idea of "probabilistic epigenesis."

CONCLUSIONS

Our conceptualization of career intervention has been guided by our view of career development: a developmental-contextual view that sees development as unfolding probabilistically rather than deterministically as a consequence of the dynamic interaction of individual and context. As a consequence of this view the intervenor in career development must try to understand the history, the present status, and the future goals and aspirations of the individual, as well as past, present, and future (aspired to) contexts within which the individual has been, is, or may be functioning.

Admittedly, the complexity of this task for the career development intervenor is enormous, for in addition to understanding the developing person in a changing context, he/she must also master intervention techniques appropriate to a given person and circumstance. Conceptual and methodological oversimplification is not the answer to this problem. Vocational and career development intervenors must develop the sophistication required by the complexity of their subject. Obviously, this does not require every intervenor to be equally adept at every type of intervention; specialization may not only be appropriate but necessary. Nevertheless, a commitment on the part of career development specialists to make a serious effort to understand and deal with the full complexity of individuals trying to optimize their career development across the life-span will have a beneficial effect, not only on the recipients of career intervention services, but on the entire professional field of career development intervention.

References

Aberle, D. F., & Naegele, K. D. (1952). Middle-class fathers' occupational role and attitudes toward children. *American Journal of Orthopsychiatry, 22,* 366–378.

Acock, A. C., Barker, D., & Bengtson, V. L. (1982). Mother's employment and parent-youth similarity. *Journal of Marriage and the Family, 44,* 441–455.

Adams, O., & Lefebvre, L. (1981). Retirement and mortality. *Aging and Work, 4*(2), 115–120.

Akabas, S. H., & Kurzman, P. (Eds.). (1982). *Work, workers, and work organizations: A review from social work.* Englewood Cliffs, NJ: Prentice-Hall.

Albrecht, S. L., Bahr, H. M., & Chadwick, B. A. (1977). Public stereotyping of roles, personality characteristics, and occupations. *Sociology and Social Research, 61,* 223–240.

Alessi, D., Brill, M., & Fowles, D. (1979). Productivity, job satisfaction, and the office workplace. *Civil Service Journal, 19,* 14–19.

Almquist, E. M., & Angrist, S. S. (1970). Career salience and atypicality of occupational choice among college women. *Journal of Marriage and the Family, 32,* 242–249.

Anderson, B. E., & Sawhill, I. V. (1980). Policy approaches for the years ahead. In B. E. Anderson & I. V. Sawhill (Eds.), *Youth employment and public policy* (pp. 137–155). Englewood Cliffs, NJ: Prentice-Hall.

Anderson, J. G., & Evans, F. B. (1976). Family socialization and educational achievement in two cultures: Mexican-American and Anglo-American. *Sociometry, 39,* 209–222.

Archer, S. L. (1985). Career and/or family: The identity process for adolescent girls. *Youth and Society, 16,* 289–314.

Archer, S. L., & Waterman, A. S. (1983). Identity in early adolescence: A developmental perspective. *Journal of Early Adolescence, 3,* 203–214.

Atchley, R. C. (1976). *The sociology of retirement.* New York: Schenkman.

Auster, C. J., & Auster, D. (1981). Factors influencing women's choice of nontraditional careers: The role of family, peers, and counselors. *The Vocational Guidance Quarterly, 29,* 253-263.

Bachman, J. G. (1970). *Youth in transition: Volume II, The impact of family background and intelligence on tenth-grade boys.* Ann Arbor: Institute for Social Research.

Bachman, J. G., O'Malley, P. M., & Johnston, J. (1978). *Youth in transition: Vol. VI, Adoles-*

175

cence to adulthood—Change and stability in the lives of young men. Ann Arbor: Institute for Social Research.

Bacon, C., & Lerner, R. M. (1975). Effects of maternal employment status on the development of vocational-role perception in females. *Journal of Genetic Psychology, 126,* 187–193.

Baer, D. M. (1976). The organism as host. *Human Development, 19,* 87–98.

Bakan, D. (1966). *The duality of human existence.* Chicago: Rand McNally.

Baltes, P. B. (1968). Longitudinal and cross-sectional sequences in the study of age and generation effects. *Human Development, 11*(3), 145–171.

Baltes, P. B. (Ed.). (1978). *Life-span development and behavior* (Vol. 1). New York: Academic Press.

Baltes, P. B. (1979). On the potential and limits of child development: Life-span developmental perspectives. *Newsletter of the Society for Research in Child Development* (Summer), 1–4.

Baltes, P. B. (1983). Life-span developmental psychology: Observations on history and theory revisited. In R. M. Lerner (Ed.), *Developmental psychology: Historical and philosophical perspectives* (pp. 79–111). Hillsdale, NJ: Lawrence Erlbaum Associates.

Baltes, P. B., & Baltes, M. M. (1980). Plasticity and variability in psychological aging: Methodological and theoretical issues. In G. E. Gurski (Ed.), *Determining the effects of aging on the central nervous system* (pp. 41–66). Berlin: Schering AG, (Oraniendruck).

Baltes, P. B., Baltes, M. M., & Reinert, G. (1970). The relationship between the time of measurement and age in cognitive development of children: An application of cross-sectional sequences. *Human Development, 13,* 258–268.

Baltes, P. B., & Brim, O. G., Jr. (Eds.). (1979). *Life-span development and behavior* (Vol. 2). New York: Academic Press.

Baltes, P. B., & Brim, O. G., Jr. (Eds.). (1980). *Life-span development and behavior* (Vol. 3). New York: Academic Press.

Baltes, P. B., & Brim, O. G., Jr. (Eds.). (1982). *Life-span development and behavior* (Vol. 4). New York: Academic Press.

Baltes, P. B., & Brim, O. G., Jr. (Eds.). (1983). *Life-span development and behavior* (Vol. 5). New York: Academic Press.

Baltes, P. B., & Brim, O. G., Jr. (Eds.). (1984). *Life-span development and behavior* (Vol. 6). New York: Academic Press.

Baltes, P. B., Cornelius, S. W., & Nesselroade, J. R. (1978). Cohort effects in behavioral development: Theoretical and methodological perspectives. In W. A. Collins (Ed.), *Minnesota symposium on child psychology* (Vol. 11, pp. 1–63). Hillsdale, NJ: Lawrence Erlbaum Associates.

Baltes, P. B., Cornelius, S. W., & Nesselroade, J. R. (1979). Cohort effects in developmental psychology. In J. R. Nesselroade & P. B. Baltes (Eds.), *Longitudinal research in the study of behavior and development* (pp. 61–88). New York: Academic Press.

Baltes, P. B., & Danish, S. J. (1980). Intervention in life-span development and aging: Issues and concepts. In R. R. Turner & H. W. Reese (Eds.), *Life-span developmental psychology: Intervention* (pp. 49–78). New York: Academic Press.

Baltes, P. B., Featherman, D. L., & Lerner, R. M. (Eds.). (1986). *Life-span development and behavior* (Vol. 7). Hillsdale, NJ: Lawrence Erlbaum Associates.

Baltes, P. B., & Nesselroade, J. R. (1973). The developmental analysis of individual differences on multiple measures. In J. R. Nesselroade & H. W. Reese (Eds.), *Life-span developmental psychology: Methodological issues* (pp. 219–251). New York: Academic Press.

Baltes, P. B., Reese, H. W., & Lipsitt, L. P. (1980). Life-span developmental psychology. *Annual Review of Psychology, 31,* 65–110.

Baltes, P. B., Reese, H. W., & Nesselroade, J. R. (1977). *Life-span developmental psychology: Introduction to research.* Monterey, CA: Brooks/Cole.

Baltes, P. B., & Schaie, K. W. (Eds.). (1973). *Life-span developmental psychology: Personality and socialization.* New York: Academic Press.

Baltes, P. B., & Schaie, K. W. (1974). The youth of the twilight years. *Psychology Today, 7,* 35-40.

Baltes, P. B., & Schaie, K. W. (1976). On the plasticity of intelligence in adulthood and old age: Where Horn and Donaldson fail. *American Psychologist, 31,* 720-725.

Banducci, R. (1967). The effects of mother's employment on achievement, aspirations, and expectations of the child. *Personnel and Guidance Journal, 46,* 263-267.

Bandura, A. (1969). *Principles of behavior modification.* New York: Holt, Rinehart & Winston.

Bandura, A. (1978). The self-system in reciprocal determinism. *American Psychologist, 33,* 344-358.

Barker, R. G. (1968). *Ecological psychology: Concepts and methods for studying the environment of human behavior.* Stanford, CA: Stanford University Press.

Barker, R. G., & Gump, P. V. (1964). *Big school, little school.* Stanford, CA: Stanford University Press.

Barker, R. G., & Wright, H. F. (1955). *Midwest and its children.* Evanston, IL: Row Peterson.

Barnaby, J. F. (1980). Lighting for productivity gains. *Lighting and Design and Applications, 10,* 20-28.

Baruch, G. K. (1972). Maternal influences upon college women's attitudes toward women and work. *Developmental Psychology, 6,* 32-37.

Beatty, R. W., & Beatty, J. R. (1982). Job evaluation and discrimination: Legal, economic, and measurement perspectives on comparable worth and women's pay. In H. J. Bernardin (Ed.), *Women in the workforce* (pp. 205-234). New York: Praeger.

Beehr, T. A., & Newman, J. E. (1978). Job stress, employee health, and organizational effectiveness: A facet analysis, model, and literature review. *Personnel Psychology, 31,* 665-699.

Bell, R. Q. (1968). A reinterpretation of the direction of the effects in studies of socialization. *Psychological Review, 75,* 81-95.

Bell, R. Q., & Harper, L. V. (Eds.). (1977). *Child effects on adults.* Hillsdale, NJ: Lawrence Erlbaum Associates.

Belsky, J. (1984). The determinants of parenting: A process model. *Child Development, 54,* 83-96.

Bengtson, V. L., & Troll, L. E. (1978). Youth and their parents: Feedback and intergenerational influence in socialization. In R. M. Lerner & G. B. Spanier (Eds.), *Child influences in marital and family interaction* (pp. 215-240). New York: Academic Press.

Berger-Gross, V., Kahn, M. W., & Weare, C. R. (1983). The role of anxiety in the career decision making of liberal arts students. *Journal of Vocational Behavior, 22,* 312-323.

Berzonsky, M. D. (1982). Inter and intraindividual differences in adolescents storm and stress: A life-span developmental view. *Journal of Early Adolescence, 2*(3), 211-217.

Bijou, S. W. (1976). *Child development: The basic stage of early childhood.* Englewood Cliffs, NJ: Prentice-Hall.

Bijou, S. W., & Baer, D. M. (1961). *Child development. Volume 1: A systematic and empirical theory.* New York: Appleton-Century-Crofts.

Biller, H. B. (1971). *Father, child, and sex roles.* Lexington, MA: Heath.

Birk, J. M., Tanney, M. F., & Cooper, J. F. (1979). A case of blurred vision: Stereotyping in career information illustrations. *Journal of Vocational Behavior, 15,* 247-257.

Blau, P. M., & Duncan, O. D. (1967). *The American occupational structure.* New York: Wiley.

Blau, P. M., Gustad, S. W., Jessor, R., Parnes, H. S., & Wilcock, R. C. (1956). Occupational choice: A conceptual framework. *Industrial Labor Relations Review, 9,* 531-543.

Block, J. H. (1973). Conceptions of sex roles: Some cross-cultural and longitudinal perspectives. *American Psychologist, 28,* 512-526.

Bogie, D. W. (1977). Regional variation in occupational plans among high-school seniors. *Growth and Change, 8*(3), 46-52.

Borgen, W. A., & Young, R. A. (1982). Career perceptions of children and adolescents. *Journal of Vocational Behavior, 21,* 37-42.

Brainerd, C. J. (1978). The stage question in cognitive-developmental theory. *The Behavioral and Brain Sciences, 2,* 173-182.

Brainerd, C. J. (1979). Further replies on invariant sequences, explanation, and other stage criteria. *The Behavioral and Brain Sciences, 2,* 137-154.

Bratcher, W. E. (1982). The influence of the family on career selection: A family systems perspective. *The Personnel and Guidance Journal, 61,* 87-91.

Brenner, M. H. (1973). *Mental illness and the economy.* Cambridge: Harvard University Press.

Brent, S. B. (1984). *Psychological and social structure: Their organization, activity, and development.* New York: Lawrence Erlbaum Associates.

Brim, O. G. (1966). Socialization through the life cycle. In O. G. Brim, Jr., & S. Wheeler (Eds.), *Socialization after childhood: Two essays* (pp. 1-49). New York: Wiley.

Brim, O. G., Jr. (1976). Theories of male mid-life crisis. *The Counseling Psychologist, 6,* 2-9.

Brim, O. G., Jr., & Kagan, J. (1980). Constancy and change: A view of the issues. In O. G. Brim, Jr., & J. Kagan (Eds.), *Constancy and change in human development* (pp. 1-25). Cambridge, MA: Harvard University Press.

Brim, O. G., Jr., & Ryff, C. D. (1980). On the properties of life events. In P. B. Baltes & O. G. Brim, Jr. (Eds.), *Life-span development and behavior* (Vol. 3, pp. 368-388). New York: Academic Press.

Bronfenbrenner, U. (1979). *The ecology of human development.* Cambridge, MA: Harvard University Press.

Bronfenbrenner, U. (1983). The context of development and the development of context. In R. M. Lerner (Ed.), *Developmental psychology: Historical and philosophical perspectives* (pp. 147-184). Hillsdale, NJ: Lawrence Erlbaum Associates.

Bronfenbrenner, U., & Crouter, A. C. (1982). Work and family through time and space. In S. B. Kamerman & C. D. Hayes (Eds.), *Families that work: Children in a changing world* (pp. 39-83). Washington, DC: National Academy of Sciences.

Brookes, M. J., & Kaplan, A. (1972). The office environment: Space, planning, and affective behavior. *Human Factors, 14,* 373-391.

Brookins, G. K. (1984, July). *Maternal employment.* Presentation at Summer Institute on Individual Development and Social Change, Center for Advanced Study in Behavioral Sciences, Palo Alto, CA.

Brooks-Gunn, J., & Ruble, D. N. (1983). The experience of menarche from a developmental perspective. In J. Brooks-Gunn & A. C. Petersen (Eds.), *Girls at puberty: Biological, psychological and social perspectives* (pp. 155-178). New York: Plenum.

Buchmann, A. M. (1983). Maximizing post-retirement labor market opportunities. In H. S. Parnes (Ed.), *Policy issues in work and retirement* (pp. 109-129). Kalamazoo, MI: Upjohn Institute for Employment Research.

Bühler, C. (1959). *Der menschliche Lebenslauf als psychologisches Problem* (2nd ed.). Göttingen: Hogrefe.

Buss, A. H., & Plomin, R. (1984). *Temperament: Early development personality traits.* Hillsdale, NJ: Lawrence Erlbaum Associates.

Callahan, E. J., & McCluskey, K. A. (Eds.). (1983). *Life-span developmental psychology: Nonnormative life events.* New York: Academic Press.

Campbell, D. P. (1974). *Strong Vocational Interest Blank, Manual for the Strong Campbell Interest Inventory—T325 (Merged Form).* Stanford: Stanford University Press.

Campbell, D. T., & Stanley, J. C. (1963). *Experimental and quasi-experimental designs for research.* Chicago: Rand McNally.

Campbell, R. E. (1969). Vocational ecology: A perspective for the study of careers. *The Counseling Psychologist, 1,* 20-23.

Campbell, R. E., & Cellini, J. V. (1981). A diagnostic taxonomy of adult career development problems. *Journal of Vocational Behavior, 19,* 175-190.

Caplan, R. D., Cobb, S., French, J. R. P., Jr., Harrison, R. V., & Pineau, S. R., Jr. (1980). *Job demands and worker health: Main effects and occupational differences.* Ann Arbor: Institute for Social Research, University of Michigan.

Cartwright, L. F. (1972). Conscious factors entering into decision of women to study medicine. *Journal of Social Issues, 28,* 201-215.

Cattell, R. B. (1952a). *Factor analysis.* New York: Harper.

Cattell, R. B. (1952b). P-technique factorization and determination of individual dynamic structure. *Journal of Clinical Psychology, 8,* 5-10.

Cattell, R. B. (1963). The structuring of change in P-technique and incremental R-technique. In C. W. Harris (Ed.), *Problems in measuring change* (pp. 167-198). Madison: University of Wisconsin Press.

Cattell, R. B. (1966). Patterns of change: Measurement in relation to state-dimension, trait change, lability, and process concepts. In R. B. Cattell (Ed.), *Handbook of multivariate experimental psychology* (pp. 355-402). Chicago: Rand McNally.

Cattell, R. B. (1970). Separating endogenous, exogenous, ecogenic, and epogenic component curves in developmental data. *Developmental Psychology, 3,* 151-162.

Cattell, R. B., & Scheier, I. H. (1961). *The meaning and measurement of neuroticism and anxiety.* New York: Ronald Press.

Chandler, T. A., Sawicki, R. F., & Stryffeler, J. M. (1981). Relationships between adolescent sexual stereotypes and working mothers. *Journal of Early Adolescence, 1,* 72-83.

Cherniss, C. (1980). *Professional burnout in human service organizations.* New York: Praeger.

Chomsky, N. (1965). *Aspects of the theory of syntax.* Cambridge, MA: MIT Press.

Chomsky, N. (1966). *Cartesian linguistics.* New York: Harper & Row.

Clarke, A. M., & Clarke, A. D. B. (Eds.). (1976). *Early experience: Myth and evidence.* New York: Free Press.

Clogg, C. C. (1981). New developments in latent structure analysis. In D. M. Jackson & E. F. Borgotta (Eds.), *Factor analysis and measurement in sociological research* (pp. 215-245). Beverly Hills, CA: Sage.

Cohen, S., Glass, D. C., & Singer, J. E. (1973). Apartment noise, auditory discrimination, and reading ability in children. *Journal of Experimental and Social Psychology, 9,* 407-422.

Collins, W. A. (Ed.). (1982). *The concept of development: The Minnesota symposia on child psychology* (Vol. 15). Hillsdale, NJ: Lawrence Erlbaum Associates.

Cooper, C. L., & Payne, R. (Eds.). (1978). *Stress at work.* New York: Wiley.

Corlett, E. N., & Richardson, J. (Eds.). (1981). *Stress, work design, and productivity.* New York: Wiley.

Costa, P. T., Jr., McCrae, R. R., & Holland, J. L. (1984). Personality and vocational interests in an adult sample. *Journal of Applied Psychology, 69*(3), 390-400.

Crites, J. O. (1962). Parental identification in relation to vocational interest development. *Journal of Educational Psychology, 53,* 262-270.

Crites, J. O. (1965). Measurement of vocational maturity in adolescence: I. Attitude Test of the Vocational Development Inventory. *Psychological Monographs, 79* (2, Whole No. 595).

Crites, J. O. (1969). *Vocational psychology.* New York: McGraw-Hill.

Crites, J. O. (1971). *The maturity of vocational attitudes in adolescence.* (APGA Inquiry Series, No. 2). Washington, DC: The American Personnel and Guidance Association.

Crites, J. O. (1973). *Career maturity inventory.* Monterey, CA: California Test Bureau/ McGraw-Hill.

Crites, J. O. (1976). A comprehensive model of career development in early adulthood. *Journal of Vocational Behavior, 9,* 105-118.

Crites, J. O. (1983). Research methods in vocational psychology. In W. B. Walsh & S. H. Osipow (Eds.), *Handbook of vocational psychology, Vol. 1: Foundations* (pp. 305-353). Hillsdale, NJ: Lawrence Erlbaum Associates.

Cronbach, L. J., & Furby, L. (1970). How should we measure "change" or should we? *Psychological Bulletin, 74,* 68-80.

Crouter, A. C., Belsky, J., & Spanier, G. B. (1984). The family context of child development: Divorce and maternal employment. In G. Whitehurst (Ed.), *The annals of child development* (pp. 201-238). Greenwich, CT: JAI Press.

Cumming, E., & Henry, W. E. (1961). *Growing old: The process of disengagement.* New York: Basic Books.

Danish, S. J., D'Augelli, A. R., & Ginsberg, M. R. (1984). Life development intervention: The promotion of mental health through the development of competence. In S. D. Brown & R. W. Lent (Eds.), *Handbook of counseling psychology* (pp. 520-544). New York: Wiley.

Danish, S. J., Smyer, M. A., & Nowak, C. A. (1980). Developmental intervention: Enhancing life-event processes. In P. B. Baltes & O. G. Brim, Jr. (Eds.), *Life-span development and behavior* (Vol. 3, pp. 340-366). New York: Academic Press.

Dannefer, D. (1984). Adult development and social theory: A paradigmatic reappraisal. *American Sociological Review, 49,* 100-116.

Datan, N., & Ginsberg, L. H. (Eds.). (1975). *Life-span developmental psychology: Normative life crises.* New York: Academic Press.

Datan, N., & Reese, H. W. (Eds.). (1977). *Life-span developmental psychology: Dialectical perspectives on experimental psychology.* New York: Academic Press.

Davis, A. (1944). Socialization and the adolescent personality. *Forty-third Yearbook of the National Society for the Study of Education* (Vol. 43, Part I). Chicago: University of Chicago Press.

Dellas, M., & Gaier, E. L. (1975). The self and adolescent identity in women: Options and implications. *Adolescence, 10,* 399-407.

Dellas, M., Gaier, E. L., & Emihovich, C. A. (1979). Maternal employment and selected behaviors and attitudes of preadolescents and adolescents. *Adolescence, 14*(55), 579-589.

Dewey, J., & Bentley, A. F. (1949). *Knowing and the known.* Boston: Beacon.

Dillard, J. M., & Campbell, N. J. (1981). Influences of Puerto Rican, black, and anglo parents' career behavior on their adolescent childrens' career development. *The Vocational Guidance Quarterly, 30,* 139-148.

Dixon, R. A., Lerner, R. M., & Hultsch, D. F. (in preparation). *Teleology and the study of human development: Contextual and dialectical approaches.*

Dobson, C., & Morrow, P. C. (1984). Effects of career orientation on retirement attitudes and retirement planning. *Journal of Vocational Behavior, 24,* 73-83.

Dohrenwend, B. P., & Dohrenwend, B. S. (1981). Some possible relations between stressful work events, other life events, and psychopathology. In G. Gardell & G. Johansson (Eds.), *Working life: A social science contribution to work reform* (pp. 159-176). Kalamazoo, MI: Upjohn Institute for Employment Research.

Douvan, E., & Adelson, J. (1966). *The adolescent experience.* New York: Wiley.

Dudley, G. A., & Tiedeman, D. V. (1977). *Career development: Exploration and commitment.* Muncie, IN: Accelerated Development, Inc.

Duncan, O. D., Featherman, D. L., & Duncan, B. (1972). *Socioeconomic background and occupational achievement.* New York: Seminar Press.

Dusek, J. B., & Flaherty, J. F. (1981). The development of the self-concept during the adolescent years. *Society for Research in Child Development Monograph, 46,* (No. 191).

Eckensberger, L. H. (1973). Methodological issues in cross-cultural research in developmental psychology. In J. R. Nesselroade & H. W. Reese (Eds.), *Life-span developmental psychology: Methodological issues* (pp. 43–64). New York: Academic Press.

Eisdorfer, C., & Cohen, D. (1983). Health and retirement, retirement and health: Background and future directions. In H. S. Parnes (Ed.), *Policy issues in work and retirement* (pp. 57–73). Kalamazoo, MI: Upjohn Institute for Employment Research.

Elder, G. H., Jr. (1974). *Children of the Great Depression.* Chicago: University of Chicago Press.

Elder, G. H., Jr. (1979). Historical change in life patterns and personality. In P. B. Baltes & O. G. Brim, Jr. (Eds.), *Life-span development and behavior* (Vol. 2, pp. 117–159). New York: Academic Press.

Elliott, G. R., & Eisdorfer, C. (Eds.). (1982). *Stress and human health: Analysis and implications of research.* New York: Springer.

Epstein, C. F. (1970). *Woman's place: Options and limits in professional careers.* Berkeley: University of California Press.

Erikson, E. H. (1950). *Childhood and society.* New York: Norton.

Erikson, E. H. (1959). Identity and the life cycle. *Psychological Issues, 1,* 18–164.

Erikson, E. H. (1963). *Childhood and society* (2nd ed.). New York: Norton.

Erikson, E. H. (1968). *Identity: Youth and crisis.* New York: Norton.

Erikson, E. H. (1975). *Life history and the historical moment.* New York: Norton.

Feather, N. T., & Davenport, P. R. (1981). Unemployment and depressive affect: A motivational and attributional analysis. *Journal of Personality and Social Psychology, 41,* 422–436.

Featherman, D. L. (1983). Life-span perspectives in social science research. In P. B. Baltes & O. G. Brim, Jr. (Eds.), *Life-span development and behavior* (Vol. 5, pp. 1–59). New York: Academic Press.

Featherman, D. L., & Hauser, R. M. (1976). Sexual inequalities and socio-economic achievement in the U.S., 1962–1973. *American Sociological Review, 41,* 462–483.

Featherman, D. L., & Lerner, R. M. (1985). Ontogenesis and sociogenesis: Problematics for theory about development across the lifespan. *American Sociological Review, 50,* 659–676.

Finnegan, M. C., & Soloman, L. Z. (1981). Work attitudes in windowed versus windowless environments. *Journal of Social Psychology, 115,* 291–292.

Fitzgerald, L. F., & Betz, N. E. (1983). Issues in the vocational psychology of women. In W. B. Walsh & S. H. Osipow (Eds.), *Handbook of vocational psychology* (Vol. I, pp. 83–159). Hillsdale, NJ: Lawrence Erlbaum Associates.

Fitzgerald, L. F., & Crites, J. O. (1980). Toward a career psychology of women: What do we know? What do we need to know? *Journal of Counseling Psychology, 27*(1), 44–62.

Flavell, J. H. (1970). Cognitive changes in adulthood. In L. R. Goulet & P. B. Baltes (Eds.), *Life-span developmental psychology: Research and theory* (pp. 248–253). New York: Academic Press.

Flavell, J. H. (1971). Stage-related properties of cognitive development. *Cognitive Psychology, 2,* 421–453.

Fox, M. F., & Hesse-Biber, S. (Eds.). (1984). *Women at work.* Palo Alto, CA: Mayfield.

Frankenhaeuser, M. (1981). Coping with job stress—A psychobiological approach. In B. Gardell & G. Johansson (Eds.), *Working life: A social science contribution to work reform* (pp. 213–234). New York: Wiley.

Frankenhaeuser, M., & Gardell, B. (1976). Underload and overload in working life: Outline of a multidisciplinary approach. *Journal of Human Stress, 2,* 35–46.

French, J. R. P., Jr., Caplan, R. D., & Harrison, R. V. (1982). *The mechanisms of job stress and strain.* New York: Wiley.

Fretz, B. (1981). Evaluating the effectiveness of career interventions. *Journal of Counseling Psychology, 28,* 77–90.

Fretz, B. R., & Leong, T. L. (1982). Vocational behavior and career development, 1981: A review. *Journal of Vocational Behavior, 21,* 123–162.

Freud, S. (1923). *The ego and the id.* London: Hogarth Press.

Freud, S. (1954). *Collected works, standard edition.* London: Hogarth Press.

Freudenberger, H. J., & Richelson, G. (1980). *Burnout: The high cost of achievement.* Garden City, NJ: Anchor Press.

Friedman, R., & Wallace, M. (1968). Vocational choice and life goals. In C. Bühler & F. Massarik (Eds.), *The course of human life* (pp. 246–267). New York: Springer.

Frost, F., & Diamond, E. E. (1979). Ethnic and sex differences in occupational stereotyping by elementary school children. *Journal of Vocational Behavior, 15,* 43–54.

Galton, F. (1874). *English men of science: Their nature and nurture.* London: MacMillan.

Gandy, G. L. (1974). Ordinal position research related to vocational interests. *Journal of Counseling Psychology, 21,* 281–287.

Garbarino, J., & Asp, C. E. (1981). *Successful schools and competent students.* Lexington, MA: Lexington Books.

Garbin, A. P., & Stover, R. G. (1980). Vocational behavior and career development, 1979: A review. *Journal of Vocational Behavior, 17,* 125–170.

Gardell, B., & Johansson, G. (Eds.). (1981). *Working life: A social science contribution to work reform.* New York: Wiley.

Gibson, E. J. (1982). The concept of affordances in development: The renascence of functionalism. In W. A. Collins (Ed.), *The concept of development. The Minnesota symposia on child psychology* (Vol. 15, pp. 55–81). Hillsdale, NJ: Lawrence Erlbaum Associates.

Gibson, J. J. (1979). *The ecological approach to visual perception.* Boston: Houghton-Mifflin.

Ginzberg, E. (1984). Career development. In D. Brown, & L. Brooks (Eds.), *Career choice and development* (pp. 169–191). San Francisco: Jossey-Bass.

Ginzberg, E., Berg, I., Brown, C., Herma, L., Yohalem, A., & Gorelick, S. (1966). *Life styles in educated women.* New York: Columbia University Press.

Ginzberg, E., Ginsburg, S. W., Axelrad, S., & Herma, J. L. (1951). *Occupational choice: An approach to a general theory.* New York: Columbia University Press.

Ginzberg, E., & Yohalem, A. M. (1966). *Educated American women: Life-styles and self-portraits.* New York: Columbia University Press.

Gold, D., & Andres, D. (1978). Developmental comparisons between ten year old children with employed and nonemployed mothers. *Child Development, 49,* 75–84.

Goldstein, B., & Oldham, J. (1979). *Children and work: A study of socialization.* New Brunswick, NJ: Transaction Books.

Gollin, E. S. (1981). Development and plasticity. In E. S. Gollin (Ed.), *Developmental plasticity: Behavioral and biological aspects of variations in development* (pp. 231–251). New York: Academic Press.

Gore, S. (1978). The effect of social support in moderating the health consequences of unemployment. *Journal of Health and Social Behavior, 19,* 157–165.

Gottfredson, G. D. (1977). Career stability and redirection in adulthood. *Journal of Applied Psychology, 62,* 436–445.

Gottfredson, L. S. (1981). Circumscription and compromise: A developmental theory of occupational aspirations. *Journal of Counseling Psychology, 28,* 545–579.

Gottfredson, L. S. (1983). Creating and criticizing theory. *Journal of Vocational Behavior, 23,* 203–212.

Gottlieb, G. (1970). Conceptions of prenatal behavior. In L. R. Aronson, E. Tobach, D. S. Lehrman, & J. S. Rosenblatt (Eds.), *Development of evolution of behavior: Essays in memory of T. C. Schneirla* (pp. 111–137). San Francisco: W. H. Freeman.

Gottlieb, G. (1976a). The roles of experience in the development of behavior and the nervous system. In G. Gottlieb (Ed.), *Neural and behavioral specificity: Studies on the development of behavior and the nervous system* (Vol. 3, pp. 25–54). New York: Academic Press.

Gottlieb, G. (1976b). Conceptions of prenatal development: Behavioral embryology. *Psychological Review, 83,* 215–234.

Gottlieb, G. (1983). The psychobiological approach to developmental issues. In M. M. Haith & J. J. Campos (Eds.), *Handbook of child psychology: Infancy and biological bases* (4th ed., Vol. 2, pp. 1–26). New York: Wiley.

Gould, R. L. (1972). The phases of adult life: A study in developmental psychology. *American Journal of Psychiatry, 129,* 521–531.

Goulet, L. R., & Baltes, P. B. (Eds.). (1970). *Life-span developmental psychology: Research and theory.* New York: Academic Press.

Greenblatt, M., Becerra, R., & Serafetinides, E. (1982). Social networks and mental health: An overview. *American Journal of Psychiatry, 139,* 157–165.

Greenhaus, J. H., & Simon, W. E. (1977). Career salience, work values, and vocational indecision. *Journal of Vocational Behavior, 10,* 104–110.

Greenough, W. T., & Green, E. J. (1981). Experience and the changing brain. In J. L. McGaugh & S. B. Kiesler (Eds.), *Aging: Biology and behavior* (pp. 159–200). New York: Academic Press.

Gribbons, W. D., & Lohnes, P. R. (1964). Relationships among measures of readiness for vocational planning. *Journal of Counseling Psychology, 11,* 13–19.

Gribbons, W. D., & Lohnes, P. R. (1965). Shifts in adolescents' vocational values. *Personnel and Guidance Journal,* 248–252.

Grimm, V. E., & Nachmias, C. (1977). The effect of cognitive style and manifest anxiety on intellectual and vocational interest in adolescents. *Journal of Vocational Behavior, 10*(2), 146–155.

Gross, M. (1967). *Learning readiness in two Jewish groups.* New York: Center for Urban Education.

Grotevant, H. D. (1979). Environmental influences on vocational interest development in adolescents from adoptive and biological families. *Child Development, 50,* 854–860.

Grotevant, H. D., & Durrett, M. E. (1980). Occupational knowledge and career development in adolescence. *Journal of Vocational Behavior, 17,* 171–182.

Grotevant, H. D., & Thorbecke, W. L. (1982). Sex differences in styles of occupational identity formation in late adolescence. *Developmental Psychology, 18,* 396–405.

Hall, C. S., & Lindzey, G. (1978). *Theories of personality* (3rd ed.). New York: Wiley.

Hamburger, V. (1957). The concept of development in biology. In D. B. Harris (Ed.), *The concept of development* (pp. 49–58). Minneapolis: University of Minnesota Press.

Harris, D. B. (Ed.). (1957). *The concept of development.* Minneapolis: University of Minnesota Press.

Harrison, R. V. (1978). Person-environment fit and job stress. In C. L. Cooper & R. Payne (Eds.), *Stress at work* (pp. 175–202). New York: Wiley.

Hauser, R. M. (1971). *Socioeconomic background and educational performance.* Washington, DC: Rose Monograph Series, American Sociological Association.

Havighurst, R. J. (1951). *Developmental tasks and education.* New York: Longmaus, Green.

Havighurst, R. J. (1964). Youth in exploration and man emergent. In H. Borow (Ed.), *Man in a world at work* (pp. 215–236). Boston: Houghton-Mifflin.

Havighurst, R. J. (1982). The world of work. In B. B. Wolman (Ed.), *Handbook of developmental psychology* (pp. 771–787). Englewood Cliffs, NJ: Prentice-Hall.

Hawkins, J. G., Bradley, R. W., & White, G. W. (1977). Anxiety and the process of deciding about a major and vocation. *Journal of Counseling Psychology, 24,* 398–402.

Hennig, M. M. (1974). Family dynamics and the successful women executive. In R. B. Kundsin (Ed.), *Women and success: The anatomy of achievement* (pp. 88–93). New York: Morrow.

Herr, E. L., & Cramer, S. H. (1984). *Career guidance and counseling through the life span: Systematic approaches* (2nd ed.). Boston: Little, Brown.

Herr, E. L., Good, R. H., McCloskey, G., & Weitz, A. D. (1982). Secondary school curriculum and career behavior in young adults. *Journal of Vocational Behavior, 21,* 243–253.

Hodgson, J. W., & Fisher, J. L. (1979). Sex differences in identity and intimacy development in college youth. *Journal of Youth and Adolescence, 8,* 37–50.

Hoffman, L. W. (1974a). The education of women, employment, and fertility. *Merrill-Palmer Quarterly, 20,* 99–119.

Hoffman, L. W. (1974b). Effects of maternal employment on the child: A review of the research. *Developmental Psychology, 10,* 204–228.

Hoffman, L. W. (1979). Maternal employment: 1979. *American Psychologist, 34,* 859–865.

Hoffman, L. W. (1985, April). *Maternal employment and social change.* Paper presented at The Pennsylvania State University, Department of Individual and Family Studies, University Park, PA.

Hoffman, L. W., & Nye, F. I. (Eds.). (1974). *Working mothers.* San Francisco: Jossey-Bass.

Holahan, C. J., & Moos, R. H. (1981). Social support and psychological distress: A longitudinal analysis. *Journal of Abnormal Psychology, 90,* 365–370.

Holland, J. L. (1959). A theory of vocational choice. *Journal of Counseling Psychology, 6,* 35–45.

Holland, J. L. (1971). *A counselor's guide for use with the Self-Directed Search.* Palo Alto: Consulting Psychologists Press.

Holland, J. L. (1973). *Making vocational choices: A theory of careers.* Englewood Cliffs, NJ: Prentice-Hall.

Holland, J. L., & Gottfredson, G. D. (1981). Using a typology of persons and environments to explain careers: Some extensions and clarifications. In D. H. Montross & C. J. Shinkman (Eds.), *Career development in the 1980s: Theory and practice* (pp. 5–27). Springfield, IL: Charles C. Thomas.

Holland, J. L., & Holland, J. E. (1977). Vocational indecision: More evidence and speculation. *Journal of Counseling Psychology, 24*(5), 404–414.

Holland, J. L., & Nichols, R. C. (1964). Explorations of a theory of vocational choices: III. A longitudinal study of change in major field of study. *Personnel and Guidance Journal, 43,* 235–242.

Hollingshead, A. B. (1949). *Elmstown youth.* New York: Wiley.

Holmes, T. H., & Rahe, R. H. (1967). The social readjustment rating scale. *Journal of Psychosomatic Research, 11,* 213–218.

Holtzman, W. H. (1962). Methodological issues in P-technique. *Psychological Bulletin, 59,* 243–256.

Horn, J. L., & McArdle, J. J. (1980). Perspective on mathematical/statistical model building (MASMOB) in research on aging. In L. W. Poon (Ed.), *Aging in the 1980s: Psychological issues* (pp. 503–541). Washington, DC: APA.

Horner, M. S. (1972). Toward an understanding of achievement-related conflicts in women. *The Journal of Social Issues, 28,* 157–175.

Hoyer, W. J. (1974). Aging as intraindividual change. *Developmental Psychology, 10,* 821–826.

Huba, G. J., & Harlow, L. L. (1986). Robust estimation for causal models: A comparison of methods in some developmental data sets. In P. B. Baltes, D. L. Featherman, & R. M. Lerner (Eds.), *Life-span development and behavior* (Vol. 7, pp. 69–112). Hillsdale, NJ: Lawrence Erlbaum Associates.

Huston-Stein, A., & Higgins-Trenk, A. (1978). Development of females from childhood through adulthood: Career and feminine orientations. In P. B. Baltes (Ed.), *Life-span development and behavior* (Vol. 1, pp. 258–296). New York: Academic Press.

Inhelder, B., & Piaget, J. (1958). *The growth of logical thinking from childhood to adolescence.* New York: Basic Books.

Jackson, R. M., & Meara, N. M. (1981). Father identification, achievement, and occupational behavior of rural youth: 10-year follow-up. *Journal of Vocational Behavior, 19,* 212-226.

Jaffee, A., Adams, W., & Meyers, S. (1968). *Negro higher education in the 1960s.* New York: Praeger.

Jepsen, D. A. (1984). The developmental perspective on vocational behavior: A review of theory and research. In S. D. Brown & R. W. Lent (Eds.), *Handbook of counseling psychology* (pp. 178-215). New York: Wiley-Interscience.

Jones, O. M., Hansen, J. C., & Putnam, P. A. (1976). Relationship to self-concept and vocational maturity preferences of adolescents. *Journal of Vocational Behavior, 8,* 31-40.

Jordaan, J. P., & Heyde, M. B. (1979). *Vocational maturity during the high school years.* New York: Teachers College Press.

Josselson, R., Greenberger, E., & McConochie, D. (1977a). Phenomenological aspects of psychosocial maturity in adolescence. Part I. Boys. *Journal of Youth and Adolescence, 6,* 25-55.

Josselson, R., Greenberger, E., & McConochie, D. (1977b). Phenomenological aspects of psychosocial maturity in adolescence. Part II. Girls. *Journal of Youth and Adolescence, 6,* 145-167.

Kagan, J. (1966). Reflection-impulsivity: The generality and dynamics of conceptual tempo. *Journal of Abnormal Psychology, 71,* 17-24.

Kagan, J. (1980). Perspectives on continuity. In O. G. Brim, Jr., & J. Kagan (Eds.), *Constancy and change in human development* (pp. 26-74). Cambridge, MA: Harvard University Press.

Kagan, J. (1983). Developmental categories and the premise of connectivity. In R. M. Lerner (Ed.), *Developmental psychology: Historical and philosophical perspectives* (pp. 29-54). Hillsdale, NJ: Lawrence Erlbaum Associates.

Kahn, R. L. (1981). *Work and health.* New York: Wiley.

Kahn, R., Hein, K., House, J., Kasl, S., & McLean, A. (1982). Report on stress in organizational settings. In G. R. Elliott & C. Eisdorfer (Eds.), *Stress and human health: Analysis and implications for research* (pp. 81-117). New York: Springer.

Kandel, D., & Lesser, G. S. (1969). Parent-adolescent relationships and adolescent independence in the United States and Denmark. *Journal of Marriage and the Family, 31,* 348-358.

Kapes, J. T., & Strickler, R. E. (1975). A longitudinal study of change in work values between ninth and twelfth grades as related to high school curriculum. *Journal of Vocational Behavior, 6,* 81-93.

Kaplan, B. (1966). The study of language in psychiatry: The comparative developmental approach and its application to symbolization and language in psychopathology. In S. Arieti (Ed.), *American Handbook of Psychiatry* (Vol. 3, pp. 659-688). New York: Basic Books.

Kaplan, B. (1983). A trio of trials. In R. M. Lerner (Ed.), *Developmental psychology: Historical and philosophical perspectives* (pp. 185-288). Hillsdale, NJ: Lawrence Erlbaum Associates.

Katz, M. (1963). *Decisions and values: A rationale for secondary school guidance.* New York: College Entrance Examination Board.

Kelso, G. I. (1977). The relation of school grade to ages and stages of vocational development. *Journal of Vocational Behavior, 10,* 287-301.

Kendall, P. C., Lerner, R. M., & Craighead, W. E. (1984). Human development and intervention in childhood psychopathology. *Child Development, 55,* 71-82.

Kessen, W. (1962). "Stage" and "structure" in the study of children. In W. Kessen & C. Kuhlman (Eds.), Thought in the young child: Report of a conference on intellective development with particular attention to the work of Jean Piaget. *Monographs of the Society for Research in Child Development, 27*(3), 65–86.

Kidd, J. M. (1984). The relationship of self and occupational concepts to the occupational preferences of adolescents. *Journal of Vocational Behavior, 24,* 48–65.

Kingson, E. R. (1981). The health of very early retirees. *Aging and Work, 4*(1), 11–22.

Kingson, E. R. (1982). Critique of early retirement study disputed. *Aging and Work, 5*(2), 93–110.

Kohlberg, L. (1968). Early education: A cognitive-developmental view. *Child Development, 39,* 1013–1062.

Kohlberg, L. (1969). Stage and sequence: A cognitive-developmental approach to socialization. In J. Goslin (Ed.), *Handbook of socialization theory and research* (pp. 347–480). Chicago: Rand McNally.

Kohn, M. L. (1969). *Class and conformity: A study in values.* Homewood, IL: Dorsey Press.

Kohn, M. L. (1984). The effects of social class on parental values. In P. Voydanoff (Ed.), *Work and family: Changing roles of men and women* (pp. 119–132). Palo Alto, CA: Mayfield.

Kohn, M. L., & Schooler, C. (1973). Occupational experience and psychological functioning: An assessment of reciprocal effects. *American Sociological Review, 38,* 97–118.

Kohn, M. L., & Schooler, C. (1978). The reciprocal effects of substantive complexity of work and intellectual flexibility: A longitudinal assessment. *American Journal of Sociology, 84,* 24–52.

Kohn, M. L., & Schooler, C. (1983). *Work and personality: An inquiry into the impact of social stratification.* Norwood, NJ: Ablex.

Kopp, C. B. (1982). Antecedents of self-regulation: A developmental perspective. *Developmental Psychology, 18,* 199–214.

Krausz, M. (1982). Policies of organizational choice at different vocational life stages. *Vocational Guidance Quarterly, 31,* 60–68.

Krumboltz, J. D. (1981). A social learning theory of career selection. In D. H. Montross & C. J. Shinkman (Eds.), *Career development in the 1980s: Theory and practice* (pp. 43–66). Springfield, IL: Charles C. Thomas.

Krumboltz, J. D., & Baker, R. D. (1973). Behavioral counseling for vocational decisions. In H. Borow (Ed.), *Career guidance for a new age* (pp. 235–283). Boston: Houghton Mifflin.

Kuhn, T. (1962). *The structure of scientific revolutions.* Chicago: University of Chicago Press.

Kuhn, T. S. (1970). *The structure of scientific revolutions* (2nd ed.). Chicago: University of Chicago Press.

Kutner, N., & Brogan, D. (1979, August). *Occupational role innovation and secondary career choice among women medical students.* Paper presented at the annual meetings of the American Sociological Association, Boston.

Labouvie, E. W. (1980). Identity versus equivalence of psychological measures and constructs. In L. W. Poon (Ed.), *Aging in the 1980s: Psychological issues* (pp. 493–502). Washington, DC: APA.

Labouvie, E. W., Bartsch, T. W., Nesselroade, J. R., & Baltes, P. B. (1974). On the internal and external validity of simple longitudinal designs: Drop-out and retest effests. *Child Development, 45,* 282–290.

Labouvie, G. V., Frohring, W., Baltes, P. B., & Goulet, L. R. (1973). Changing relationships between recall performance and abilities as a function of stage learning and timing of recall. *Journal of Educational Psychology, 64,* 191–198.

Lamiell, J. T. (1981). Toward an idiothetic psychology of personality. *American Psychologist, 36,* 276–289.

Lebo, M. A., & Nesselroade, J. R. (1978). Intraindividual differences of mood change during pregnancy identified in five P-technique factor analyses. *Journal of Research in Personality, 12,* 205–224.

Leibson, D. E. (1981). How Corning designed a "talking" building to spur productivity. *Management Review, 70,* 8-13.

Lerner, J. V. (1983). The role of temperament in psychosocial adaptation in early adolescents: A test of a "goodness of fit" model. *Journal of Genetic Psychology, 143,* 149-157.

Lerner, J. V., Baker, N., & Lerner, R. M. (1985). A person-context goodness of fit model of adjustment. In P. C. Kendall (Ed.), *Advances in cognitive-behavioral research and therapy* (Vol. 4, pp. 111-136).

Lerner, J. V., & Galambos, N. L. (1985a). Maternal role satisfaction, mother-child interaction, and child temperament. *Developmental Psychology, 21,* 1157-1164.

Lerner, J. V., & Galambos, N. L. (1985b). Child development and family change: The influences of maternal employment on infants and toddlers. In L. P. Lipsitt & C. Rovee-Collier (Eds.), *Advances in infancy research* (Vol. IV, pp. 39-86). Norwood, NJ: Ablex.

Lerner, J. V., & Lerner, R. M. (1983). Temperament and adaptation across life: Theoretical and empirical issues. In P. B. Baltes & O. G. Brim, Jr. (Eds.), *Life-span development and behavior* (Vol. 5, pp. 197-231). New York: Academic Press.

Lerner, R. M. (1976). *Concepts and theories of human development.* Reading, MA: Addison-Wesley.

Lerner, R. M. (1978). Nature, nurture, and dynamic interactionism. *Human Development, 21,* 1-20.

Lerner, R. M. (1979). A dynamic interactional concept of individual and social relationship development. In R. L. Burgess & T. L. Huston (Eds.), *Social exchange in developing relationships* (pp. 271-305). New York: Academic Press.

Lerner, R. M. (1980). Concepts of epigenesis: Descriptive and explanatory issues. A critique of Kitchener's comments. *Human Development, 23,* 63-72.

Lerner, R. M. (1981). Adolescent development: Scientific study in the 1980s. *Youth and Society, 12,* 251-275.

Lerner, R. M. (1982). Children and adolescents as producers of their own development. *Developmental Review, 2,* 342-370.

Lerner, R. M. (1984). *On the nature of human plasticity.* New York: Cambridge University Press.

Lerner, R. M. (1985). Individual and context in developmental psychology: Conceptual and theoretical issues. In J. R. Nesselroade & A. von Eye (Eds.), *Individual development and social change: Explanatory analysis* (pp. 155-187). New York: Academic Press.

Lerner, R. M. (1986). *Concepts and theories of human development* (2nd ed.). New York: Random House.

Lerner, R. M., & Busch-Rossnagel, N. A. (Eds.). (1981a). *Individuals as producers of their development: A life-span perspective.* New York: Academic Press.

Lerner, R. M., & Busch-Rossnagel, N. A. (1981b). Individuals as producers of their development: Conceptual and empirical bases. In R. M. Lerner & N. A. Busch-Rossnagel (Eds.), *Individuals as producers of their development: A life-span perspective* (pp. 1-36). New York: Academic Press.

Lerner, R. M., & Hultsch, D. F. (1983). *Human development: A life-span perspective.* New York: McGraw-Hill.

Lerner, R. M., Hultsch, D. F., & Dixon, R. A. (1983). Contextualism and the character of developmental psychology in the 1970s. *Annals of the New York Academy of Sciences* (pp. 101-128).

Lerner, R. M., & Kauffman, M. B. (1985). The concept of development in contextualism. *Developmental Review, 5,* 309-333.

Lerner, R. M., Lerner, J. V., Windle, M., Hooker, K., Lenerz, K., & East, P. L. (1986). Children and adolescents in their contexts: Tests of a goodness of fit model. In R. Plomin & J. Dunn

(Eds.), *The study of temperament: Changes, continuities, and challenges* (pp. 99–114). Hillsdale, NJ: Lawrence Erlbaum Associates.

Lerner, R. M., & Ryff, C. D. (1978). Implementation of the life-span view of human development: The sample case of attachment. In P. B. Baltes (Ed.), *Life-span development and behavior* (Vol. 1, pp. 1–44). New York: Academic Press.

Lerner, R. M., Skinner, E. A., & Sorell, G. T. (1980). Methodological implications of contextual/dialectic theories of development. *Human Development, 23,* 225–235.

Lerner, R. M., & Spanier, G. B. (Eds.). (1978). *Child influences on marital and family interaction: A life-span perspective.* New York: Academic Press.

Lerner, R. M., & Spanier, G. B. (1980). *Adolescent development: A life-span perspective.* New York: McGraw-Hill.

Levi, L., Frankenhaeuser, M., & Gardell, B. (1982). Report on work stress related to social structures and processes. In G. R. Elliott & C. Eisdorfer (Eds.), *Stress and human health: Analysis and implications of research* (pp. 119–146). New York: Springer.

Levinson, D. J., Darrow, C. N., Klein, E. B., Levinson, M. H., & McKee, B. (1974). The psychosocial development of men in early adulthood and the midlife transition. In D. F. Ricks, A. Thomas, & M. Roff (Eds.), *Life history research in psychopathology* (Vol. 3, pp. 243–258). Minneapolis: University of Minnesota Press.

Levinson, D. J., Darrow, C. N., Klein, E. B., Levinson, M. H., & McKee, B. (1978). *The seasons of a man's life.* New York: Knopf.

Lewin, K. (1935). *A dynamic theory of personality.* New York: McGraw-Hill.

Lewis, M., & Rosenblum, L. A. (Eds.). (1974). *The effect of the infant on its caregiver.* New York: Wiley.

Lewontin, R. C. (1981). On constraints and adaptation. *The Behavioral and Brain Sciences, 4,* 244–245.

Liebow, E. (1983). Chapters 3 & 4 discussion. In H. S. Parnes (Ed.), *Policy issues in work and retirement* (pp. 91–97). Kalamazoo, MI: Upjohn Institute for Employment Research.

Liem, R., & Rayman, P. (1982). Health and social costs of unemployment: Research and policy considerations. *American Psychologist, 37,* 1116–1123.

Ling, T. M. (Ed.). (1955). *Mental health and human relations in industry.* New York: Paul B. Hoeber.

Lokan, J. J., & Biggs, J. B. (1982). Student characteristics and motivational and process factors in relation to styles of career development. *Journal of Vocational Behavior, 21,* 1–16.

Lokan, J. J., Boss, M. W., & Patsula, P. J. (1982). A study of vocational maturity during adolescence and locus of control. *Journal of Vocational Behavior, 20,* 331–342.

Looft, W. R. (1973). Socialization and personality throughout the life-span: An examination of contemporary psychological approaches. In P. B. Baltes & K. W. Schaie (Eds.), *Life-span developmental psychology: Personality and socialization* (pp. 26–52). New York: Academic Press.

Louis, M. R. (1980). Toward an understanding of career transitions. In C. B. Derr (Ed.), *Work, family, and the career: New frontiers in theory and research* (pp. 200–218). New York: Praeger.

Lueptow, L. B., McClendon, M. J., & McKeon, J. W. (1979). Father's occupation and son's personality: Findings and questions for the emerging linkage hypothesis. *The Sociological Quarterly, 20,* 463–475.

Lynch, E. M. (1980). *Decades—Lifestyle changes in career expectations.* New York: AMACOM.

Maccoby, E. E. (Ed.). (1966). *The development of sex differences.* Stanford, CA: Stanford University Press.

Maccoby, E. E., & Jacklin, C. N. (1974). *The psychology of sex differences.* Stanford, CA: Stanford University Press.

Mac Donald, K. (1985). Early experience, relative plasticity, and social development. *Developmental Review, 5,* 99-121.

MacKay, W. R., & Miller, C. A. (1982). Relations of socioeconomic status and sex variables to the complexity of worker functions in the occupational choices of elementary school children. *Journal of Vocational Behavior, 20,* 31-39.

Maier, K. E., & Ferguson, G. S. (1983). *Annotated bibliography of office design literature.* Department of Man-Environment Relations, The Pennsylvania State University, University Park, PA.

Maier, N. R. F., & Schneirla, T. C. (1935). *Principles of animal behavior.* New York: McGraw-Hill.

Marcia, J. E. (1966). Development and validation of ego identity status. *Journal of Personality and Social Psychology, 3*(5), 551-558.

Marcia, J. E. (1967). Ego identity status: Relationship to change in self-esteem, "general maladjustment," and authoritarianism. *Journal of Personality, 35*(1), 119-133.

Marcia, J. E. (1980). Identity in adolescence. In J. Adelson (Ed.), *Handbook of adolescent psychology* (pp. 158-187). New York: Wiley.

Markham, S. (1983). I can be a bum: Knowledge about abilities and life style in vocational behavior. *Journal of Vocational Behavior, 23,* 72-86.

Marx, M. (1956). Sources of confusion in attitudes toward clinical theory. *Journal of General Psychology, 55,* 19-30.

Maslach, C. (1976). Burned out. *Human Behavior, 5,* 16-22.

Matteson, D. R. (1975). *Adolescence today: Sex roles and the search for identity.* Homewood, IL: Dorsey.

McCandless, B. R. (1970). *Adolescents.* Hinsdale, IL: Dryden.

McClendon, M. J. (1976). The occupational status attainment processes of males and females. *American Sociological Review, 41,* 52-46.

McHale, S., & Lerner, R. M. (1985). Stages of development. In T. Husen & T. N. Postlethwaite (Eds.), *International Encyclopedia of Education: Research and studies* (pp. 2327-2331). Oxford, England: Pergamon Press.

McKinley, D. G. (1964). *Social class and family life.* New York: Free Press.

McNeill, D. (1966). Developmental psycholinguistics. In F. Smith & G. A. Miller (Eds.), *The genesis of language: A psycholinguistic approach* (pp. 15-84). Cambridge, MA: MIT Press.

Mednick, M. T. (1982). Women and the psychology of achievement: Implications for personal and social change. In H. J. Bernardin (Ed.), *Women in the workforce* (pp. 48-69). New York: Praeger.

Miller, D. C., & Form, W. H. (1951). *Industrial sociology.* New York: Harper & Row.

Miller, J., Schooler, C., Kohn, M. L., & Miller, K. A. (1979). Women and work: The psychological effects of occupational conditions. *American Journal of Sociology, 85,* 66-94.

Miller, N. E., & Dollard, J. (1941). *Social learning and imitation.* New Haven: Yale University Press.

Minkler, M. (1981). Research on the health effects of retirement: An uncertain legacy. *Journal of Health and Social Behavior, 22,* 117-130.

Minuchin, P. P., & Shapiro, E. K. (1983). The school as a context for social development. In P. H. Mussen (Ed.), *Handbook of child psychology* (4th ed., Vol. 4, pp. 197-274). New York: Wiley.

Mischel, W. (1977). On the future of personality measurement. *American Psychologist, 32,* 246-254.

Mitchell, A. M., Jones, G. B., & Krumboltz, J. D. (Eds.). (1979). *Social learning theory and career decision making.* Cranston, RI: Carroll.

Molenaar, P. C. M. (1985). A dynamic factor model for the analysis of multivariate time series. *Psychometrika, 50,* 181-202.

Morrison, M. H. (1983). Health circumstances a major factor in retirement decision. *Aging and Work, 6,* 89–92.

Mortimer, J. T. (1974). Pattern of intergenerational occupational movements: A smallest-space analysis. *American Journal of Sociology, 5,* 1278–1295.

Mortimer, J. T. (1975). Occupational value socialization in business and professional families. *Sociology of Work and Occupation, 2,* 29–53.

Mortimer, J. T. (1976). Social class, work and family: Some implications of the father's occupation for family relationships and son's career decisions. *Journal of Marriage and the Family, 38,* 241–254.

Mortimer, J. T., & Kumka, D. (1982). A further examination of the "occupational linkage hypothesis." *The Sociological Quarterly, 23,* 3–16.

Mortimer, J. T., & London, J. (1984). The varying linkages of work and family. In P. Voydanoff (Ed.), *Work and family* (pp. 20–35). Palo Alto, CA: Mayfield.

Munley, P. H. (1975). Erik Erikson's theory of psychosocial development and vocational behavior. *Journal of Counseling Psychology, 22,* 314–319.

Munley, P. H. (1977). Erikson's theory of psychosocial development and career development. *Journal of Vocational Behavior, 10,* 261–269.

Nagel, E. (1957). Determinism and development. In D. B. Harris (Ed.), *The concept of development* (pp. 15–24). Minneapolis, MI: University of Minnesota Press.

Neapolitan, J. (1980). Occupational change in mid-career: An exploratory investigation. *Journal of Vocational Behavior, 16,* 212–225.

Nelson, J. A. N. (1978). Age and sex differences in the development of children's occupational reasoning. *Journal of Vocational Behavior, 13,* 287–297.

Nemerowicz, G. M. (1979). *Children's perception of gender and work roles.* New York: Praeger.

Nesselroade, J. R. (1983). *Some implications of the trait-state distinction for the study of aging: Still labile after all these years.* Paper presented at the annual meeting of the American Psychological Association, Anaheim, CA.

Nesselroade, J. R., & Baltes, P. B. (1974). Adolescent personality development and historical change: 1970–1972. *Monographs of the Society for Research in Child Development, 39* (1, Serial No. 154).

Nesselroade, J. R., & Baltes, P. B. (Eds.). (1979). *Longitudinal research in the study of behavior and development.* New York: Academic Press.

Nesselroade, J. R., & Bartsch, T. W. (1977). Multivariate perspectives on the construct validity of the trait-state distinction. In R. B. Cattell & R. M. Dreger (Eds.), *Handbook of modern personality theory* (pp. 221–238). Washington, DC: Hemisphere.

Nesselroade, J. R., & Ford, D. H. (1985). P-technique comes of age: Multivariate, replicated, single-subject designs for studying older adults. *Research on Aging, 7,* 46–80.

Nesselroade, J. R., & Reese, H. W. (Eds.). (1973). *Life-span developmental psychology: Methodological issues.* New York: Academic Press.

Nesselroade, J. R., Stigler, S. M., & Baltes, P. B. (1980). Regression toward the mean and the study of change. *Psychological Bulletin, 88,* 622–637.

Nesselroade, J. R., & von Eye, A. (Eds.). (1985). *Individual development and social change: Explanatory analysis.* New York: Academic Press.

Nye, F. I. (1974). Effects on mother. In L. W. Hoffman & F. I. Nye (Eds.), *Working mothers* (pp. 207–225). San Francisco: Jossey-Bass.

Ogbu, J. V. (1981). Origins of human competence: A cultural-ecological perspective. *Child Development, 52,* 413–429.

Olneck, M. R., & Bills, D. B. (1979). Family configuration and achievement: Effects of birth order and family size in a sample of brothers. *Social Psychology Quarterly, 42,* 135–148.

Orlofsky, J. L., Marcia, J. E., & Lesser, I. M. (1973). Ego identity status and the intimacy vs.

isolation crisis of young adulthood. *Journal of Personality and Social Psychology, 27,* 211-219.

Osipow, S. H. (1973). *Theories of career development* (2nd ed.). Englewood Cliffs, NJ: Prentice-Hall.

Osipow, S. H. (1975). The relevance of theories of career development to special groups: Problems, needed data, and implications. In S. Picou & R. Campbell (Eds.), *Career behavior of special groups* (pp. 9-22). Columbus, OH: Merrill.

Osipow, S. H. (1979). Occupational mental health: Another role for counseling psychologists. *The Counseling Psychologist, 8,* 65-70.

Osipow, S. H. (1982). Research in career counseling: An analysis of issues and problems. *The Counseling Psychologist, 10*(4), 27-38.

Osipow, S. H. (1983). *Theories of career development* (3rd ed.). Englewood Cliffs, NJ: Prentice-Hall.

Osuji, O. N. (1976). Patterns of occupational drive aspirations in conditions of economic and technological underdevelopment. *Journal of Vocational Behavior, 8,* 133-144.

Overton, W. F. (1973). On the assumptive base of the nature-nurture controversy: Additive versus interactive conceptions. *Human Development, 16,* 74-89.

Overton, W. F. (1978). Klaus Riegel: Theoretical construction to concepts of stability and change. *Human Development, 21,* 360-363.

Overton, W. F. (1984). World views and their influence on scientific research: Kuhn, Lakatos, Lauden. In H. W. Reese (Ed.), *Advances in child development and behavior* (Vol. 8, pp. 191-226). New York: Academic Press.

Overton, W. F., & Reese, H. W. (1973). Models of development: Methodological implications. In J. R. Nesselroade & H. W. Reese (Eds.), *Life-span developmental psychology: Methodological issues* (pp. 65-86). New York: Academic Press.

Overton, W. F., & Reese, H. (1981). Conceptual prerequisites for an understanding of stability-change and continuity-discontinuity. *International Journal of Behavioral Development, 4,* 99-123.

Parnes, H. S. (1981). *Work and retirement: A longitudinal study of men.* Cambridge, MA: MIT Press.

Parnes, H. S. (1983). Health, pension policy and retirement. *Aging and Work, 6,* 93-103.

Pepper, S. C. (1942). *World hypotheses: A study in evidence.* Berkeley, CA: University of California Press.

Perun, R. J., & Del Vento Bielby, D. (1981). Toward a model of female occupational behavior: A human development approach. *Psychology of Women Quarterly, 6,* 234-252.

Pervin, L. A. (1968). Performance and satisfaction as a function of individual-environment fit. *Psychological Bulletin, 69,* 56-68.

Peterson, G. W., Rollins, B. C., Thomas, D. L., & Heaps, L. K. (1982). Social placement of adolescents: Sex-role influences on family decisions regarding the careers of youth. *Journal of Marriage and the Family, 44,* 647-658.

Piaget, J. (1950). *The psychology of intelligence.* New York: Harcourt Brace.

Piaget, J. (1968). *Six psychological studies.* New York: Random House Jovanovich.

Piaget, J. (1970). Piaget's theory. In P. H. Mussen (Ed.), *Carmichael's manual of child psychology* (3rd ed., Vol. 1, pp. 703-732). New York: Wiley.

Pleck, J. H. (1984). The work-family role system. In P. Voydanoff (Ed.), *Work and family* (pp. 8-19). Palo Alto, CA: Mayfield.

Plomin, R., & Fulker, D. (in press). Behavioral genetics and development in early adolescents. In R. M. Lerner & T. T. Foch (Eds.), *Biological-psychological-social interactions in early adolescents: A life-span perspective.* Hillsdale, NJ: Lawrence Erlbaum Associates.

Podd, M. H., Marcia, J. E., & Rubin, B. M. (1970). The effects of ego identity and partner perception on a prisoner's dilemma game. *Journal of Social Psychology, 82,* 117-126.

Powell, B., & Steelman, L. C. (1982). Testing an undertested comparison: Maternal effects on sons' and daughters' attitudes toward women in the labor force. *Journal of Marriage and the Family, 44,* 349–355.

Powell, K. (1963). Personalities of children and childrearing attitudes of mothers. In F. I. Nye & L. W. Hoffman (Eds.), *The employed mother in America* (pp. 125–141). Chicago: Rand McNally.

Prediger, D. J. (1974). The role of assessment in career guidance. In E. L. Herr (Ed.), *Vocational guidance and human development* (pp. 325–349). Boston: Houghton Mifflin.

Princeton Manpower Symposium. (1968). *The transition from school to work.* Princeton, NJ: Industrial Relations Section, Princeton University.

Pryor, R. G. L. (1980). Some types of stability in the study of students' work values. *Journal of Vocational Behavior, 16,* 146–157.

Purifoy, F. E., & Koopmans, L. H. (1980). Androstemedione, T and Free T concentrations in women of various occupations. *Social Biology, 26,* 179–188.

Rabin, A. I. (1965). *Growing up in the Kibbutz.* New York: Springer.

Rainwater, L. (1984). Mothers' contribution for the family money economy in Europe and the United States. In P. Voydanoff (Ed.), *Work and family: Changing roles of men and women* (pp. 73–88). Palo Alto, CA: Mayfield.

Reese, H. W. (1982). Behavior analysis and developmental psychology: Discussant comments. *Human Development, 35,* 352–357.

Reese, H. W., & Overton, W. F. (1970). Models of development and theories of development. In L. R. Goulet & P. B. Baltes (Eds.), *Life-span developmental psychology: Research and theory* (pp. 116–145). New York: Academic Press.

Rehberg, R. A., & Westby, D. L. (1967). Parental encouragement, occupation, education, and family size: Artifactual or independent determinants of adolescent educational expectations? *Social Forces, 45,* 362–374.

Ridgeway, C. (1978). Parental identification and patterns of career orientation in college women. *Journal of Vocational Behavior, 12,* 1–11.

Riegel, K. F. (1975). Toward a dialectical theory of development. *Human Development, 18,* 50–64.

Riegel, K. F. (1976). The dialectics of human development. *American Psychologist, 31,* 689–700.

Riley, M. W. (1978). Aging, social change, and the power of ideas. *Daedalus,* Fall, 39–52.

Riley, M. W. (1979). Introduction: Life-course perspectives. In M. W. Riley (Ed.), *Aging from birth to death* (pp. 3–13). Washington, DC: American Association for the Advancement of Science.

Riley, M. W., Johnson, M. E., & Foner, A. (Eds.). (1972). *Aging and society: A sociology of age stratification.* New York: Russell Sage Foundation.

Robbins, P. I. (1978). *Successful midlife career change: Self-understanding and strategies for action.* New York: AMACOM.

Roberts, M. L., & Nesselroade, J. R. (1983). *State variability in a locus of control measure: P-technique factor analyses of short-term change.* Unpublished manuscript, The Pennsylvania State University.

Roe, A. (1956). *The psychology of occupations.* New York: Wiley.

Roe, A. (1964). Personality structure and occupational behavior. In H. Borow (Ed.), *Man in a world at work* (pp. 196–214). Boston: Houghton Mifflin.

Rogosa, D. (1979). Causal models in longitudinal research: Rationale, formulation and interpretation. In J. R. Nesselroade & P. B. Baltes (Eds.), *Longitudinal research in the study of behavior and development* (pp. 263–302). New York: Academic Press.

Rogosa, D., Brandt, D., & Zimowski, M. (1982). A growth curve approach to the measurement of change. *Psychological Bulletin, 92,* 726–748.

Rosenberg, M. (1957). *Occupation and values.* Glencoe, IL: Free Press.

Ruggie, M. (1984). *The state and working women: A comparative study of Britain and Sweden.* Princeton, NJ: Princeton University Press.

Russo, N. F. (1979). Overview: Sex roles, fertility and the motherhood mandate. *Psychology of Women Quarterly, 4*(1), 7-15.

Sameroff, A. L. (1975). Transactional models in early social relations. *Human Development, 18,* 65-70.

Scarr, S. (1982). Development is internally guided, not determined. *Contemporary Psychology, 27,* 852-853.

Scarr, S. (1984, Spring). *The danger of having pet variables.* Presidential address, Division on Developmental Psychology Newsletter.

Scarr, S., & McCartney, K. (1983). How people make their own environments: A theory of genotype → environment effects. *Child Development, 54,* 424-435.

Schaie, K. W. (1965). A general model for the study of developmental problems. *Psychological Bulletin, 64,* 92-107.

Schaie, K. W. (1982, April). *New directions for an applied developmental psychology of adulthood.* Invited lecture presented at Eastern Psychological Association meeting, Baltimore.

Schaie, K. W. (1982, May). *Historical time and cohort effects.* Paper presented at the West Virginia University Conference on Life-span Developmental Psychology, Morgantown, WV.

Schaie, K. W., & Baltes, P. B. (1975). On sequential strategies in developmental research: Description or explanation? *Human Development, 18,* 384-390.

Schaie, K. W., Labouvie, G. V., & Buech, B. V. (1973). Generational and cohort-specific differences in adult cognitive functioning: A fourteen-year study of independent samples. *Developmental Psychology, 9,* 151-166.

Schein, E. H. (1971). The individual, the organization, and the career: A conceptual scheme. *Journal of Applied Behavioral Science, 7,* 401-426.

Schein, E. H. (1978). *Career dynamics: Matching individual and organizational needs.* Reading, MA: Addison Wesley.

Scheller, R. (1976). *Psychologie der Berufswahl und der beruflichen Entwicklung.* Stuttgart: Verlag Kohlhammer.

Schenk, D. C., & Emerick, R. (1976). The young male adolescent's perception of early child-rearing effects of socioeconomic status and family size. *Sociometry, 39,* 39-52.

Schneirla, T. C. (1956). Interrelationships of the innate and the acquired in instinctive behavior. In P. P. Grasse (Ed.), *L'Instinct dans le comportement des animaux et de l'homme* (pp. 387-452). Paris: Masson & Cie.

Schneirla, T. C. (1957). The concept of development in comparative psychology. In D. B. Harris (Ed.), *The concept of development* (pp. 78-108). Minneapolis: University of Minnesota Press.

Schulenberg, J. E. (1984). *Dimensions of intra-individual variability and inter-individual similarities in work values: P-technique factor analyses of short-term change.* Unpublished Master's thesis, The Pennsylvania State University.

Schulenberg, J. E., & Garbarino, J. (1985). Academic and vocational development in schools and at work. In J. Garbarino (Ed.), *Adolescent development: An ecological perspective* (pp. 378-427). Columbus, OH: Charles E. Merrill.

Schulenberg, J. E., Vondracek, F. W., & Crouter, A. C. (1984). The influence of the family on vocational development. *Journal of Marriage and the Family, 46,* 129-143.

Schulenberg, J. E., Vondracek, F. W., & Nesselroade, J. R. (1985). *Patterns of short-term changes in individuals' work values: P-technique factor analyses of intraindividual variability.* Unpublished manuscript, The Pennsylvania State University.

Schwartz, G. E. (1982). Testing the biopsychosocial model: The ultimate challenge facing behavioral medicine? *Journal of Consulting and Clinical Psychology, 50*(6), 1040-1053.

Sears, S. (1982). A definition of career guidance terms: A National Vocational Guidance Association perspective. *Vocational Guidance Quarterly, 31,* 137–143.

Shappell, D. L., Hall, L. G., & Tarrier, R. B. (1971). Perceptions of the world of work: Inner-city versus suburbia. *Journal of Counseling Psychology, 18,* 55–59.

Sherraden, M. W. (1980). Youth employment and education: Federal programs from the New Deal through the 1970s. In R. C. Rist (Ed.), *Confronting youth unemployment in the 1980s: Rhetoric versus reality* (pp. 17–39). New York: Pergamon Press.

Simpson, R. L. (1962). Parental influence, anticipatory socialization, and social mobility. *American Sociological Review, 27,* 517–522.

Smith, E. J. (1981). The working mother: A critique of the research. *Journal of Vocational Behavior, 19,* 191–211.

Smith, E. J. (1983). Issues in social minorities' career behavior. In W. B. Walsh & S. H. Osipow (Eds.), *Handbook of vocational psychology* (Vol. 1, pp. 116–122). Hillsdale, NJ: Lawrence Erlbaum Associates.

Smuts, R. W. (1971). *Women and work in America.* New York: Schocken Books.

Snyder, M. (1981). On the influence of individuals on situations. In N. Cantor & J. F. Kihlstrom (Eds.), *Personality, cognitive, and social interaction* (pp. 309–329). Hillsdale, NJ: Lawrence Erlbaum Associates.

Sonnenfeld, J., & Kotter, J. P. (1982). The maturation of career theory. *Human Relations, 35*(1), 19–46.

Sorell, G. T., & Nowak, C. A. (1981). The role of physical attractiveness as a contributor to individual development. In R. M. Lerner & N. A. Busch-Rossnagel (Eds.), *Individuals as producers of their development: A life-span perspective* (pp. 389–446). New York: Academic Press.

Spence, J. T., & Helmreich, R. L. (1980). Masculine instrumentality and feminine expressiveness: Their relationships with sex role attitudes and behaviors. *Psychology of Women Quarterly, 5,* 147–153.

Spenner, K. I. (1981). Occupations, role characteristics and intergenerational transmission. *Sociology of Work and Occupation, 8,* 89–112.

Squires, G. D. (1979). *Education and jobs: The imbalancing of social machinery.* New Brunswick, NJ: Transaction Books.

Standley, K., & Soule, B. (1974). Women in male-dominated professions: Contrasts in their personal and vocational histories. *Journal of Vocational Behavior, 4,* 245–258.

Stark, P. A., & Traxler, A. J. (1974). Empirical validation of Erikson's theory of identity crises in late adolescence. *The Journal of Psychology, 86,* 25–33.

Stein, A. H. (1973). The effects of maternal employment and educational attainment on the sex-typed attributes of college females. *Social Behavior and Personality, 1,* 111–114.

Stein, A. H., & Bailey, M. M. (1973). The socialization of achievement orientation in females. *Psychological Bulletin, 80,* 345–366.

Steinberg, L. D. (1983). The varieties and effects of work during adolescence. In M. Lamb, A. Brown, & B. Rogoff (Eds.), *Advances in developmental psychology* (Vol. 3, pp. 1–38). Hillsdale, NJ: Lawrence Erlbaum Associates.

Steinberg, L. D., Greenberger, E., Garduque, L., & McAuliffe, S. (1982). High school students in the labor force: Some costs and benefits to schooling and working. *Education and Policy Analysis, 4,* 363–372.

Stokols, D. (1978). Environmental psychology. *Annual Review of Psychology, 29,* 253–295.

Stokols, D. (1981a, August). *Environmental psychology: A coming of age.* G. Stanley Hall Lecture presented at the Annual Meeting of the American Psychological Association, Los Angeles, CA.

Stokols, D. (1981b). Group X place transactions: Some neglected issues in psychological research on settings. In D. Magnussen (Ed.), *Toward a psychology of situations: An interactional perspective* (pp. 393–450). Hillsdale, NJ: Lawrence Erlbaum Associates.

Super, D. E. (1951). Vocational adjustment: Implementing a self-concept. *Occupations, 30,* 88–92.

Super, D. E. (1953). A theory of vocational development. *American Psychologist, 8,* 185–190.

Super, D. E. (1955). The dimensions and measurement of vocational maturity. *Teachers College Record, 57,* 151–163.

Super, D. E. (1957). *The psychology of careers.* New York: Harper & Row.

Super, D. E. (1970). *Manual of the work values inventory.* Boston: Houghton Mifflin.

Super, D. E. (1977a). The identity crisis of counseling psychologists. *The Counseling Psychologist, 7*(2), 13–15.

Super, D. E. (1977b). Vocational maturity in midcareer. *Vocational Guidance Quarterly, 25,* 294–302.

Super, D. E. (1980). A life-span, life-space approach to career development. *Journal of Vocational Behavior, 16,* 282–298.

Super, D. E. (1981). A developmental theory: Implementing a self-concept. In D. H. Montross & C. J. Shinkman (Eds.), *Career development in the 1980s: Theory and practice* (pp. 28–42). Springfield, IL: Charles C. Thomas.

Super, D. E. (1983). Assessment in career guidance: Toward truly developmental counseling. *Personnel and Guidance Journal, 63,* 555–562.

Super, D. E., Crites, J. O., Hummel, R. C., Moser, H. P., Overstreet, P. L., & Warnath, C. F. (1957). *Vocational development: A framework for research.* New York: Teacher's College, Columbia University.

Super, D. E., & Knasel, F. G. (1981). Career development in adulthood: Some theoretical problems and a possible solution. *British Journal of Guidance and Counseling, 9,* 194–201.

Super, D. E., & Nevill, D. D. (1984). Work role salience as a determinant of career maturity in high school students. *Journal of Vocational Behavior, 25,* 30–44.

Super, D. E., & Overstreet, P. L. (1960). *The vocational maturity of ninth grade boys.* New York: Teachers College Press.

Tangri, S. S. (1972). Determinants of occupational role innovation among college women. *Journal of Social Issues, 28,* 177–199.

Tenzer, A. (1977). Parental influences on the occupational choice of career women in male-dominated and traditional occupations. *Dissertation Abstracts International, 38,* 2014.

Thomas, A., & Chess, S. (1977). *Temperament and development.* New York: Brunner/Mazel.

Thomas, A., & Chess, S. (1980). *The dynamics of psychological development.* New York: Brunner/Mazel.

Thomas, A., & Chess, S. (1981). The role of temperament in the contributions of individuals to their development. In R. M. Lerner & N. A. Busch-Rossnagel (Eds.), *Individuals as producers of their development: A life-span perspective* (pp. 231–255). New York: Academic Press.

Thomas, L. E. (1980). Typology of mid-life career changes. *Journal of Vocational Behavior, 16,* 173–182.

Thorndike, E. L. (1905). *The elements of psychology.* New York: Seiler.

Tiedeman, D. V., & O'Hara, R. P. (1963). *Career development: Choice and adjustment.* New York: College Entrance Examination Board.

Tilly, L. A. (1985). Family, gender, and occupation in industrial France: Past and present. In A. S. Rossi (Ed.), *Gender and the life course* (pp. 193–212). New York: Aldine.

Tinsley, H. E. A., & Heesacker, M. (1984). Vocational behavior and career development, 1983: A review. *Journal of Vocational Behavior, 25,* 139–190.

Tinsley, H. E. A., Kass, R. A., Moreland, J. R., & Harren, V. A. (1983). A longitudinal study of female college students' occupational decision making. *The Vocational Guidance Quarterly, 32,* 89-102.

Tobach, E. (1978). The methodology of sociobiology from the viewpoint of a comparative psychologist. In A. L. Caplan (Ed.), *The sociobiology debate* (pp. 411-423). New York: Harper & Row.

Tobach, E. (1981). Evolutionary aspects of the activity of the organism and its development. In R. M. Lerner & N. A. Busch-Rossnagel (Eds.), *Individuals as producers of their development: A life-span perspective* (pp. 37-68). New York: McGraw-Hill.

Tobach, E., & Schneirla, T. C. (1968). The biopsychology of social behavior of animals. In R. E. Cooke & S. Levin (Eds.), *Biologic basis of pediatric practice* (Vol. I, pp. 68-82). New York: McGraw-Hill.

Toulmin, S. (1981). Epistemology and developmental psychology. In E. S. Gollin (Ed.), *Developmental plasticity: Behavioral and biological aspects of variations in development* (pp. 253-267). New York: Academic Press.

Turner, R. J. (1981). Social support as a contingency in psychological well-being. *Journal of Health and Social Behavior, 22,* 357-367.

Urban, H. B., & Looft, W. R. (1973). *Issues in human development intervention.* Paper presented at the conference: Applied Human Development: Issues in Intervention, The Pennsylvania State University.

Vaillant, G. E. (1977). *Adaptation to life.* Boston: Little Brown.

Vaitenas, R., & Wiener, Y. (1977). Developmental, emotional, and interest factors in voluntary mid-career change. *Journal of Vocational Behavior, 11,* 291-304.

Verger, D. M. (1968). Birth order and sibling differences in interests. *Journal of Individual Psychology, 24,* 56-59.

Vinovskis, M. A. (in press). The historian and the life course: Reflections on recent approaches to the study of American family life in the past. In P. B. Baltes, D. L. Featherman, & R. M. Lerner (Eds.), *Life-span development and behavior* (Vol. 8). Hillsdale, NJ: Lawrence Erlbaum Associates.

Vogel, S. R., Broverman, I. K., Broverman, D. M., Clarkson, T. E., & Rosenkrantz, P. S. (1970). Maternal employment and perception of sex roles among college students. *Developmental Psychology, 3,* 384-391.

Vondracek, F. W., & Lerner, R. M. (1982). Vocational role development in adolescence. In B. B. Wolman (Ed.), *Handbook of developmental psychology* (pp. 602-614). Englewood Cliffs, NJ: Prentice-Hall.

Vondracek, F. W., Lerner, R. M., & Schulenberg, J. E. (1983a). The concept of development in vocational theory and intervention. *Journal of Vocational Behavior, 23,* 179-202.

Vondracek, F. W., Lerner, R. M., & Schulenberg, J. E. (1983b). On aspiring to present a developmental theory of occupational aspirations: A reader's guide to Gottfredson. *Journal of Vocational Behavior, 23,* 213-218.

Vondracek, F. W., & Schulenberg, J. E. (in press). Career development in adolescence: Some conceptual and intervention issues. *The Vocational Guidance Quarterly.*

Vondracek, S., & Kirchner, E. (1974). Vocational development in early childhood: An examination of young children's expressions of vocational aspirations. *Journal of Vocational Behavior, 5,* 251-260.

Waddington, C. H. (1957). *The strategy of genes.* London: George Allen & Unwin.

Waite, C. J. (1981). U.S. women at work. *Population Bulletin, 36*(2), Washington, DC: Population Reference Bureau.

Waldman, E. (1985). Today's girls in tomorrow's labor force: Projecting their participation and occupations. *Youth and Society, 16*(3), 375-392.

Warren, G. D., Winer, J. L., & Dailey, K. C. (1981). Extending Holland's theory to the later years. *Journal of Vocational Behavior, 18,* 104-114.

Waterman, A. S. (1982). Identity development from adolescence to adulthood: An extension of theory and a review of research. *Developmental Psychology, 18*(3), 341–358.

Waterman, A. S., & Goldman, J. A. (1976). A longitudinal study of ego identity development at a liberal arts college. *Journal of Youth and Adolescence, 5,* 361–369.

Watson, R. I. (1977). Psychology: A perspective science. In J. Bronzek & R. B. Evans (Eds.), *R. I. Watson's selected papers on the history of psychology* (pp. 95–112). Hanover, NH: University of New Hampshire Press.

Weeks, M. O., Thornburg, K. R., & Little, L. F. (1977). The impact of exposure to nontraditional vocational role models on the vocational role preferences of five-year-old children. *Journal of Vocational Behavior, 10,* 139–145.

Weiner, Y., Vardi, Y., & Muczyk, J. (1981). Antecedents of employees mental health—the role of career and work satisfaction. *Journal of Vocational Behavior, 19,* 50–60.

Weiss, R. S. (1979). Growing up a little faster: The experience of growing up in a single-parent household. *Journal of Social Issues, 35,* 135–142.

Weitz, S. (1977). *Sex roles.* New York: Oxford University Press.

Werner, H. (1948). *Comparative psychology of mental development.* New York: International Universities Press.

Werner, H. (1957). The concept of development from a comparative and organismic point of view. In D. B. Harris (Ed.), *The concept of development* (pp. 125–148). University of Minnesota Press.

Werner, H., & Kaplan, B. (1963). *Symbol formation.* New York: Wiley.

Wicker, A. W., McGrath, J. E., & Armstrong, G. E. (1972). Organization size and behavior setting capacity as determinants of member participation. *Behavioral Science, 17,* 499–513.

Wijting, J. P., Arnold, C. R., & Conrad, K. A. (1978). Generational differences in work values between parents and children and between boys and girls across grade levels 6, 9, 10, and 12. *Journal of Vocational Behavior, 12,* 245–260.

Wohlwill, J. F. (1973). *The study of behavioral development.* New York: Academic Press.

Wohlwill, J. F., & Heft, H. (1978). Environmental fit for the developing child. In H. McGurk (Ed.), *Ecological factors in human development* (pp. 125–138). Amsterdam: North Holland.

Wohlwill, J. F., & Heft, H. (in press). The physical environment and the development of the child. In D. Stokols, & I. Altman (Eds.), *Handbook of environmental psychology.* New York: Wiley.

Young, R. A. (1983). Career development of adolescents: An ecological perspective. *Journal of Youth and Adolescence, 12,* 401–417.

Zagar, R., Arbit, J., Falconer, J., & Friedland, J. (1983). Vocational interests and personality. *Journal of Occupational Psychology, 56,* 203–214.

Zajonc, R. B. (1976). Family configuration and intelligence. *Science, 192,* 227–235.

Zajonc, R. B., & Markus, G. B. (1975). Birth order and intellectual development. *Psychological Review, 82,* 74–85.

Zaslow, M., Rabinovich, B., & Suwalsky, J. (1983). *The impact on the child of maternal employment: An examination of mediating variables.* Paper presented at the Boulder lecture series on Developmental Plasticity "Social Context and Human Development," Boulder, CO.

Zevon, M. A., & Tellegen, A. (1982). The structure of mood change: An idiographic/nomothetic analysis. *Journal of Personality and Social Psychology, 43,* 111–112.

Zytowski, D. G. (1969). Toward a theory of career development for women. *Personnel and Guidance Journal, 47,* 660–664.

Zytowski, D. G. (1970). The concept of work values. *Vocational Guidance Journal, 18,* 176–186.

Author Index

Spanier, G. B., 27, 101, 131, 132
Spence, J. T., 129
Spenner, K. I., 52, 60, 62, 172
Squires, G. D., 59
Standley, K., 53, 54
Stanley, J. C., 104
Stark, P. A., 142
Steelman, L. C., 136
Stein, A. H., 132, 136
Steinberg, L. D., 59, 100, 101
Stigler, S. M., 94, 104, 107
Stokols, D., 36, 40, 43, 56
Stover, R. G., 5
Strickler, R. E., 116
Stryffeler, J. M., 136
Super, D. E., 2, 3, 4, 6, 7, 9, 15, 16, 19, 23,
   35, 44, 68, 78, 86, 97, 115, 117, 118,
   155, 160, 165

T

Tangri, S. S., 54, 136
Tanney, M. F., 127
Tarrier, R. B., 134
Tellegen, A., 116, 117
Tenzer, A., 53
Thomas, A., 78, 79, 80, 81
Thomas, D. L., 53
Thomas, L. E., 147, 148
Thorbecke, W. L., 90, 132, 142, 143, 144, 165
Thornburg, K. R., 140
Tiedeman, D. V., 2, 19, 71
Tilly, L. A., 126, 127
Tinsley, H. E. A., 86, 87, 88, 89, 94, 97
Tobach, E., 31, 71, 79
Toulmin, S., 71
Traxler, A. J., 142
Troll, L. E., 76, 172
Turner, R. J., 150

U

Urban, H. B., 155

V

Vaillant, G. E., 3
Vaitenas, R., 95, 96, 148
Vardi, Y., 151

Verger, D. M., 55
Vinovskis, M. A., 114
Vogel, S. R., 136
Vondracek, F. W., 3, 5, 6, 7, 8, 9, 19, 40, 41, 42,
   46, 54, 56, 69, 112, 118, 144, 162, 167
Vondracek, S., 140
von Eye, A., 108

W

Waddington, C. H., 33
Waite, C. J., 128
Waldman, E., 127, 128, 129
Wallace, M., 68
Warnath, C. F., 3, 9
Warren, G. D., 148
Waterman, A. S., 86, 132, 140, 141, 142, 143,
   144, 145, 165
Watson, R. I., 19
Weare, C. R., 142
Weeks, M. O., 140
Weiss, R. S., 56
Weitz, A. D., 165
Weitz, S., 53
Werner, H., 18, 25, 31
Westby, D. L., 54
White, G. W., 142
Wicker, A. W., 57
Wiener, Y., 95, 96, 148, 151
Wijting, J. P., 98
Wilcock, R. C., 35
Windle, M., 10
Winer, J. L., 148
Wohlwill, J. F., 30, 35, 36, 39, 40, 43, 57, 88
Wright, H. F., 57

Y

Yohalem, A. M., 132, 136
Young, R. A., 40, 87, 101

Z

Zagar, R., 90
Zajonc, R. B., 55, 56
Zaslow, M., 98
Zevon, M. A., 116, 117
Zimowski, M., 107
Zytowski, D. G., 116, 133

Subject Index